Barometers of Change

Seymour B. Sarason

Barometers of Change

Individual, Educational, and Social Transformation

Jossey-Bass Publishers
San Francisco

Substantial discounts on bulk quantities of Jossey-Bass books are available to corporations, professional associations, and other organizations. For details and discount information, contact the special sales department at Jossey-Bass Inc., Publishers (415) 433-1740; Fax (800) 605-2665.

For sales outside the United States, please contact your local Simon & Schuster International Office.

 Manufactured in the United States of America on Lyons Falls Pathfinder Tradebook. This paper is acid-free and 100 percent totally chlorine-free.

Library of Congress Cataloging-in-Publication Data

Sarason, Seymour Bernard, date.
    Barometers of change : individual, educational, and social
transformation / Seymour B. Sarason. — 1st ed.
      p.   cm.
    Includes bibliographical references and index.
    ISBN 0-7879-0198-9
    1. Social change—United States.   2. Education—Social aspects—
United States.   3. United States—Social conditions.   I. Title.
HN57.S28   1996
303.4'0973—dc20
                                                     95-26191
                                                       CIP

HB Printing   10 9 8 7 6 5 4 3 2 1   FIRST EDITION

Contents

*This book is dedicated
with boundless love to
Julie, Paul, and Nathaniel*

Preface

. . . .

In 1980, historian Carl Schorske's *Fin-De-Siècle Vienna* (1980) was published. Why write about Vienna at the end of the nineteenth century? Schorske's area of expertise was modern European intellectual history. He had, he tells us, no special training or expertise as a historian of the Habsburg Empire.

In the late 1940s, Schorske started to outline a course in modern European intellectual history "designed to help students to understand the large, architectonic correlations between high culture and sociopolitical change" (pg. xviii). The course development went well until he ran into what Nietzsche and the Marxists called "decadence."

> European high culture entered a whirl of infinite inno-
> vation, with each field proclaiming independence of the
> whole and each part in turn falling into additional parts.
> Into the ruthless centrifuge of change were drawn the
> very concepts by which cultural phenomena might be
> fixed in thought. Not only the producers of culture but
> also its analysts and critics fell victim to the fragmenta-
> tion. The many categories devised to define or govern
> any one of the trends in post–Nietzschean culture—
> irrationalism, subjectivism, abstractionism, anxiety, tech-
> nologism—neither possessed the surface virtue of lending

themselves to generalization nor allowed any convincing dialectical integration into the historical process as previously understood. Every search for a plausible twentieth-century equivalent to such sweeping but heuristically indispensable categories as "the Enlightenment" seemed doomed to founder on the heterogeneity of the cultural substance it was supposed to cover. Indeed, the very multiplicity of analytic categories by which modern movements defined themselves had become, to use Arnold Schoenberg's term, "a death-dance of principles" [p. xix].

Schorske goes on to say, "What was the historian to do in the face of this confusion? It seemed imperative to respect the historical development of each constituent branch of modern culture (social thought, literature, architecture, etc.), rather than to hide the pluralized reality behind homogenizing definitions. I therefore turned for help to my colleagues in other disciplines. Their intellectual situation, however, only compounded the problem" (p. xix–xx). What Schorske found was frustrating in the extreme. When he spoke to his colleagues (at Berkeley and elsewhere) about the fields of greatest interest to him (social thought, literature, architecture, philosophy, and music and other arts) he found that scholarship in the 1950s had turned away from history as a basis for self-understanding, and parallel with that, had moved in directions that markedly weakened their "social relatedness." In literature, the New Critics adopted an "atemporal, internalistic formal analytic" approach. In political science, the normative concerns of traditional political philosophy, with its pragmatic concerns for questions of public policy, "began to give way to ahistorical and politically neutralizing reign of the behaviorists." In economics, mathematically oriented theorists "expanded their dominion at the expense of older, socially minded institutionalists and of public policy Keynesians." In music, a "new cerebrality" had begun to erode musicology's historical concerns. And in philosophy, the traditional questions, the "old" enduring questions, were eschewed in favor of questions about the nature of language and logic, as if philosophy was to be an arm of scientific thinking. Philosophy broke ties "both to history and to the discipline's own past."

What intrigued Schorske was that in post World War II America a variety of ideas and trends that were so much a feature of end-of-the-century Vienna had suffused a number of disciplines in the American University. It was this observation that led Schorske to spend years studying that Vienna: capital of an empire that was coming apart at the seams, a turbulent decline in large part initiated in the 1848 war in which Austria was the loser; a pluralistic, conflict-ridden Vienna. Schorske felt justified in suggesting that the political and intellectual life in post World War II America reflected a "crisis of a liberal polity as a unifying context for the simultaneous transformation in the separate branches of culture. The fact that Freud and his contemporaries [not only psychoanalysts] aroused new interest in America in itself suggested Vienna as a unit of study" (p. xxv).

All of the above is stated very succinctly in Schorske's brief introductory chapter. Clearly, he saw that post World War II America was in a process of transformation.

Schorske's "problem" arose when he began to teach his course on modern European intellectual history. My "problem" arose in the 1960s when I tried to make unified sense out of the welter of seemingly discrete trends and happenings that made that decade a legend. By "make sense" I mean two things. First, I wondered, how did seemingly discrete trends, events, and happenings appear to be coalescing, and if they were, were they expressive of shared feelings and ideas, however differently verbalized? Second, could I profitably mine my own past adult life—beginning in the 1930s—to glean aspects of the sociohistorical context from which the sixties emerged? In books and articles I wrote after that decade, these two questions were implicitly in the background, sometimes explicitly in the foreground. I was always aware, however, that I was intimidated by the fear, not without basis, that much of what I observed and thought was in the realm of personal opinion, a frail reed upon which to depend for general conclusions. And, yet, the more I thought, read, and pondered, the more convinced I became that what I wanted to say needed to and should have been said. It is not that what I had to say was new—it was not—but rather that it had not been said enough, certainly not enough to counter the ahistorical stance endemic in the university, although Schorske saw that stance emerging in the 1950s, and he was not, as a decade later I was not, untroubled by what he was observing and being told by his ahistorical colleagues.

My books *Work, Aging, and Social Change* (1977) and *The Making of an American Psychologist* (1988), and my more recent book of essays, *Psychoanalysis, General Custer, and the Verdicts of History* (1994), were efforts to begin to clarify my "problem." The present book of essays is still another effort at presentation and clarification. If I am agonizingly aware that I have no corner on knowledge, truth, and wisdom, I am not at all defensive about the contents of these essays. They are honest expressions of my thinking, as they may also be a symptom of chutzpah because nothing in my formal education and training, or in the professional roles I have been in, has "credentialed" me to write about social change. This book will be published after I have become seventy seven years of age. Time is not on my side, which is to say that whatever credentials some would say I should have in order to tackle the nature of post World War II social change, I have neither the time or inclination to obtain. That in large part explains why I wrote these essays as individual pieces, each dealing with an aspect of that change. They share several common themes which, I trust, will be evident, but each essay can stand by itself.

The essays in this book were not informed by any desire to construct or test any formal theory. I am not a theoretician, by talent or by interest. I am an observer of the social scene, trying to make sense of why and how America changed in my lifetime, and by "make sense" I mean doing it in a way that will allow readers to determine whether it makes sense to them too in light of what they

have experienced and concluded; whether it helps them see relationships that they may not have thought about and that deserve
reflection; whether because of age they fell victim to ignoring that
their present contains the lineal psychological descendants of a not-
distant past that they themselves cannot understand without knowing how that past is in the present.

No reader will deny that his or her past is relevant to his or her
present "psychology." That is precisely the principle I would hope
that readers would become aware of and apply when they seek to
explain today's social scene, rather than, as too many readers will
have done, explaining it only in light of the compelling present and
the very near past. If the unexamined life is not worth living, then
leaving your society unexamined, its past ethos and vicissitudes relegated to the museum of history to which you are not inclined to go,
is doing no favor to the worth of your society. Vienna at the end of
the nineteenth century is not America at the end of the twentieth
century. But I agree completely with Schorske that the America of
today, like an earlier Vienna, has been undergoing a social transformation in a major way. One can hope that what happened in
Vienna and the rest of Europe after the turn of the century will not
happen here. As I am at pains to say in these essays, the present is
pregnant with many futures, not one. How the post World War II
social change gets played out I make no predictions about. I could,
at the point of a gun, envision a gloomy future or a more hopeful
one. Of one thing I am sure: that future will in part depend on
whether increasing numbers of people depart from the intellectually simple, ahistorical stance. That is why in several of these essays
I repeat Mencken's caveat that for every important problem there
is a simple answer that is wrong.

Acknowledgments

In the course of thinking about and writing the essays in this book,
Michael Klaber was helpful both as a dear friend and as a very astute
and idea-producing sounding board. Needless to say, it will be apparent

to the scholarly reader that much of what I have to say has been said or adumbrated in the past by others too numerous to mention. I trust that no reader will accuse me of the Henry Ford stance that history is bunk. Again needless to say, I am indebted to Lisa Pagliaro, who in small and large ways makes it impossible for me "just" to say thanks for her secretarial assistance. Even though "secretarial assistance" is factual, using the term is another instance of the factual obscuring the truth. Finally, it is with gratitude that I acknowledge Lesley Iura for her editorial suggestions.

New Haven, Conn.   Seymour B. Sarason
January 1996

The Author

．．．．．．．．．．．．．．．．．．．．．．．．．．．．．．．．

Seymour B. Sarason is professor of psychology emeritus in the Department of Psychology and at the Institute for Social and Policy Studies at Yale University. He founded, in 1962, and directed, until 1970, the Yale Psycho-Educational Clinic, one of the first research and training sites in community psychology. He received his Ph.D. degree (1942) from Clark University and holds honorary doctorates from Syracuse University, Queens College, Rhode Island College, and Lewis and Clark College. He has received an award for distinguished contributions to the public interest and several awards from the divisions of clinical and community psychology of the American Psychological Association, as well as two awards from the American Association on Mental Deficiency.

Sarason is the author of numerous books and articles. His more recent books include *The Making of an American Psychologist: An Autobiography* (1988); *The Predictable Failure of Educational Reform: Can We Change Course Before It's Too Late?* (1990); *The Challenge of Art to Psychology* (1990); *You Are Thinking of Teaching? Opportunities, Problems, Realities* (1993); *The Case for Change: Rethinking the Preparation of Educators* (1993); *Letters to a Serious Education President* (1993); *Psychoanalysis, General Custer, and the Verdicts of History and Other Essays on Psychology in the Social Scene* (1994); and *Parental Involvement and the Political Principle: Why the Existing Governance Structure of Schools Should Be Abolished* (1995). He has made contributions in such fields as mental retardation, culture and personality, projective techniques, teacher training, the school culture, and anxiety in children.

Barometers of Change

1

. . . .

Introduction

The Past in the Present

In 1988 I published my autobiography *The Making of an American Psychologist*. Although I intended it as autobiography, I knew at the outset that the last thing the reading public needed was a clinical account of the complexities of my mind, personality, sources of guilt and shame, and the like. Those complexities are the same as those of everyone else, an assumption I have never had reason to question. What I wanted to do was show how a particular psychologist who grew up in a distinctive time and era in a distinctive society came to think and act as he did. My interest was in time, place, era—that is, the externals, so to speak, that impacted on me and guaranteed that I would become an *American* and an *American* psychologist, not a British, French, or Japanese psychologist. That is not to say that an American psychologist has no intellectual-conceptual-substantive kinship to a "foreign" psychologist, but rather that being an American psychologist is a difference that makes a difference. All of us know that principle, without resort to comparison among people in different countries. If we have lived our lives in Manhattan, we have no doubt that we see ourselves and the world differently than we would if we had spent our lives in another city. We are increasingly told that if you work within the confines of the beltway, called Washington, D.C., you acquire an outlook different from the one you would acquire in Albany, Trenton, or Sacramento. When you send your child to a private rather than a public school, it is because you believe or hope that he or she will acquire an outlook that is different in important ways from the outlook he or she would acquire in the public school.

In the course of growing up, no one had to tell me that America was a large, complex country comprised of regions and groups each of which had distinctive characteristics that "somehow or other" were assimilated by those in the regions or groups. I put quotes around "somehow or other" because that is what fascinated me about myself and about others elsewhere. In cultural-crazy-quilt America, how did I come to think as I do or did? Why and in what ways have I changed? At the core of one's identity is a kernel of psychological constancy, that is, you feel you have always been the kind of person you are, that basically and privately you have always been "this way." And yet, you know that a lot about you has changed because of where you have been and moved from, the institutions of which you have been a part, the people you have known and been influenced by, and the events (local, national, and international) that have caused you to see yourself and the world differently than before. That is why the word "making" is in the title of that earlier book. My emphasis was on the aspects of American society that entered into the manufacture of me, and I gave what I hoped was enough very personal material to allow the reader to know that I knew the manufacturing process was of and about a particular human being. As I indicated to the reader of that book, I truly believe that if you know I am an American male, a New Yorker to boot, possessing a physical handicap, and Jewish, you know or can intuit a good deal about me, some of it invalid but much of it on target. In any event, given my purpose I did not feel it was necessary to spill my psychological guts. I did precisely that when I was psychoanalyzed, soon after which I realized that nothing in the analysis illuminated how being brought up in America at a certain time and era was no less impactful than the personalities of my parents, siblings, and an extended family with "only in America" characteristics. To my analyst (a superb one), my psyche—

better yet, my intrapsychic goings on—was center stage. How my psyche was impacted on by being born into, reared, and educated in America was for all explanatory purposes not on that stage.

In the course of writing that book I realized that far more important, to me at least, than how I became the psychologist I did were the ways in which America had changed in my lifetime—more important and more interesting, certainly more complex to understand. As one becomes truly, demographically old it is understandable, perhaps inevitable, to start "summing up," constructing a narrative that explains why you became what you are: the roads taken or not, the impact of diverse relationships, the mistakes you think you made, the gratification from reaching your mark or sadness that you did not, the role of luck or serendipity, and a lot more in the nature of "those are the cards I was dealt, that is the way I played them; I won some deals and I lost some deals." In my case, for the last decade or so, trying to sum up the significances of and relationships among the social changes I witnessed has been a major preoccupation. I was born at the end of World War I; I have vague memories of the twenties (the "jazz age," café, night club society); I remember the fantastic excitement when Lindbergh flew over the ocean, then the stock market crash, the Great Depression, World War II, the cold war, the Korean War, the Vietnam War, racial issues, the women's liberation movement, assassinations—need I say more? Those were not items in books. However you define real, they were real for me. But they were largely discrete events; I saw and sought no pattern. The conclusion that perhaps the world was going to hell—or perhaps flirting with that possibility—was a tempting one, but only if I was semisecure that underlying those events was a pattern in line with that conclusion.

I have no such security today. I am gun-shy of grand theories that purport to explain social change, although most of them have kernels of compelling truths, such as Marx, Spengler, and Toynbee. Reading these and other theorists I am struck by three of their characteristics. First, they seek to predict the long-term future. Second, the forces they regard as powering social change are unstoppable, permitting them to say what will inevitably be apparent in the distant future. Third, they do not end up with but rather begin with values and assumptions about what the good society should be.

The first characteristic is foolhardy. The second I regard as largely wrong because it rests on the assumption that contingency is no factor in societal affairs. These theorists never would, I assume, make that assumption about individual lives, but they do make it about a whole society—and some of them do not restrict themselves to one society but take on the whole world. It is one thing to say that the forces that power social change are unstoppable; it is quite another thing to say that how they get played out is predictable. So, for example, from our earliest national days it was made clear that America would someday have its comeuppance for legitimating slavery. How and if that bill would be paid was unpredictable; the only thing that could be said was that it would be high. Would it have been as high as it is if Lincoln had lived? Or would it have made no difference in how things got played out? One could retort by saying that the question is on all fours with the question, "What if Cleopatra had a long nose?" But if neither question is answerable, it does not invalidate the role of contingency in the direction, pace, and consequences of social change.

The third characteristic may be the most problematic of all. When you start with values, explicit or implicit, you tend to be drawn to data or examples that confirm your values and you tend to ignore or misweigh those factors that would disconfirm those values (or assumptions) or that would require you to temper your certainty about how things *will* be played out. That is a problem for every social theorist. Misreading or misweighing the strength with which different groups hold or oppose a particular value is why long-term predictions are so frequently grossly wrong. For example, I am not aware that anyone ever predicted that the end of apartheid in South Africa would come about peacefully and legally. On the contrary, it was expected to come about by a civil war or some version of a bloodbath. It has not happened that way, and the explanation is and will turn out to be complex, to indulge understatement. That the personality, status, and history of Nelson Mandela have to be part of that explanation is obvious, and the kind of contingency of which historians are quite aware. But it is equally obvious that what Mandela stands for, his values, were not alien to those of his racial constituencies or to a significant fraction of whites, among whom there undoubtedly were some, to say the least, who experienced a conflict or ambivalence about their values. And that is the point: the forecasters misread or misweighed the strength and prevalence of those values as they envisioned what would happen when push came to shove. The relation of values to action depends on many factors not the least of which is whether those values are, if only on the level of rhetoric, in the people's phenomenology. It is when the conflict of values among the players is sharp, absolute, and irreconcilable that bloodbaths and civil wars occur—witness the American Civil War, the history of Northern Ireland, and the Arab-Israeli conflicts. If the forecasters in and out of South Africa were wrong about how the seemingly irreconcilable values would get played out, it was in part (and only in part) because they underestimated the degree to which democratic values were held in the different segments of the population. That, I hasten to add, does not mean that it will continue to be played out as it so far has been. Precisely because those values are not Platonic essences uncomplicated by ambivalence due to other conflicting values, the playing out of the social drama is not something about which I, for one, am unequivocally sanguine. As a friend of mine said, "I do not believe in God but I sure as hell hope and pray that He takes good care of Mandela's health at the same time that He strikes dead any would-be assassin." Hopes expose our values, and in the case of South Africa it appears that many of its citizens had and have hopes the strength and prevalence of which were underestimated. I consider hopes one of the important barometers of the course of social change.

In any one century there is more than one watershed, a point after which a social change becomes apparent and few things remain what they had been before. World War I was such a watershed. The cream of European youth was slaughtered in great numbers, the communists in Russia seized control of the government, Germany underwent socioeconomic convulsions, the United States emerged for the first time as a superpower, and a peace treaty was signed that redrew the map of parts of Europe, Africa, the mideast, and parts of Asia. You did not have to be particularly astute to anticipate that the postwar period would be stormy.

World War I was not a "world" war the way World War II was. World War II was truly global, larger, and in the case of the United States, caused 10 percent of the population—a rather mind-boggling number—to spend time in service. Unlike World War I, the number of those who were not in service but were directly impacted by the war was enormous. Everyone agreed that the postwar society (and the rest of the world) *should* not be like the prewar one that had "caused" the Great Depression, refused to play a forceful role in foreign affairs, and mammothly misweighed or minimized or, for some people, looked favorably upon Hitler's and Mussolini's actions—that is, that they brought order out of chaos and were staunchly anti–Soviet Union, which some people said was our real enemy. But agreement that the postwar society would and should be different was on vague moral grounds, not on substantive or programmatic ones. You could say that people wanted or hoped for a different state of affairs but that their wanting and hoping lacked concreteness, let alone specificity. "We will be smarter and wiser, we will shape our future, we will not be prisoners of our past"—that encapsulates what people envisioned for postwar days. Whatever changes were necessary would be made *after* the war. Indeed, during the first two years of the war it was a waste of time to think about the country after the war because it seemed as if Hitler, Mussolini, and the Japanese militarists would be victorious. The task was to win the war, regardless of what that required of everyone. If we won, we could then think about what smarter and wiser meant in action.

What was happening during the war years? What *then* were the discrete events and trends that already were barometers of a social change the broad outlines of which could not be clear, depending as they did on how things got played out, how the different trends would coalesce to produce a general social change. Single barometers have meaning, but in terms of what we ordinarily mean by social change, that meaning is altered when the barometer is perceived as in some way related to the meaning and implications of other single barometers of a change. By "perceived" I mean that groups who heretofore saw their outlook and advocacy as peculiar to themselves now see kinship to other groups and their claims. And that coalescence also has the effect of coalescing those segments of society that oppose what they see as undesirable change. Social change is divisive. No one likes being asked, required, or forced to change what he/she considers right, natural, and proper— a fact as bedrock valid as any fact in human affairs. We are used to hearing that war is the continuation of politics by other means. Social change is a continuation of social battles and war by other means, sometimes without the weapons of "real" war and sometimes with them—for example, when President Eisenhower sent troops to protect the entry of black children into a segregated Little Rock high school, and when President Kennedy threatened Governor Wallace of Alabama with federal troops if he continued to resist school integration.

The disruption of lives of millions of *individuals*; a similar disruption in millions of *families*; racial conflicts and riots; a dramatic increase in the number of working women and their acceptance into the military; mass migrations from rural areas to urban manufacturing centers in need of workers; a dramatic increase in the diversity (religious, ethnic, socioeconomic background) of students on college campuses for special training-educational programs supported by the military; similar opportunities afforded by and within the military for work opportunities not previously available to many soldiers (this and the previous point causing these young people to change their postwar plans); the sexual frustrations (the limited outlets for sexual expression put their mark, as they always do, on servicemen as well as on their loved ones back home and, not paradoxically, on those individuals who had sexual experiences and liaisons in and around military bases in the United States and in foreign lands, with diverse consequences for their attitudes toward sexuality and for relationships back home); and finally, the fears, frustrations, and attitudinal changes (sexual and otherwise) of loved ones back home—a lot was going on in those war years that set the stage for a postwar social change the substance and pace and direction of which were hardly, if at all, sensed or discussed for the understandable reason that we were engaged in a total war; indeed, we were infinitely more clear about what social change could mean if we lost the war. For purposes of emphasis I remind the reader that for the first two years of the war it was very far from clear that the allied countries could stop the Nazi and Japanese juggernauts. It was Samuel Johnson who said that nothing focuses the mind more than the knowledge that you will be executed tomorrow. The absorbing focus on the war left no room or time to reflect on what was happening within the society. Survival and victory were the names of the game. That is what is meant when World War II is called a "popular" war, an appellation I find somewhat oxymoronic.

The above is by way of explaining why in the essays to follow the different aspects of the post World War II social change are seen primarily but not exclusively in light of what happened during the war years. I intend no simple cause-and-effect relationship and I do not suggest that what America was before the war played little role. Social change is not a process of coalescence that has anything to do with the calendar. To say that there has been a social change in the post World War II era is not to say that very crucial aspects of our history and culture have not endured. That we did not become a "born again" nation is well illustrated every day by the polemics and controversies surrounding issues of public policy, for example, abortion, sexual lifestyles and behavior, individual responsibility, federal versus state powers, gender discrimination, racial conflicts and inequities, educational policy and reform, family values, and more. If I set limits to the range of these essays, it is because I lived through the war years (and the preceding Great Depression) and was mightily affected by them although at the time I hardly sensed their potential significances. It was not until the war ended that those significances began to dawn on me. With the cessation of the war, I left a position in the nowhere of rural Connecticut for one at Yale, a move that was a direct consequence of what World War II meant and would mean for higher education, a move that requires me now to explain why education (colleges, universities, *and* the public schools) is an important theme in some of the essays.

There are many windows and sites that allow you to catch glimpses of the different aspects of social change. None rival the educational setting, at least for its post World War II social change, a fact or possibility that the social sciences scandalously ignored. That is especially true for our colleges and universities, which were transformed by the GI Bill of Rights, a piece of legislation that truly deserves the label "hallmark." "Transform" is a more apt term than "change." These educational centers grew in size of student body, faculty, budgets, special enclaves for research and professional train-ing, new fields of inquiry, and sources of funding. Those were obvi-ous changes, but the consequences of those changes transformed the culture of these sites: their attitudes, outlooks, behavioral and programmatic regularities, allegiances, personal relationships, and sense of community and institutional purpose. In an essay in a pre-vious book (Sarason, 1994), I gave an extended description of how some of these aspects were apparent at Yale, which sought neither to increase much in size nor to stray from its basic traditions. But in many other institutions, especially public universities (even new ones), all of the aspects I have mentioned were plain to see. If in the essays to follow I frequently refer to the GI Bill, it is because the transformations it brought about were not only a direct result of the war and a reflection of an altered societal zeitgeist and worldview, but also because they were barometers of what *might* be coming down the social road.

Imagine that we have found, like the Dead Sea Scrolls, an unpublished study that had carefully noted, counted, and comprehensively described during the *prewar* period the points and nature of the contacts between the university and the "outside world," such as who initiated those contacts, for what purposes, and with what consequences for the internal culture of the university, as well as other related "variables." And then further imagine that for each of the ten years *after* the war, someone had the good sense, or the beneficence of a divine scientific Providence, to do essentially the same kind of study.[1] It would be an exaggeration to say that comparing the results of the two studies would be like comparing the differences between night and day, but it would be impossible to deny that a transformation had occurred. (Perhaps not impossible. There are people who say that the Nazi Holocaust is a myth!) It was not a transformation only *within* the university but a *transactional* (bidirectional) process in which the inside and outside were changing each other. The social change had begun, and barometers of that change were registering the change in ways distinctive for institutions of higher education. We were not then wise enough to devise or heed those barometers, and even today, as those years and transactions fade from memory and are relegated to the Museum of History, our current wisdom is no basis for congratulations. There are a few exceptions, among which Robert Nisbet's *The Degradation of the Academic Dogma* (1971) is to me the most interesting and instructive.

---

[1] The study by the Lynds (1956, 1982) of "Middletown" before the Great Depression and later when it was still a social reality comes to mind. And if you read Robert Lynd's *Knowledge for What?* (1970), written before we entered the war, you may be struck, as I was, by its prodromal features in that these features became part and parcel of the postwar university-society relationship.

If in my adult life I have always been in and around the univer-sity, I have at the same time been in and around the public schools in one or another capacity. The public school has never been an institution of significant interest to the social sciences, although that kind of interest was precisely what John Dewey pleaded for in his presidential address to the American Psychological Association in 1899. Indeed, that address, apart from any other of his writings on education, foreshadows the substance, direction, and concerns that our society is only now beginning to intuit, and I say intuit because to say comprehend would be hyperbole. That its relation to the societal surround and the quantity and quality of its transac-tions have, as in the case of the university, changed dramatically in the post World War II era is a glimpse of the obvious. And that is the point: the post World War II social changes were manifest early in the public schools, especially in our cities and large metropoli-tan areas, and those manifestations had their sources in World War II. The baby boom; an increase in juvenile delinquency; racial mil-itancy and conflict before and after the 1954 desegregation deci-sion; a women's liberation movement that began to change the composition of the pool of teachers; a dramatic increase in geo-graphical mobility within our cities and to the suburbs; and early on the articulation of fear in (among others) the scientific, business, political, and military communities that our public schools could not be relied on to maintain the country's intellectual-research-sci-entific leadership in a very dangerous and unpredictable world; the rise in divorce and teenage pregnancy—all of these phenomena "showed up" in our schools, but there were no barometers to sug-gest to us that not only was a social change occurring, its conse-quences for the school by no means murky, but we also would have done well to think about what they portended and what actions we might have taken.

The more I have reflected on my prewar and postwar years, and as I have read the history of other social changes in earlier times and in other countries, the more convinced I am of a conclusion that I regard as having the status of a law: social change, the coalescence of seemingly discrete, relatively circumscribed changes, is only recognized after that coalescence hits us, so to speak, in the face, that is, after it has a direction and force that pervades the society. Whether it can be otherwise I have my doubts. That we might be able to devise barometers that would allow us to recognize social change in its early phases is potentially and theoretically possible. But that possibility is reduced to nil as long as we regard schools (and universities) in terms of the usual imagery that gets conjured up when we say they are educational institutions, imagery that almost totally prevents the recognition that they are cultures within a local, state, and national culture. As long as we think about schools in terms of classrooms, teachers, principal, curriculum, specialized personnel, and test scores, we are blind to or downplay some other obvious and no less significant features: each school contains at least three generations of people, while a school system contains more than three generations; a school is embedded in a bureaucratic and corporatelike structure and ethos; a school system is in fact the creation and responsibility of local and state bureaucratic-political structures that have their own distinctive features. Like the university, in the post World War II years all of these structures have bidirectional connections with the federal government and all that implies; they also, again like the university, have become plaintiffs or defendants in our judicial system; they are interconnected with colleges and universities in myriads of ways. And all of this in a society like no other on this earth, a society which in its comparatively short history has one feature, I would say a unique one, that is hard to deny—really, impossible to deny: America has always been changing at a rate unequaled in human history, or at least in the history of the Western world. *The importance of that point cannot be overestimated, because given how schools are cultures within cultures, systems within systems, institutions in a box in a very complicated flowchart of institutions, it has to be the case that they are unexcelled barometers, very early barometers, revealing barometers of social change.* That is why I began my list of features with the "generations" factor, because when that factor is seen in light of other features on the list, the number of generations, each of whom experienced an America different in ways from that of other generations, increases.

My experience in and around public schools began before the post World War II social change was seen as a social change. When I reflect on those early experiences I cringe, I start outlining a course on Humbleness 101, because *now* it is obvious to me that the earliest outcroppings of the social change were plain to see in the schools but I had no barometers to call my attention to what those outcroppings *might* mean or what their underlying relationships *might* be.

I have in previous books written about the public schools largely from the stance of how they do or do not change, and how they should change. Nothing in what I have said here is for the purpose of convincing the reader that how our schools should change should be given more attention than it currently receives. The schools are getting a lot of attention in that regard, although I have made it clear (Sarason, 1990) that our efforts are not likely to succeed, and why I have been driven (internally kicking and screaming) to conclude that our current efforts will at best have minimal, positive consequences and will at worst see the dismantling of the public school system as we have known it. (Some would rejoice at that dismantling, but without exception they would confirm Mencken's priceless observation that for every important problem there is a simple explanation that is wrong.) Nothing in what I have said here has any *direct* bearing on social change. My purpose rather has been to suggest that if you want to understand the post World War II social change, and if you want to understand where that change *might* be taking us (the italics are to emphasize contingency), then you can do no better than begin to ponder how to devise and develop barometers of social change in schools.

There is a thriving industry of economists, statisticians, and kindred souls whose sole aim is to develop barometers of economic change and to correlate those barometers with each other. These barometers are almost always based on impersonal data, with the implicit assumption that they reflect activities and behaviors of people that have an "average" psychological meaning. On Wall Street, with the creation of the market for derivatives, they have devised barometers that border on the bizarre and even to sophisticated traders are semi-intelligible. The point is that there are many arenas for which people spend their careers devising barometers of change. Some of these barometers have to do with social change— the Federal Census, for example—but few have seen fit to devise barometers of social change for schools, colleges, and universities. I emphasize this omission because my experience in and around these sites over the past half century has forced me to say that these institutions may well be the best early detectors of social change. But as long as the social sciences devalue these sites as laboratories for their theories and research, that potential can neither be tested nor exploited.

We should of course be anxious about the inadequacies of our schools as they are judged by conventional criteria for student performance. There are many reasons why I have since 1965, both orally and in print, predicted with 100 percent accuracy the decline in student performance. What I did not see clearly in 1965, what it took me a long time to see, is that the decline was, to an undetermined extent, both cause and effect of the social change. There used to be a time when it was argued that schools should be agencies for social change, that is, not preservers of the status quo. The advocates of such agency, however persuasive and certainly well-intentioned, met with no success. What they never considered was the possibility that just as social change is something you can count on, schools inevitably play a cause and effect role in that social change, which is not to say that the consequences of that role have been and will be those the advocates would approve, but that is another story.

Only a few essays in this book directly or indirectly involve our educational institutions, because one of my purposes was to try to identify some of the discrete changes each of which we today know were harbingers of what may be coming down the social road. My other major purpose was to try to understand why and how these discrete changes coalesced as they did to allow us to say that there has been a momentous post World War II social change. This I could not do without speculation, conjecture, and taking the risk of assuming that although I lived through it all my interpretations are not far off the mark.

If there is any central "actor" in the stories the different essays tell, it is World War II and the years immediately following. That presents a problem to the younger reader, who may have been born after that period. Beginning in the early sixties, I was made aware that when I referred to *the* war I had to make sure that I told my students that I was not referring to the Korean War. For the students, World War II was already in the history books and was in no discernible way in their present. They had no trouble whatsoever agreeing that their childhood experiences and familial relationships were in one way or another "in" their psychological memory and makeup. But that their social world was uninterpretable apart from World War II presented problems to them. Few of them had had the need and desire—and of course the modal history course was no spur—to read about those war years—the kind of need, desire, and curiosity that makes possible the forging of connections between past and present, connections that give meaning to the overworked metaphor of the seamless web. To Armenians, the Turkish slaughter of their population decades ago is part of their ethnic identity; it is not a footnote in history. To a fair number of Americans, both black and white, the Civil War is not over—witness the recent controversy in Georgia about displaying the Confederate flag. And of course to Americans generally, among both young and old the Vietnam War is still in the living present. And to Jews generally the Nazi Holocaust is associated with the importuning "Never again. We will not forget." In each of these examples, history is a conscious variable because each of these groups "lost." We didn't lose World War II. We were victorious. What is there to remember and why? To that question I have devoted these essays, knowing full well that I have limitations of knowledge and of conceptual scope. I am no theorist. I have tried to make sense of a life during which, depending on your point of view, I had the fortune or misfortune to live. I am quite aware that despite agonizing awareness of my limitations— and that is an expression of realistic modesty—I am the kind of person who *must* try to make sense of my past and present worlds. Obsessive-compulsiveness is not, for me at least, without interesting virtues.

2

. . . .

The Coalescing of Discrete Trends

The perception of social change, or the conclusion that you may be noting a social change, always involves a relationship among more than one event or happening. You do not perceive event X and conclude that it is a barometer of social change. Instead, when event X causes you to see it as possibly related to events Y and Z, you may conclude that something has happened, or has already begun to happen, that signals an ongoing social change. That conclusion may be justified or not, but it is always a deduction from more than one event. I say deduction or conclusion because the different events, singly or together, in no way contain the conclusion. Indeed, the words "deduction" and "conclusion" may be inappropriate because they suggest an orderly, rational thinking process whereas, I think, it is an intuitive one; it "occurs" to you, "pops into your head," so to speak, usually accompanied by a feeling of surprise, following which what might be called a cognitive process takes over, a process of questioning, a mulling over, a seeking for the covert significances of the describable events. This is a variant of the "appearance and reality" dichotomy. The different events appear to be unrelated, but your conclusion indicates that there is a "reality" undergirding these events that suggests they are of a piece. Your conclusion may say what that piece is, but far more often than not it will be an example of Mencken's caveat that for every complex problem there is a simple answer that is wrong.

In any event, to conclude that possibly you have perceived a barometer of a social change is to say that among an undetermined but growing number of people there has been a change in attitude, values, and outlooks, a change in the perception of what in the past had been considered right, natural, and proper, that is, conventional. What is distinctive is the sense—and it is usually no more than a sense, a conjecture, a vague feeling—that the social barometer is dynamic, not static, that it is pointing to an ongoing change the course and strength of which are not predictable.

It is frequently the case that you come to a second conclusion: you do not like or approve of what the change signifies now and portends for the future. Implicit in that conclusion is that those you perceive as illustrative of that change approve of the change. There is or will be conflict about and polarization around what is desirable for the welfare of the individual *and* of the society. The perception of social change is always about both individuals and the collectivity. The diagnosis of a social change is not, like a clinical diagnosis, only about individuals, which is why the process of social change is inevitably stormy and upsetting. What is at stake are opposing answers to the question: what kind of a society do we want to have?[1]

Back in the late fifties and early sixties parents began to be confronted with this situation: their son or daughter was coming home from college over a holiday, accompanied by an opposite-sex partner and telling his or her parents that the two would be sleeping together. Some parents had heard "stories" like that, but most had not. The parental reaction was strong, to indulge understatement. What was going on in the college dorms? Who was supervising these

---

[1]The reader has probably heard the joke about the man who decides to see a therapist and spends the first forty-five minutes describing his major problems and his understanding of them, following which the heretofore silent therapist says, "Those are not your problems. Your real problem is you hate your mother." As is the case with satire, the joke contains the kernels of two truths. The first is that we seek to relate and explain disparate phenomena by nonobservable processes. The second, of course, is that Mencken's caveat is confirmed. I shall have more to say about a particular type of clinical diagnosis in later pages.

dorms? Were the college authorities unaware, or were they con-
doning it by ignoring it? Could it be that "my" child is also into
drugs as some of the mass media had begun to report? Were college
campuses satellites of San Francisco's Haight-Ashbury version of
Babylon? These and other questions plagued parents. What initially
was perceived by them as a change in their child became a barometer of a change involving other people's children as well. They and
their children saw the world very differently. And they could not
see how they could reconcile the two contrasting views of what was
right, natural, and proper, that is, how life should be lived. And not
infrequently they blamed themselves for having been blind to an
ongoing social change that most of them considered catastrophic
for the society.

   This scenario is an example of arriving at a conclusion about
social change that was disconcerting to many parents. But what
about changes they favored? I refer to the rise of black assertiveness
and militancy against discrimination and oppression. Most of these
parents, as well as people in general, were politically liberal, even
leftist, and as a matter of principle were opposed to discrimination
and segregation in all of its manifestations. A just society should and
would redress these grievances, which is why the 1954 school desegregation decision was greeted with joy and relief. But that was a judicial decision involving defendants and plaintiffs acting in accord
with agreed-upon legal processes. How did most of these people react
when diverse groups, black and white, carried out demonstrations,
challenged existing practices, flouted police tactics, and more? In the
main they were supportive. They were also surprised because they
had been unaware of the degree of assertiveness and militancy that
had developed in these groups, that is, a readiness and willingness to
take bold actions. They were also surprised at the strength of the
reaction of those opposed to the court's decision, that is, the actions
these people were ready to take, and did take, to circumvent the
decision. The sources of their surprise forced on them the conclusion that a social change was occurring, that it would not be a

peaceful affair, that the proponents for militancy, mostly young people, included more than blacks, and that the sites where the change
would be manifested varied considerably, from churches to schools
to workplaces to recreation and sports facilities to housing. If it was
a conclusion derived from what they saw, read, and heard, they
inchoately sensed that this was no passing phenomenon.

I have used these two examples as very condensed illustrations
of how at a particular time the perception of apparently disparate
social phenomena caused many people to conclude that a social
change was taking place. What did these people mean by social
change? What were the referents for those words? I ask these questions because in my experience conclusions about a social change
usually pay far more attention to its explicit or observable features
than to its implicit ones and it is the implicit that gives direction
to the change's future course and permits one to see connections
that, when made, illuminate what that future course might be. The
explicit features are what you see people doing and saying that you
regard, positively or negatively, as a break with the past. The implicit features are the attitudes, feelings, and values behind or underneath the observable actions. A conclusion about social change
always says something about its implicit features. So, in my first
example the parental response to the sexual activity of their son or
daughter could be summed up in these ways: This is not the child I
sent off to college. Where did my child get these ideas? What made
my child think we would approve? What is going on in my child's
mind? What are we dealing with? When parents learned from
friends that they too were confronting the same problem, it led to
the conclusion that some kind of social change was occurring, but
it clarified little about the young people's phenomenology. Even
when parents became aware, as they quickly did, that the change
in attitude toward sexual activity was only one of several barometers of a social change in the outlook of young people, parents
remained puzzled and uncomprehending. This was to be called the
generation gap.

Why were parents so puzzled and resistant? Explanations have focused on their resistance: no one warmly embraces a change that is a clear break with his or her past. Why then did young people very warmly embrace change that represented a break with their pasts? Not only warmly embraced it, but fought for its triumph. That was what was surprising to parents, which is why they plagued themselves with the question: why were we so unaware of what young people had been hearing, thinking, feeling, interpreting? As one parent said at the time, "We not only missed the boat, but we did not know there was a boat that was sailing." That is a revealing remark in two respects. First, it acknowledges that the social change they had perceived had begun prior to their recognition of the change. Second, it assumes that if the change had been recognized earlier, it could have been blunted or diluted in strength, or even nipped in the bud. The first point is clearly valid. The second is very problematic and probably in large part invalid. Let me explain by personal example.

I lived through the Great Depression and my college years were in that period. Why was the disaster such a surprise? What were the barometers of the change to come to which experts and nonexperts alike had been insensitive? These were the questions asked in courses in economics, history, and politics. Immersed as I was in radical politics, I of course had a ready answer: the self-defeating dynamics of capitalism. Depression, small or great, was a built-in feature of capitalism. To someone like me who was trying to make sense of what I was experiencing and who wanted to prevent future disasters, the Marxist explanation provided answers. In my courses I got other answers: the excesses of frenzied speculation in real estate and the stock market, the plummeting health of the agricultural economy, tariff walls that disrupted international trade, failure to pay attention to the iron laws of supply and demand, and an unwarranted belief that the country was on an upwards and onwards course to utopia. In brief, with the benefit of hindsight it was clear that there had been barometers of social change but they were either ignored or misread, or the connections among them were never discerned.

These barometers and the Marxist answers had several common features. The first was that the Great Depression could not have been anticipated by only one barometer of change or by a handful of barometers. The second was that the different barometers gave different readings or data about different groups in different arenas or sites. What relationship could have been discerned between what was happening on farms and what was happening on Wall Street? The third feature was that each barometer said something about the psychological outlook of those about whom the barometer was constructed even though that barometer did not give psychological readings. For example, the agricultural barometer *implied* much about the psychological outlooks of farmers but said nothing directly about those outlooks. Similarly, the statistical barometers for Wall Street implied a lot about psychological outlooks but said nothing directly about them.

The explanations rested on one fact and one assumption: the fact was, we had not had a large number of high-quality barometers of change, and the assumption was that if we had had such barometers, society would have been alerted to the looming disaster. The fact is valid; the experts were asleep at the switch. The assumption is far more problematic, because it is undergirded by the belief that connections among barometers are knowable even though the barometers are suggesting ongoing changes that vary markedly in appearance, strength, and familiarity. By familiarity I mean that *what is familiar after the social change has taken place (in its early or later phases) may not have been familiar while the changes were occurring.* Far from being familiar, some barometers may be uncovered only by hindsight. But the implications of the assumption are problematic for still another reason. Let us assume we can get agreement and make the compelling case that we know all of the barometers (and their connections) that could have told us that the Great Depression was likely. (Sixty five years after the catastrophe such agreement is still not possible, not among economists, political scientists, and others.) It does not follow that those barometers, at least some of them, are valid for similar purposes in the succeeding era, *precisely because the social change literally changed the social ball game and changed it in ways that make some barometers misleading for the succeeding era.* What is perversely fascinating about social change is that we are always playing catch-up ball, that is, using what we think we have learned from the past to understand the present, which the past has shaped in ways to which our barometers are insensitive. We are then surprised when we are jolted into the awareness that our accustomed ways of seeing our world did not prepare us for changes we *now* are glimpsing. It is not that we are dense, unperceptive, or stupid, but rather that the barometers (again, some of them) we have learned to employ have prevented us from seeing what is *now* obvious to us: a change was occurring and we did not recognize it.

Let us go back to the Marxists and the Great Depression. The Marxists had long predicted that the inner social class and the economic contradictions of capitalism would cause its demise. For them the Great Depression, which became international in scope, was the initial death rattle; the death of capitalism was in no distant future. Crucial to their argument was not only that the economic system was collapsing, indeed had collapsed, but that the collapse had already produced and would continue to produce a change in the psychological readiness of people to scrap the system. They could and did point to various events as barometers of a new awareness in people of their need for revolutionary action. They correlated the economic and political barometers of collapse with reports of the actions of individuals and groups who were clamoring for change, a prelude to the storming of the barricades. They considered these actions as barometers of a new way of thinking.

Why were they so wrong? Why did they so egregiously misread the significances of those psychological barometers? The short answer is that they were ideologues who saw what they wanted to see and were rendered incapable of interpreting the psychological changes as other than signs or seeds of revolutionary action. The fact is that many people who clearly were not Marxists looked at the economic and psychological barometers and were as egregiously wrong as the Marxists. I refer to those who viewed the beginning of the catastrophe as a temporary phenomenon, a glitch in the system, that would right itself and there would be a return to past ways of thinking. There were others who sensed—and in the earliest phases of the Great Depression it was only a "sense"—that a change in attitude and mood had already taken place. That change can be wrapped up in two statements: first, the federal government should no longer, as it traditionally did in the past, be a relatively indifferent and passive observer of the plight of its citizens when that plight is not of their making. And second, never again should this be allowed to happen. In light of the history of a country that had witnessed other depressions, albeit less severe but nevertheless severe, those were revolutionary statements, although not in the Marxist sense but in the sense that they called for an alteration in the obligations of government to its citizens. Even so, the strength and direction of that change were poorly grasped in the first half of the Great Depression. It became crystal clear when the Social Security Act came before Congress and met strong opposition from those who, although they read the barometers in much the same way as the act's proponents, saw the act as undercutting and vitiating the American tradition of individualism and individual responsibility. The act passed the senate by one vote.

I have used two examples and the case of the Great Depression to make several points. First, we become aware of a social change after it has begun. Second, that delay is in large part due to the fact that unlike conventional barometers of observables (such as unemployment, crime, divorce, and drop-out rates), barometers for changes in thinking, values, and outlook are in principle and method untrustworthy. Third, *whatever we or history regard as a social change represents a coalescence of different social phenomena reflected in different barometers, and it is that coalescence from which the social change gains a force, a percolating force, that cannot be extinguished, that leaves its stamp on the society.* That does not mean that its strength and direction cannot be altered in any way, but rather that the society will never "go back" to the way things were.

This last point is one of the reasons I used the two examples at the beginning of this essay. In the late fifties and early sixties, parents and other adults had become aware that young people had unconventional views of sexual relationships, and that the black community—largely but not exclusively its young—was no longer passively and peacefully accepting its "accustomed" role. On the surface the two changes had no relationship to each other. What did the fight against racial discrimination have to do with the sexual activity of young white people? The answer is, nothing, but only if you stick to barometers of the observables: more and more young people were departing from convention, and more and more blacks were demonstrating with an unfamiliar militancy. Each barometer was literally a counting or measuring rod, and they were counting very different occurrences. But if you had had a barometer that told you what these two groups were thinking and feeling, you might have discerned that they had in common the desire to feel and be free, to be unconstrained by conventional criteria of what was right, natural, and proper. Each group in its own way was rejecting those criteria. They had common cause. I am in no way suggesting that they became allies in any formal sense of the word. Neither group had the formal properties of a group; each contained a wide diversity of people, an array of subgroups, a crazy quilt of individuals. But they were living at the same time in the same society, in which messages of freedom were beginning to be heard from, for example, the women's liberation and civil rights movements. I am talking of the late fifties and early sixties. We are used to hearing that the fifties were "silent." That is true only if you mean that older generations were vastly underestimating, indeed were virtually ignorant of, what younger people were hearing, thinking, and feeling. What was happening at Columbia and Berkeley went unnoticed; cadres at each of these urban campuses already were well known to each other. It was in those years when the different agendas of different individuals and small groups began to overlap, that heterogeneity in outlook began to be replaced by "common cause." The effect was multiplicative, not additive.

The concept of social change means nothing if it does not refer to a changing outlook that has percolated into and been absorbed by many individuals and groups. That is why devising and interpreting barometers of social change is such a problematic process even when the social change has been perceived. Why does the accuracy of weather forecasts get increasingly unreliable when predictions are made for two or more days after tomorrow, even though over the decades meteorologists have increased and refined their different indices of atmospheric change, a refinement based on the most detailed analyses of past sources of unreliability? Like those who seek to understand and predict social change, meteorologists have a long history of being surprised by what they did or did not predict in the past. The answer meteorologists give to the question is that what we call weather is comprised of so many different factors or variables—energy, altitude, direction, pressure, and God knows what—that it would require hundreds, perhaps thousands, of the most avant-garde computers to make sense of the connections among factors, both known and as yet unknown. So, for example, they know that beginning in midsummer, hurricanes will start forming in the Caribbean. On what day conditions will give rise to the earliest seeds of a hurricane; when, if, and where the seeds will become a tropical storm; whether and when the storm will become a hurricane; what its speed and direction will be; and so on and so forth—the only thing meteorologists know with anything resembling "accuracy" is that hurricanes will originate in the Caribbean in the summer.

The analogy breaks down in one respect: a hurricane is a visible, concrete phenomenon that recurs. If you have seen one you have seen them all may not be strictly true, but you get the point. Social change X in one era is not like social change Y in another;

one is quite different from the other in substance, direction, and consequences, and the origins of each also differ. A hurricane during the years of the Great Depression cannot be implicated in a hurricane that occurred in the sixties. But the social changes ushered in by the Great Depression were very much implicated in the social changes of the late fifties and beyond. And those changes played a role in shaping the social changes brought about by our entry into World War II.

In regard to explaining the sixties, science–technology pales in comparison to the role of an ecological variable that was sudden in time and revolutionary in its immediate and long-term consequences: our entry into World War II. The words "World War II" have no specific, concrete, psychological referents. They are words we use to signify the coalescence of a mass of events and processes, a coalescence that separates present from past and that has predictable and unpredictable, nonreversible consequences for everyone and everything. It signifies cataclysm and catastrophe. If it is not in any conventional linguistic or psychological sense a psychological variable, its impact on psyches cannot be overestimated. If it impacts differentially on individual psyches, it is also the case that individuals cannot or do not grasp the dimensions and consequences of the cataclysm (that is, unseeable dimensions and consequences that will be no less salient or that will become salient for their lives). Ecological variables are not *seeable*; they have to be conceptualized, imagined. They are not things or people. They are, initially at least, a cloud chamber of correlated and uncorrelated, impersonal goings on.

It is fair to say that on Sunday, December 7, 1941, every adult American, regardless of individual differences, was asking four questions: How did this come about? What does it mean? What does it portend? How should I think about it? If you had asked individuals what they meant by "it," they would have been unable to answer the question because "it" is a word intended to have a concrete referent, an impersonal referent, and in that sense each person knew that

World War II was not an "it." We are not schooled to think about
an "it" we cannot see except by giving it meaning in terms of our
individual lives, which thereby hugely constricts our understanding
of the dimensions and consequences of the "it." It is an understandable form of trivialization, excusable in individuals but not in those
who seek to understand how the "out theres" of people influence
their "in heres," how ecological variables influence psyches—silently,
subtly, inevitably—independent of individual differences.

Let me start with the predictable consequences of World War II.
The most obvious is that millions of people would no longer be
doing what they had been doing or had hoped to do. In a population
of somewhat more than 150 million people, 15 million became part
of the armed services. It is not playing loose with words or concepts
to say that that number represented a form of mammoth, unsought
emigration. You do not have to be a psychologist to say that such a
disruption in lives would have consequences not only for those who
entered military service but for those they left behind (such as parents, wives, lovers, children, and friends). For each person World
War II was personalized in a circumscribed way. Practically no one
saw "it" as having differential effects on identifiable *groups* in the
society (such as blacks, women, diverse professional groups, and
those living in rural areas). No one said about these identifiable
groups, "People in these groups will change in ways that will alter
their view of themselves in relation to the larger society, alterations
that are both predictable and unpredictable, intended and unintended. These alterations will be inevitable and irreversible. Their
dynamics, course, and pace will not be visible initially, but at some
point they will be, and in ways that will be psychologically salient
for everyone. We will not understand any of this by looking at individuals unless we look at them from the standpoint of the place their
group has in the larger society. If the impact on these groups will be
discernibly and markedly different, it is highly likely that those differences will have similar consequences for the larger society."

It is far beyond my purposes here to describe the differential impacts of World War II on major societal groups. Scores of books have been written about how that war affected women, racial-ethnic minorities, professions, and those in the military. It is my purpose to suggest that, however different the impact, in each group it engendered some common "themes." A better way to put it is to say that in each group an altered world view was emerging, inchoate and hardly articulated, and reflecting new axioms about what life is and should be. That these themes were embedded in what on the surface were very different phenomenologies made them difficult to be discerned from the standpoint of psychologies in which ecological variables have no formal role and a concept like worldview has no standing. There were several such themes.

1.   This is a stupid, immoral world in which the individual is akin to a snowflake in a storm. If this is the way things have been, then things have to change. This is the "never again" theme, a rejection of old rhetoric and stances, a willing, indeed eager, embracing of "fundamental" change. This has to be seen in relation to an ecological variable preceding World War II: the Great Depression.

2.   What we want and expect out of life we want *now*, not in a distant future. Life is short and unpredictable. My late travel agent's logo was: See the world before you leave it. This theme is: Experience the world—the quicker the better—before you leave it. Time perspectives were changing. Delayed gratification of desires, goals, and status was not congenial to this changing time perspective.

3.   "We" deserve, need, and expect a new lease on life, an expanded lease, a lease that is not a gift but a right. We (especially the military and blacks) have paid our dues and we expect something in return. And for those (such as women) to whom the war had given a new lease, not only was that lease renewable, but it would have to be expanded. This is the "expectation" or "rights" theme.

4.   This theme is a composite of interrelated themes: I want to go home again. I should want to go home again. I do not want to go home again. You can't go home again. Many who were adults during the war years had read Thomas Wolfe's novels and identified

with his ever-present central character's longings, loneliness, and search for intimacy. What the war years did was enormously exacerbate the saliency of his portraits in that the need for intimacy, the need to break out from the prison of unwanted privacy, *and the willingness to do so* took on a force that heretofore it had lacked. The search for meaning was the search for intimacy, and if that search required unconventional actions, so be it.

5.   We are morally obliged to prevent our children from experiencing what we have experienced and continue to experience. They must not be what we are. They deserve a new world, not our old one. They must not live slotted, pigeonholed, frustrated lives. Our world was a screwed-up, unhappy one and that should not be their world. This is the "pursuit of happiness and fulfillment" theme for the coming generations.

I have labeled these ideas "themes," but that implies a degree of clarity and articulation I do not intend. They were stirrings in what may be called a readiness to depart from the past. If you peruse the social science literature about the war years, including clinical psychological–psychiatric journals, these stirrings are hardly noted. What you get are descriptions and explanations of disruptions in lives in terms of extant theories of individual development and adaptation. You learn a great deal about individual differences, how differences in pasts produced differences in presents. But you find little about these stirrings, all of which were concerned with the *future*, and for two reasons. First, as I have said, these stirrings were inchoate. Second, our psychologies in no way sensitized us to these stirrings that were reflective of changes in worldview far more than they were reflective of what we ordinarily mean by personality dynamics. The barometers of individual change are not those of changes in worldview.

In stating these themes I in no way intend to make value judgments. Nor do I mean to suggest that they inevitably led to the sixties. What I do suggest is that in different groups with very different phenomenologies and pasts, these stirrings were in the air, so to

speak. That these stirrings had and would have *individual* consequences is a given. Whether the stirrings in these groups would
have a *societal* impact would depend on whether postwar events
would serve to coalesce the stirrings in the different groups. The
present is not pregnant with *a* future, it is pregnant with many
futures. And that is what I am saying about the stirrings aroused by
World War II.

When in the late fifties and early sixties adults became aware of
a change in the sexual activities of young people and in the growing militancy of the black community, they could not and did not
relate those changes to the consequences of World War II. They
were not alone; generally speaking, social scientists did not make
the connection. Like the so-called lay citizen, the social scientists
were no less surprised by what was beginning to happen; they were
no less ahistorical, even though one of the most indisputable conclusions derived from human history is that a war in which most or
all of a society are directly or indirectly involved will forever change
that society both in direct and subtle ways. The subtle ways are akin
to the "timed-release" features of many medications, that is, their
effects are slow and cumulative and are intended to abort or stop a
disease process. The timed-release features of wars are not stoppable.

What I have been saying will be reacted to by some people as
unjustifiably fatalistic. Others may read into it that mine is an
antichange, status quo position. Some may see both. I must remind
such critics that the recognition that a social change is occurring is
the recognition that there are opponents and proponents of that
change, which gives added force to what is happening. It is a time
when positions are sharply drawn, there are no shades of gray, and,
crucially, the controversy-conflict becomes more widespread as the
self-interests of diverse groups cause them to take sides. Social
change, once it is sensed, recognized, articulated, and labeled, is no
local affair; it is a systemic one. It is not a fad or fashion that will
soon be replaced by new ones. It is a passionate affair because both
opponents and proponents believe that what is at stake is what is

right, natural, and proper for them as individuals and for the future of the society. And all of this takes place *after* the seeds of social change have begun to sprout. But there is another feature that adds fuel to the fire: there are always people, including public figures, who by background and tradition should be expected to be opponents, but instead, surprisingly, they support the proponents, lending the proponents a legitimacy they did not expect. To say that social change is unstoppable is not to say it cannot be influenced in any way. But to say that it can be influenced does not in any way mean that the social clock can be reset. One way or another, society will reflect features of that change.

The fact is that the examples I have used all contained features on which I looked favorably, albeit in varying degrees. And that is the point: it was hard for me to view any of the changes as unalloyed blessings, as having only intended consequences, as if the law of un-intended consequences had been repealed. The origins of my skep-ticism—of my inability to be a true believer—go back to my youth when I was willingly indoctrinated into the necessity and glories of the Russian revolution. To put it very briefly, the Lenin-Trotsky–led revolution capitalized (obviously no pun intended) on a long-brew-ing series of social changes that were manifested in different ways in different groups, changes that were vastly underestimated by their opponents, who took steps that not only exacerbated those differ-ential effects but also began to coalesce the different proponents of change. The revolution was justified, morally and politically, as the only way Russia could become a socially just society. (That is pre-cisely the guts of the argument the Chinese Communists used to jus-tify their seizing power.) My teachers of radical politics told me that the revolution was on the way to accomplish some of its intended purposes. The problem was, they said, that someone as evil as Stalin had become Lenin's successor. That was an unintended consequence. If Trotsky had been his successor, the revolution would have had no or few unintended catastrophic consequences. The revolution was a glorious culmination of ongoing social changes. Stalin was an aber-ration. That was not supposed to happen. It was as simple as that!

Trotskyists and Stalinists were deadly enemies. (Stalin arranged to have Trotsky murdered in Mexico.) But they had one thing in common: they were true believers in that they could not seriously entertain the possibility that something as complicated as a revolution would have any significant unintended consequences. They literally believed they could control events and their effects, that they could "read" the moods and predispositions of the people. I did not remain a true believer for very long.

Let us take a more recent example the substance and consequences of which we are still confronting. I refer to the 1954 school desegregation decision. It has been said that the Supreme Court reads the newspapers, that is, there are times that their decisions have been influenced, in part at least, by their perception of a social change. That is why such an effort was made within the court to make the decision unanimous. They knew well that a social change was taking place about racial discrimination. A split or close decision would be grist for the mill of those wanting no change, and it would undercut the moral and political position of proponents of change. What they sought was a decision that in the most clear way would give voice and support to an ongoing social change that at the time was discernible but by no means had the characteristics of a movement. It was a legal decision but also a moral-political-social one.

I, like many people, greeted the decision with joy. But unlike most other proponents my joy was tempered by foreboding. By what way of thinking could one expect the decision to have only desirable consequences? Or expect the intended desirable consequences to be achieved without serious unintended consequences beyond the doors of the school? Could the intended consequences be carried out in the spirit of the court's words "with due deliberate speed" without serious conflicts that would have unpredictable unintended effects? Had the court opened up a Pandora's box the contents of which the court would not have to deal with, that is, they would become the responsibility of other authorities?

I use the word foreboding advisedly. I was no seer. My crystal ball was cloudy. I just could not see how the intended change would not spill over into other social arenas in ways that I for one might not like. My foreboding was mightily reinforced by proponents who reacted to me with impatience and even disdain, viewing me as a congenital pessimist whose liberalism was skin deep and who was reacting to the political excesses of his youth. As one friend said to me, "In your Trotskyist days you heard the party's leaders say that you cannot make an omelette without cracking a few eggs, and you cannot carry out a revolution without cracking a few heads." What bothered me was not cracking a few heads but the possibility of spoiling the whole meal. Foreboding is an uneasy, plaguing, disquieting feeling about an unknowable future. I had that feeling in spades. What I lacked was any barometer of what was brewing outside of the educational arena, such as among blacks, women, and young people, and in an escalating rate of juvenile crime and the beginnings of a "drug culture." Yes, I expected that the polarizations the 1954 decision caused would be severe, that they would be so in both the north and the south, that traditional housing patterns would be challenged, that the inadequacies of our schools would become more apparent, that busing would become part of the problem and not of the solution, that politics as usual would become somewhat less usual. But I had no basis for entertaining the *possibility* that what would happen in and around our schools would get connected in any way with what was beginning to happen elsewhere in the society. It was a time of beginnings and I and almost everyone else "over thirty" were insensitive to them. But in a few short years these beginnings coalesced into a movement comprised of groups with different agendas but perceiving a basis for kinship and mutual support.

We like to believe that we understand the times we live in, which is to say we are fairly secure that we know what those times are and what they portend. It is more correct to say that we *want* to believe it in regard to individual and collective living. I would argue that we *have* to believe it if only because we cannot escape being aware that inevitably we are reacting to, analyzing, and judging our times and their implications for the future. We do not and cannot live each day at a time. What we do and think today assumes a tomorrow. We do not read the daily newspaper or listen to the news only to find out what has happened. We want to know, and we make judgments about, the implications of those happenings for our futures. And we do this unaware that we each have our own barometers of what signifies social change. There are, of course, those whose stock-in-trade is to devise means or barometers of quantity and quality so as to alert the rest of us to what we ordinarily do not attend to. The thrust of this essay has been that, devised by expert or not, the barometers of social change do not get meaningfully devised or start to register until after the social change is already under way. I do not find that dishearteningly fatalistic but rather a characteristic of social living. And it is not fatalistic because we are never indifferent to social change; we make judgments about it, be they to oppose or support the change. We are surprised, we may be angry, we may be enthusiastic, we may be puzzled, but we are never neutral. What we should guard ourselves against is a stance that uncritically assumes that the barometers we are using are obviously validly connected so as to give us a picture of the dimensions of the change. And finally, we should be aware that whether we are for or against a change, it has unintended consequences that are no more predictable than were the seeds of the change. Problem creation through problem solution is as true in social living as it is in science. The more you know, the more you have to know. Passion for or against a social change is understandable. It is also a trap.

Social change is one of those things that you inevitably confront (like death or taxes); you may support or oppose it, but with, one would hope, respect for the fact that history is the supreme court of social change, a court that not infrequently changes its mind and judgments.

3

· ·

The Individual and
the Theme of Liberation

Unlike "rock," "pencil," or "chair" the words "social change" do not have a concrete referent. Social change is not a thing or event but rather a way of noting that there has been a "before and after" alteration in the attitudes and behavior of many people in seemingly discrete areas of social relationships. What initially appears to be discrete, over time and sometimes quickly comes to be seen as related, and it is then that the concept of social change is applied, that is, after the social change has already begun. That belated diagnosis is the spur to seek commonalities in theme among what had been regarded as discrete, nonpercolating changes, and it also heightens awareness that more general change has divided the citizenry into proponents and opponents. Social change is not like an earthquake that happens suddenly and surprises everyone. Seismologists endeavor to develop barometers of future geologic convulsions, knowing that such convulsions *will* occur and that having early warning signals could dilute some of the catastrophic consequences. Following an earthquake, seismologists reassess their barometers to determine which were misleading or wrongly weighted, or to determine what new barometers or theories need to be developed.

Social changes have their opponents and proponents, the former viewing them in negative terms and the latter in positive terms. Both may use the same, if not identical, barometers as indicators of the social change, but their historical explanations may be quite different. The point that deserves emphasis is that before opponents and proponents become aware that a more general change has started, each weights poorly this or that barometer that comes to their attention, only later becoming aware that they have had no barometers at all. Social change sneaks up, so to speak, in a society; it does not erupt. If the history of a social change is one of conflict and controversy, its prehistory is more silent or unobtrusive, and it is only in retrospect that we realize that we were not paying attention—we had no barometers to signal to us—to certain alterations that were prodromal for what was coming down the social road.

Many people today point to the 1960s as the crucible years in which a social change occurred. It would be more correct to say that it was a decade during which discrete forces of change converged, when commonalities were recognized, alliances forged, and relative silence replaced by unmistakable thunder.

In the prehistory of a social change the discrete precursors are not of a piece. Indeed, they may appear to be at worst innocuous and at best beneficial, causing no one to view them as possible barometers of a social change that will be socially divisive. They are not group phenomena, as in the case of race, gender, poverty, or civil rights, but are quintessentially the behavior of individuals. To illustrate what I mean I shall discuss the post World War II meteoric rise of psychotherapy as an aid in coping with personal distress.

Psychotherapy was, of course, available before World War II. Indeed, one of the things "discovered" in World War I was that a lot of males were psychologically unfit to adjust to army life and combat. That was learned during the screening process as well as in the various arenas of the armed services. It was learned again in World War II. However, between the wars the availability of psychotherapy increased only very modestly, and if you exclude the largest metropolitan areas, the increase was minuscule.

Several factors were at work. First, plaguing personal problems were seen as truly private affairs not to be discussed with anyone except, perhaps, selected friends or relatives, and even then with great reluctance. Those problems involved guilt, shame, inadequacy, and defeat, which to many people explained why more women than men availed themselves of psychotherapy: women were prejudicially seen as the "weaker sex." Second, pre World War II psychiatry was primarily biological in orientation; psychotherapy was not its stock-in-trade. Third, as a specialty, psychiatry attracted fewer, perhaps the fewest, medical students to its ranks, and it was a devalued field in the medical community. The professions of psychology and social work did not prepare their members for the practice of psychotherapy; in most states they were legally prevented from presenting themselves to the public as practicing psychotherapy. Fourth, during the ten years of the Great Depression, the psychological problems of individuals were far less salient to them than their material existence. Even if people were inclined to seek counseling, which they were not, paying money for it was not even in the picture. Psychoanalytic therapy was available in a few large cities, but only if you were rich enough to pay twenty-five dollars (or more) an hour, four or five times a week, for two, three, or more years. Fifth, going for personal help was not only regarded as a sign of inadequacy, but it was also associated with the fear that others, like yourself, would think you were "going crazy" and that you might end up in a state mental hospital, which was viewed as not a place from which one returned discernibly better than when one entered, those being the days of electric shock, insulin and metrazol therapy, and prefrontal lobotomies, all this in overpopulated, understaffed, architecturally forbidding, Charles Adams–like buildings. (I know whereof I speak. I interned at the Worcester State Hospital, then considered one of the best in the country, as ghoulish and dispiriting a place as I have ever been in. That accounts in part for why, when I had to choose among three state institutions for my first position after receiving my doctorate in 1942 from Clark University, I chose the one that was newly built and a joy to behold.)

We entered World War II on December 7, 1941. Ten years later the psychotherapeutic landscape had dramatically changed and after that it was unrecognizable. Elsewhere (Sarason, 1988) I have discussed in detail the factors contributing to that transformation, and I use the word "transform" advisedly. Very briefly, those factors were:

1.   The rate of psychological breakdown in the armed services in World War II was not only high but overwhelmed the service's capacity to respond. Whereas such individuals had previously been cared for by medical personnel, the need was such that nonmedical personnel were recruited and "trained." Physicians with no experience in psychiatry became (by fiat) psychiatrists.

2.   The armed forces could not afford to send all or most of these casualties far from battle, let alone back to the States. They supported innovative psychotherapeutic efforts that were intensive and brief and that allowed individuals to return to their squadrons. There was little, really no, stigma attached to "breaking down" or seeking help.

3.   During the war years, psychiatrists (especially younger ones), who were less wedded to biological interventions than to psychological ones and who had never been a force in American psychiatry, assumed important positions in the armed services. After the war, many of them took positions in medical schools.

4.   Soon after the war began it became clear that it would be a long one, the number of casualties would be enormous, and existing clinic and hospital facilities for veterans would be utterly inadequate, quantitatively and qualitatively, to render appropriate care. Plans were drawn up for a mind-boggling transformation and expansion of the Veterans Administration programs and facilities.

5.   In a population of 150 million people, approximately 15 million spent time in uniform. They did not return to civilian life with the same attitudes they had before the war about seeking help for personal misery. And people who had remained in civilian life, especially those who had lost a loved one or who had a family member or close friend whose psychological stability had become impaired, had also altered their attitudes to the seeking of psy-

chotherapeutic aid. Veterans were told and even encouraged to take advantage of the new facilities that were springing up.

In earlier writings I have called the first two decades after the war "the Age of Mental Health." The war years can be considered the opening chapters of an account of how psychotherapy came to be accepted as a desirable, beneficial source of personal help. What happened after the war ended—and it happened quickly—is complicated and best subsumed under the heading "what was in the air," or zeitgeist.

There were a lot of things in the air, and if their sources varied, they nevertheless had cumulative or interactive effects. One such interactive effect involved, on the one hand, still-fresh memories of the Great Depression and the even fresher memories of the brutalities of war, and on the other hand, the fear that the transition from a wartime to a peacetime economy would be socially and economically destabilizing and fraught with threat to our political system. The future was cloudy and threatening, tempered only somewhat by relief that the war was over. However, if the transition to peacetime was not as economically and politically upsetting as feared, there was little doubt that for millions of *individuals* the transition was destabilizing. As one might expect, aspects of that difficult transition—both for veterans and for the families and friends to whom they returned—began to be portrayed in movies, novels, and the theater. And those aspects were common fare in the mass media, including television, which came on the scene in the late forties and soon dominated that scene. One of the sources feeding the mass media was a burgeoning professional literature that not only documented the frequency and disruptiveness of personal-familial-marital-parental unhappiness but also stressed the importance of psychotherapeutic interventions.

Nothing better reflects what was in the air than the creation in 1948 of the National Institute of Mental Health. The Veterans Administration, of course, had obligations only to veterans. The National Institute of Mental Health was concerned with a *national* problem: its nature, frequency, and remediation. It was not long afterwards that a noted psychiatrist wrote in an article in a popular magazine that what this country needed was a five-dollars-an-hour psychotherapy. And around that same time the newly created Ford Foundation gave large grants for the study of mental health and psychotherapy.

The change I have described was remarkable for its speed and spread. The description makes it seem like a case of demand and supply, just as in the case of television, that is, wants become needs. The supply seeks to meet the demand, and both are spurred by the equivalent of a Madison Avenue promotional campaign, except that unlike a commodity, all participants in the growth of psychotherapy sincerely promoted and sought the alleviation of personal misery. The problem was real, it was not manufactured, and a spectrum of psychotherapies gave promise of being effective, at least relatively so.

There were features of the change that went relatively unremarked. They had the nature of implicit messages either sent or interpreted, silently assimilated but not articulated. One such message was that these problems were those of individuals, each of whom had a unique social-developmental history. Wherever and however the causes of these problems originated, they were in individual psyches and they would not go away unless the individual took steps to know himself or herself better; and in taking those steps the individual would come to see that whatever the problem, blame (the "causes") would largely but by no means exclusively be assigned to external factors. There is always collusion between internal and external factors, but the shame and guilt that should spur an individual to seek help have their origins in circumstances over which the individual had little or no control. The process by which one comes to "know thyself" is one that "frees" the individual to be more "authentically" him or herself, to "actualize" heretofore "unrealized potentials." The words in quotes speak to the goals individuals were told they might or could reach in psychotherapy.

So what was one of those implicit messages? Let me put it this way: "*You* should give priority to *your* needs, *your* goals, *your* uniqueness, *your* potentials, to break the chains that fetter and plague *you*." It was a message that supported and reinforced an emphasis on self. It was an asocial message—not a message of selfishness but one that made the self the measure of living. Today we are familiar with the words "born-again Christian." In those early decades after the war, psychotherapy was promoted as a process that helped individuals experience something akin to rebirth. It was an individualism not in conflict with the rugged individualism of a long-standing American ethos. As is almost always the case when individualism is highly prized, the sense of belonging and having obligations to the collectivities to which you belong takes second place.

What I have said will not sit well with many in the mental health community. Let me emphasize two points. First, when you go back and read how the mental health community promoted psychotherapy and how it was portrayed in the various media at the time, it is hard to avoid the conclusion that the overwhelming emphasis was on the individual's psyche. It could be argued that that emphasis is a necessary precondition to the establishment or reestablishment of more productive, satisfying social relationships. If it is a necessary precondition, there was and is no persuasive evidence that whatever attitudinal changes occur in psychotherapy—and those changes do occur—transfer to and alter the individual's customary style in interpersonal relationships. Indeed, it did not take long for psychotherapists to scale back their claims and say that the major benefit of psychotherapy is in the diminishing of the strength of self-critical attitudes and an increase in the readiness to accept one's limitations. To know thyself helps you to live with yourself. The self is center stage in psychotherapy; all else is backdrop.

If the galactic growth of the psychotherapeutic endeavor signified anything, it was that a lot of people did not want to or could not live with their selves, and they responded to messages that told them they should not be content to live with those selves. For what or for whom should they live and why? These, the professionals said, were moral-philosophical questions patients had to answer for themselves. Psychotherapists were not in the business of indoctrinating or propagandizing; they were sympathetic listeners, questioners, interpreters, sounding boards. Why, for whom, and for what their patients should live were not questions with which psychotherapists felt comfortable. *In bypassing or ignoring those questions, psychotherapists were rendered insensitive to the fact that a crucial consequence of the Great Depression and World War II was that those were the questions that had become salient to "selves," questions that were difficult to face or articulate.*

I am in no way suggesting that the problems that spurred people to seek psychotherapy were unimportant or superficial. The problems were real and practical in their consequences. But they masked the fact that people's beliefs in an orderly, predictable, meaningful social world in which and to which their "selves" belonged had been challenged and, for many people, shattered. They were alone with their "selves" in an unwanted privacy. To escape from that privacy was one of the allures of psychotherapy: it would not only solve practical problems of living, it would provide justification for living, striving, and achieving, as well as a sense that you not only counted to yourself but to others as well.

But psychotherapy did not provide that justification, if only because the part of the self that sought justification hardly entered the therapeutic hour. Psychotherapists were not philosophers, let alone clerics. For justification, go read the philosophers. The fact is that that is precisely what the more-educated segment of the population found themselves doing, with consequences that contributed mightily to the ongoing social change. Let me briefly discuss this development, because it illustrates well how the psychotherapeutic emphasis on the self was missing the boat and in that respect was unwittingly contributing to a festering silence about the fragility and incompleteness of the selves it purported to understand and help.

Marital discord, unmodulated hostility, self-hatred, dissatisfaction with work, plaguing feelings of sadness and alienation from others, conflict with offspring, too little or too much sexual activity—these and more were the stuff of the self that occupied patient and therapist. What I am suggesting is that beyond and behind these concrete problems was a question as puzzling as it was inchoately and fleetingly posed: "What in hell is this world all about and where do I fit in, if I fit in at all?" This was not a parochial question limited by geographical, interpersonal, and local-social boundaries. It was a question about how one can and should understand a perplexing, chaotic, dangerous world so that one can face the future, if not unafraid, then with some kind of compass, with a sense of direction and purpose. To paraphrase a certain poet, "Life takes its final meaning in chosen death." Life is not meaningless; decide what meaning it will have for you. *What would truly be mystifying, indeed inexplicable, would be if many among the millions who grew up and lived during the Great Depression and the war years did not emerge with a worldview at the center of which was uncertainty.*

At the end of World War II, Europe was in an economic chaos and nightmare, a social psychological disaster; hundreds of thousands of its buildings had been destroyed, the fires of old ethnic and religious conflicts had been rekindled, the seeds of the cold war were starting to grow, and the dimensions of the Nazi slaughter of Jews, Gypsies, political dissidents, and Catholic and other diverse clerics had become clear. It was hard, and for some people impossible, to continue to hold to a belief in progress and a belief in the benevolence and omnipotence of God. It was easier to believe that Satan had triumphed over God than that the world had been created and was ruled by a providential divinity.

Illustrative of this loss of belief was the emergence of the "God is dead" explanation of what had happened, which came from some religious leaders trying to hold onto the belief that is bedrock to all religions: there is a God, but not the personal one to whom people prayed. Far more widespread was the existential stance that life had no transcendent meaning, was essentially meaningless, that human beings were alone on this earth and in the universe, living lives suffused with fear of nothingness, pointlessness, emptiness, and death. It was in the nature of the human animal to be and feel alone, to want to be connected but to always feeling disconnected. If it was the fate of humans to construct a justification for living, it was also their fate ultimately to find that justification illusory. As Beckett insisted in *Waiting for Godot* (1954), you may hope for salvation from God or elsewhere, but you wait in vain. The "theatre of the absurd" was born; life was absurd.

Those European (largely French) points of view found fertile soil in the United States, especially in literary circles and in the university. If it would be grossly wrong to suggest that existential philosophies occupied dinner table conversation, it would be no less wrong to say that precisely because they were taken seriously by literary people and those who taught literature, drama, philosophy, and psychology in universities, the philosophers were not influential. These imported writings were not easy reads, but their emphasis on puny, lonely man in an insensitive, disordered, and disordering world sounded chords to which many people were responsive. It should be noted that such responsiveness was also elicited among those who taught in divinity schools, where the existential stance was always a matter of discussion and controversy, a matter to which the Holocaust of the Jews (and others) gave increased poignant and inescapable significance.

One more thing: to call the cessation of hostilities in World War II "peace" is playing loose with words. There were civil wars; war between the United States and Stalin's Soviet Union seemed likely and to some inevitable; and there was the atomic bomb, which threatened human existence.

The existential philosophers were implicitly at odds with American psychotherapy, and sometimes explicitly. From the existential standpoint the "root" problem—the problem that, if it did not cause them, exacerbated all other problems of living—was where, why, and how did man exist in an uncaring, impersonal, meaning-lacking world for which the previous worldview had long seemed adaptive but that was now part of the problem and not part of the solution. Psychotherapy was a bromide, and there is a place for bromides, but it was still a bromide, which diverts attention away from where pain is.[1]

I am endeavoring to explain the significance of the meteoric rise in the seeking and provision of psychotherapy. The reader may regard what I say as in part or in whole unpersuasive. But that reader is still left with how to explain the quick and dramatic alteration in the readiness to seek psychotherapeutic help for personal problems, and it simply will not pass muster to proffer an explanation in which the selves that are the object of change have not already been changed by previous, convulsive world events that continued in subsequent decades when, as one person said, "It seems as if at any one time during the day one-half of the population is spilling its guts to the other half, who is listening and trying to be helpful." But let us go on to another significance of the psychotherapy explosion.

How and why should I go to a complete stranger who does not know me or my circumstances, tell him my troubles, and expect him to understand me? So, I tell him why I am unhappy, so what good will talking do me? When I tell him what is bothering me, he will be shocked, probably think I am crazy. And what do I tell my family and friends? That I have thoughts and feelings even they don't know about? That I need a specialist to figure out why I am miserable? And it will cost me money, which will make me more miserable. I'll live with my troubles. That is my fate. What else can I do?

Those words reflect the public's conception of an attitude toward

---

[1]In a 1948 meeting in which the virtues of psychotherapy were being discussed, I heard Victor Raimy say, "Psychotherapy is an undefinable technique applied to an unspecified problem with unpredictable outcomes." He then wryly added, "For this, rigorous training is required." Raimy was no opponent of psychotherapy, as I am not, but his words were intended as a caveat against the prevalent view that psychotherapy was the psychological equivalent of aspirin.

psychiatrists and psychotherapy before World War II. (They are attitudes and conceptions by no means infrequent today as well, despite
the psychotherapy explosion. No single aspect of a social change
takes hold in all segments of the population.) The significance of
those attitudes was twofold. First, the unwanted privacy associated
with plaguing, personal problems—a privacy to be guarded and
undivulged, if only because to disclose it to others in one's circle,
let alone to a stranger—would mean you would be negatively
judged, that is, you were "weak." Second, there was the question of
the assignment of blame: who or what "caused" these problems?
Except in very extreme cases when all blame was directed outward
or inward, causes were inevitably bidirectional, but the major ones
were attributed to the self. Weakness meant that there was something about the person—thoughts, feelings, actions, anxieties, or
fantasies—that was out of control.

There was (and is) nothing new about these two factors. It was
their combination—personal responsibility and the fear of a negative social judgment—that made seeking professional help not even
an option. Earlier, I briefly indicated how attitudes and actions
changed rather quickly as "peace" followed war. Part of that change
was reflected in several implicit and explicit messages in the promotion of psychotherapy:

1. A personal problem should be regarded as one does any
   medical problem: you go to someone trained to fix it. Going
   for help is not a sign of weakness. It should be regarded as a
   strength in that you have resolved to do something about
   your problems.

2. Psychotherapists are by selection and training special people
   in whom you can confide, who you can trust to help you to
   see yourself and your problems with greater clarity and objec-
   tivity, enabling you to see new options for action. The implication is that such help should not be expected to be
   available from family members and friends.

3. There are many people like you who need and should seek psychotherapeutic help. Your problems are not unique.

4. You did not cause or will your problems. It is far more complicated than that.

5. You should not regard your problems as hopeless. They are remediable and often solvable.

If these messages were sent, there were a lot of people ready to hear and act on them.

As long as we rivet on this or that message, we truly miss the forest for the trees, which is to say that as long as we see psychotherapy as quintessentially concerned with individuals and how to help them, we fail to see what the psychotherapy explosion was saying about the larger society. And what it signified was a belief held and promoted by the mental health community. It was more than just a belief; it was based on studies and surveys, all of which indicated that there was a staggering number of people leading quiet and not so quiet lives of psychological desperation! More than that, it was not long after the end of World War II that it became obvious that the supply of psychotherapists was minuscule compared to the number of those who sought help, which was a fraction of all those whom the mental health community deemed in need of help.

What kind of society were we living in? What did this portend? What was the attractiveness of the therapist's office? Refuge from the real conflicts with the self and others? Was it a sense of intimacy rarely experienced? Was it a longing to be with someone who would be nonjudgmental and capable of giving you undivided attention?

What kind of society were we living in where so many people lived unhappy and often unproductive lives?[2] That question hardly got raised and discussed in the mental health community. It was

[2]A few professionals questioned, on theoretical and methodological grounds, criteria of "normality" and the number of distressed people the studies and surveys suggested. Nevertheless, no critic asserted that the "mental health problem" in America was less than worrisome.

riveted on individuals. Was the psychotherapy explosion a barometer of a social change? Was it to be regarded only as a beneficial, long-overdue change in people's attitudes? Or was the sheer number of unhappy people, only a small number of whom would be able to take advantage of psychotherapy, more worrisome for the societal future than the nature, dynamics, and outcomes of individual psychotherapy? Was not psychotherapy an effort at repair, and did one not have to be all that wise to know that repair efforts are very difficult and their outcomes by no means robust? That being the case, it was knowable that an undetermined (but by no means minuscule) number of people would not be helped by psychotherapy.

For the purposes of this essay the most important feature of the psychotherapy explosion was as fateful as it was obvious: *Psychotherapy was promoted and accepted as a means whereby an individual could be liberated from an existing and unhappy psychological-social state of affairs.* Whether that state of affairs was largely (at least on the surface) intraindividual in nature (such as obsessions, compulsions, or anxiety) or interpersonal (such as marital, parental, work, or friendships), or both, psychotherapy would stimulate and reinforce the client's desire to feel more free, to be less constrained by his or her past or by his or her present circumstances, to be more open to change. *Although psychotherapy was quintessentially an individual affair, its promotion and acceptance spoke volumes about what was in the "social air."* It was far more than a barometer of individual change, it was a barometer, albeit a murky one, of a social change the substance and direction of which would depend on other ingredients that were in or would become part of the "social air."

For example, divorce is an instance in which at least one member of a marriage seeks to sever a relationship and alter a style of living, that is, to free himself or herself from what is, in the hope that what follows will be more satisfying. Following World War II the legal obstacles to divorce began to change and the divorce rate began to climb, as did the frequency of "living together" without the formality of marriage and its legal-moral obligations.[3] Those barometers of social change were regarded negatively by many, but with each passing year the number who regarded those developments as positive indicators of people's unwillingness to be bound by constricting customs zoomed. My experience is limited, and I am not aware of any relevant studies, but it has long been my impression— and I have always been in and around the psychotherapeutic–mental health community—the rate of divorce following psychotherapy was higher than in the general population, and that appeared to be as true for the psychotherapists as for their patients. Indeed, it appeared to be more true among psychotherapists. I am being descriptive, not judgmental. I am not "blaming" psychotherapy; it is more complicated than that. I am saying that these different barometers signified changes that had in common the theme of personal liberation. I am also saying that in the following decades that theme spread and gained strength as other societal changes reached the threshold of recognition.

If attitudes toward psychotherapy dramatically changed after World War II—and the liberation theme was one of its major ingredients, albeit by no means an ingredient absent outside the therapeutic arena—it is no indulgence of unwarranted speculation to suggest that the theme played a role in the contents and goals of child rearing. If any hope and resolve were explicitly articulated with the war's end, it was that coming generations not only would and should live in a new and better world but also that they should have a major voice in constructing that world. Implicit in that view

[3]In his book *Fatherless America*, Blankenhorn (1995) discusses the "fatherhood debate" occasioned by our entry into World War II, "a little remembered but important historical moment" (p. 50). His book contains revealing statistics, and what he says about what was happening to soldiers and their spouses and/or families in regard to matters marital and sexual during the war confirms in all respects what I have said here and in other essays. One example: 321,000 couples divorced in 1942; in 1945 the number was 485,000; and in 1946, the year after the war ended, the number was 610,000.

was the liberation theme: coming generations should not be expected to be bound by those diverse factors and traditions which had contributed to making the century (at its midpoint) the most bloody in history. It was not unusual to hear parents (or would-be parents) say, "I do not want my child to be brought up the way I was," or "I want my child to have a mind of his or her own," or "I want my child to become what he or she wants to become, not what I want. My child should feel free to find and go his or her own way. I want my child to feel free and to be able to experience as much of this world as possible." Those sentiments were redolent of the Declaration of Independence. The goals of life were seen to be life, liberty, and the pursuit of happiness.

Some readers may have difficulty believing that nothing I have said has been uttered in the spirit of criticism or derogation. For one thing, as I noted earlier, the liberation theme was understandable, persuasive, and yes, commendable. And, let us not forget, it was a theme that had no opponents; it was not socially divisive. It was a barometer of a change (actually, it was a barometer of several related changes) that was seen as necessary for a better world. Also, I am quite aware that my conclusions do not rest on substantial empirical "data." But that is my point: there was no reason to construct such barometers, their possible implications for the future seemed to contain no untoward possibilities. And there was no reason to seek interrelationships among barometers each of which was discrete. We become aware of a social change *after* recognition of the change is unavoidable, *after* a variety of barometer readings from diverse social arenas tell us that a coalescence of forces has occurred and is percolating throughout the society. Social change creeps up on a society. When we become aware of the change, we may think it has happened quickly, that the divisiveness concomitant with the change was "planned" by its proponents, that its roots are relatively recent origins. So, when the now legendary "sizzling sixties" erupted and the fact and dimensions of the social change became obvious, the question of where, why, and how it started became as pressing as the question of what should be done, what stance, pro or con, should be taken.

What I have endeavored to do in previous pages is to direct attention to discrete changes in the years immediately following World War II, changes noteworthy for their generally commendable intentions, but changes that later interacted with other ongoing changes to produce the divisiveness and turmoil of a social change that, as the years went on, more than a few proponents of the change had second thoughts about regarding what happened and why.

The bulk of opponents still did not understand that what is "finally" called a social change is not a willed phenomenon, except perhaps at the apogee of its obviousness or clarity (as in the sixties), but a concatenation of heretofore seemingly discrete changes no one of which was regarded as socially portentous, and their later coalescence was neither inevitable or predictable. The idea that social change is willed or predictable rests on the assumption that we live in a predictable and controllable world. That view is, of course, a ludicrous overestimation of man's capacity to be rational, objective, and wise. It also ignores the law of unintended consequences, a vulnerability that opponents and proponents of change share.

4

. . . .

The University as a
Barometer of Social Change

When we are forced to recognize that a social change has occurred, it is understandable if we see it largely in terms of the
actions of individuals; that is, we become aware that many individuals in many places are thinking, saying, and acting in similar ways
that represent an upsetting challenge to what had earlier been
regarded as right, natural, and proper. But it is also the case that
when we recognize the change, we attend to more than the behavior of individuals because we are made aware that the challenge is
coming most clearly from individuals in certain institutions. By its
very widespread, percolating nature, social change mightily involves
and influences the major formal societal institutions: their stance,
structure, traditions, and power relationships within the institution
and between it and the larger society. When the institution is identified with a particular kind of place and its physical structures—the
churches, the public school, the college, the university—and with
the individuals comprising it, we ask why the institution is reflecting the social change as it is. Our attention is directed as much, or
even less, to individuals as to the institution qua institution. Why
is it playing the role it is in supporting or opposing the social
change? How did that state of affairs come about?

It is a glimpse of the obvious to say that colleges and universities
changed remarkably in the post World War II era, and that the consequences of those changes in large part explain why in the sixties

campuses were stages on which the drama and complexity of social change were, to say the least, clear, compelling, and provocative.[1] In the following pages, I shall try to identify how and why college campuses changed in ways that initially reflected changes elsewhere and only later became themselves major actors in the social change. The reader needs to keep in mind that words like "college" and "university" refer to institutions that vary wildly on almost every variable by which institutions can be described.[2] No generalization about them is without error or inappropriateness. So, in what follows I make no attempt to take that diversity into account. I restrict myself to those colleges and universities that during the sixties clearly manifested the post World War II social change. They were not few in number. Based on the criterion of their "goings on" reported in the local and mass media, they number in the hundreds.

I begin with some characterization of these institutions in the years shortly before the war:

1.   Compared to today's colleges and universities, they were small institutions. Most of the students were male and white. Faculty were, for all practical purposes, near exclusively white and male. The top layers of administration rarely came from outside of academia; they formerly had been members of the faculty. Although the president had either the sole or major responsibility for representing the institution to the outside world, he—and it was almost always he—spent most of his time on matters internal to the university. The boards of trustees was composed of representatives who had distinguished themselves in the corporate, business, political, and religious worlds.

---

[1]Aspects of what I shall be discussing are contained in books by Nisbet (1969, 1971). Case histories illustrative of those changes have yet to be written because, I assume, such a case history would require a degree of concrete detail and confrontation of complexity as to require years of study.

[2]Someone once said that the university is the only major social institution whose internal structure and dynamics remain unstudied and unknown and where the disparity between appearance and reality, between the formal and informal, are of a nature best left to portrayal by novelists. Beginning in the sixties, such novels began to appear and their number have increased steadily up to today.

2.   Except for the small number of poor students who attended college on a scholarship, the student body came from affluent or semiaffluent families. Leaving aside the relatively few institutions created and supported by the Catholic Church, which drew a largely Catholic student body, college students were largely Protestant. (The City College of New York, which was tuition free, was the only college where the number of Jewish students was not minuscule—indeed they were in the majority.) Generally speaking, students with Jewish and other "foreign-sounding" names had a hard time getting through admissions committees. Religious intolerance and discrimination also played a large role in appointments to the faculty.

3.   These institutions could legitimately be characterized as having an informal quality in two respects. First, faculty members tended to know each other, if only because the size of the faculty was not large and members were expected to serve on committees, that is, to be part of the college community, to feel a responsibility to it, to be a responsible citizen, and that meant discharging the obligation to contribute to the institution's welfare. Second, these institutions were informal in the sense that the gulf between faculty and administration was not large; the members of both groups knew one another and that meant more than being able to recognize faces. Put another way, there were few layers of bureaucracy between faculty and the top layers of administration. The boundaries were porous.

4.   A major, if not *the* major, function of the institution was teaching undergraduates. Contributing to knowledge through research and scholarly studies was important, but these activities were coequal with, not more important than, the teaching function. Financial support for such investigations came exclusively from inside the institution. Outside sources of funding, such as foundations, were few, and the amounts available from any internal or external source were not large. There were not such things (the usual exceptions aside) as "research empires" dotting the campus, headed by one entrepreneurial faculty member.

5.   If only because of history and tradition, status and both formal and informal power resided in the faculty of the humanities. If anything, the sciences were envious of the humanities, aware as they were that a sizable part of the university budget went to the library in which faculty from the humanities did their scholarly studies, whereas the individual member of a science department could count on little or no support for his research.

6.   Just as the sciences took second place to the humanities, graduate schools took second place to undergraduate schools. Second place meant that such schools were smaller, had fewer resources, and could attract, admit, and support a smaller number of students, except again in the humanities. Graduate school was not seen as all that important for carving out a career, unless it was an academic one. In the years of the Great Depression, getting advanced degrees held out little promise of a college or university position.

7.   The major point of contact between the university and the larger society was in the professional departments or schools: social work, education, law, medicine, public health, and nursing. If these schools were seen as performing important societal functions, and in some instances esteemed, they nevertheless were seen as diverting resources away from the arts and sciences. Simply put, they were not central to the university's historical purpose, and no alumnus or alumna of the undergraduate college ever had reason to think otherwise. The undergraduate college was preeminently the place for learning, reflecting, maturing, and developing understanding and respect for the knowledge and wisdom uncovered by the human mind, past and present. It was an oasis in which the liberal arts liberated you from myth, superstition, and thoughtless ignorance. It was seen as the last time the undergraduate would have such an opportunity to learn about the best of humanity's achievements. By implication, the outside world was, if not antithetical, an obstacle to good thinking and the good life.

There were two consequences for colleges with the United

States' entry into World War II. The most immediate was the possibility that an undetermined but certainly not a small number of institutions would have to close because the draft, which had already been in existence, would take hundreds of thousands of college-age students into the armed services. (During the war years, 15 million people entered the armed services, from a population of 150 million people.) What prevented this from happening was the need of the military for scores of specialized personnel (such as engineers and medical personnel) for whom a college education (albeit a speeded-up one) was necessary. In addition, the number of officers a much-expanded military needed had to come from a college-educated pool. With governmental funding, these needs and programs allowed colleges and universities to avoid closing or financial disaster. This also meant that the demographics of the student population changed dramatically. Economic background, ethnicity, and religion were no longer significant factors in the admission process; the needs of the military took precedence over customary criteria.[3] In our so-called elite institutions, for example, many individuals were admitted who heretofore would never have been on campus (as sightseers yes, as students no!).

Another consequence was that many faculty members left their academic posts either to become officers or to take some war-related governmental position. If the size of student bodies did not dramatically decrease, that was not true for the size of faculties. Their migration from the cloisters of academia to the "real world" opened their eyes to issues and problems (scientific, educational, and social) that changed their views about the relationship between the academy and the larger society. War, total war, changes everything and everybody. Although the country was willing to do whatever was necessary to win what was going to be a long war—and in 1941 and

[3]I am being descriptive, not judgmental. That is to say, I am describing different days, not the "good old days." What I described in points 1 and 2 above could be considered the "bad old days."

1942 winning appeared to be very uncertain—few gave thought to the possibility that whatever changes were necessary would not be temporary or that when peace came there could be no return to "normalcy."[4] If during the war years there were many changes, it is understandable that people were not disposed to give thought to how those changes might have long-term consequences not all of which would be favorably accepted. The obvious point is that what we call the post World War II social change had its roots in the war years.

In the case of the university there can be no doubt that the single most important change immediately after the war was in the growth of the student body, a growth that in fact overwhelmed its physical and teaching resources. That was, of course, the result of what I consider to be one of a handful of legislative acts in the twentieth century that deserve the label "landmark." I refer to the GI Bill of Rights, which underwrote college and graduate education for millions of those who had served the country in war. That legislation also applied to individuals with advanced degrees (M.A., Ph.D., M.D.) who needed "retooling" or who wanted to change careers. What was significant was not only the increase in numbers but that the returning veterans were older than the usual student, many had married, some had children, and the diversity in their social, economic, religious, and racial backgrounds was remarkable indeed. And some came to the campus who had never dreamed they would ever be in such a place.

In general, these were not silent, conforming students who passively adjusted to the mores or traditions of the prewar college or university. You might say they were "boys" when they entered service and they were "men" when they left it: their lives had been disrupted, they had seen more than they had wanted to see, time was not on their side, and they had had their fill of military rules, regu-

---

[4]I am not aware of statistics about the degree of increase of black students entering college in the different military-supported programs. I assume that on a percentage basis the increase was large but on an absolute basis very small.

lations, and bureaucracy. If they came willingly and enthusiastically to the campus, they had no desire to stay there for long. They wanted to resume "normal" living. I am trying to describe here less their behavior than their attitudes toward themselves and the future. (An earlier essay, "Explaining the Sixties" [Sarason, 1994], contains a rather long description of what happened at Yale, where the contrast between prewar and postwar Yale was subtle but clear, that is, Yale was changing.)

Among faculties and administrators there was what you might call a "compliance" factor in that they knew and wanted to accommodate this new population whose needs were special and many. Faculty who had been involved in the war had returned and, again generally speaking, their views of the university and its relationship to the larger society had also changed. Central to that altered view was that the boundaries between the university and society had to become more porous, that is, the university had obligations to the society; the university had to become more than an oasis for thinking, reflection, and study.

Before elaborating on that I must briefly indicate what the sharp growth of the university brought in its wake because they were factors that later played a part in the role of students and faculty in the social change.

1. As a generalization it is valid to say that when an institution grows rapidly, especially *very* rapidly, the individual tends to become more anonymous: known more as a number, a label, or a name than as a person. That was especially true for students in universities where the relative and absolute increase was largest. Their opportunities for meaningful, let alone intimate, contact with faculty and administration was small—much smaller than in the prewar period when universities, especially the state ones, were not exactly what you would call sparsely populated. What began to happen was that the perceived gulf between students and the faculty and administration widened and a note of adversarialism became audible. It was not a case of open conflict but, as in the military, of

the "upper brass" not being seen as concerned with the thoughts, feelings, and attitudes of students. I am not aware of statistics about the dropout rate in those early postwar years but by the middle of the fifties the dropout rate during the first two years of college had become a topic of conversation. Unlike in the military, you could leave college with impunity. It was also the case that some students did not drop out because they had no better alternatives, career plans were murky or even nonexistent, and in the case of veterans they could count on government support for material existence.

2.   The number of faculty and administration increased. Departments (like psychology) mushroomed in size and that altered the frequency and quality of collegial relationships. Whatever the quality of informal relationships before the war, it changed remarkably after the war. Many departments became complicated organizations far more concerned with their internal tasks and problems than with what was happening elsewhere in the university. Again compared to the prewar years, contacts (personal-social or professional) between faculty members in different departments were infrequent. It was not unusual for faculty never to have met or to have known anyone in the administrative layers, layers that began to increase for several reasons: to keep records and account for government funds supporting veterans, to try to satisfy housing needs including the construction of additional facilities, to develop and run much-expanded counseling services, and more. The bureaucratization of the university had discernibly escalated.

These reasons were in their consequences matched by a factor that was totally lacking in the prewar years but that came on the scene immediately after the war. More correctly, it started during the war in a modest way and directly concerned only the war effort. I refer to research sponsored by the federal government. Let us turn to that fateful factor, because its consequences altered the university politically, structurally, academically, and culturally. And it mightily affected, albeit indirectly and unintentionally, the availability of faculty to students, an effect the significance of which did not get articulated by students until the end of the next decade.

3.   Before World War II, funds for faculty research came from two sources, the amount of available funds being modest. The first source was the university budget. The second source was foundations, the recipients tending noticeably to be individuals in the prestigious universities. For all practical purposes, that funding changed little, if anything, in the culture of these universities. During the war, and for specifically military-related problems, the government began to sponsor research in the university. Because of the contributions of science and technology to the success of the war effort, it became government policy to support basic and applied research, and within five years research was sponsored and supported by different government agencies, after which what was a steady stream became a flood of funding.

The effects were several. First, it added new administrative layers to the university: checking grant proposals, monitoring them, alerting faculty to funding sources, all of which required new personnel, additional space requirements, and of course, an escalating expenditure for paper and files. What government agencies "wanted and required" was a question that became salient in an institution unaccustomed to dealing with federal bureaucracies. Top administrators began to spend more and more time on these matters.

Second, whereas before the war a faculty person's loyalty was exclusively to profession, department, and university, those objects now competed with an outside "master," a well-heeled, well-intentioned one to be sure, but one that had to be cultivated and satisfied because its largesse enabled one to do what one wanted to do: to be independent (relatively speaking) of the department and the university and, with such funds, to pay oneself a salary during the summer months when not teaching.[5] And depending on the size of the grant, faculty members could pay for their own secretaries and even have research assistants. Not infrequently, one could have (or

[5]The one crucial exception was the planning that began sometime in 1942 about what would be required at war's end to care adequately for the staggering number of psychiatric and medical casualties. Those plans would have mammoth consequences for many parts of the university.

pay for) a reduced teaching load. More than a few researchers became administrators of programs, centers, or institutes. A grant usually contained a budget for travel, and that is when faculty began to spend time away from the campus, giving lectures and attending meetings and conventions, all of which had long been justified (as it should have been) but support for which was small and, more frequently, nonexistent.

Third, status and power within a department began to be correlated with grant size; those who had no grant had less status and power. Collegial relationships, which always had been fragile but civil, became suffused with competitiveness and conflict. By the processes of selection and self-selection, academics are individualists, but the change in sources of funding played into the excesses of individualism.

Finally, precisely because these new sources of funding were directed to the physical and social sciences, power relationships changed: the humanities lost power, and graduate schools gained a status and power they never had before.

The above effects, together with what happened on campuses during the war years, describe an institution undergoing swift change.[6] And practically everybody looked favorably on the change (as in the case of psychotherapy). Few saw the change in terms of the law of unintended consequences. The bureaucratization of the university; a large number of disaffected, anonymous students; a faculty much more concerned with research than with students; an increasing gulf between faculty and an ever-growing, complex administrative hierarchy; a student body much of which had no sense of personal mission and an administration unable to articulate (let

---

[6]There was a "market" factor. Institutions began to "raid" each other for their rising stars or "superstars," dangling as incentives higher salaries, better research support and facilities, and reduced teaching loads. The rate at which faculty changed universities was unprecedented. In that respect, the American university and the American corporation both played the personnel market in the same way. The transience and superficial loyalty of the faculty were not lost on students (both undergraduate and graduate).

alone implement) a compelling mission to students—these were not intended consequences. Were they temporary phenomena? Would their untoward effects be able to be contained within the academy? What if anything might happen if these changes began to interact with other discrete barometers of social change in the larger society? The answer to these questions was unknowable. As I have been saying, we do not recognize a social change—a coalescence of heretofore discrete changes—until it hits us in the face, and then we revisit the past to seek answers. When and how that coalescence begins to occur, and its pace, is not predictable. Social change is not like a bomb waiting to be ignited, as if one event or one discrete change is the match that ignites the social change. The present is pregnant with many futures and coincidence always plays a role.

It is beyond the scope of this essay to discuss in any detail how what was happening elsewhere in the society began to interact with changes in the university. I limit myself to several factors.

1.   The Great Depression radicalized both students and faculty. Radicalized may be too strong a word, although for some campuses that word is appropriate. President Roosevelt's New Deal saw the beginning of a road between Washington and the campus. During the war years, and especially after the war ended, that road became a kind of superhighway. The university had become a Democratic stronghold, a development that, it should be noted, gained strength by virtue of the demographic changes in students and faculty, that is, ethnic minorities with their foreign-sounding names became part of the university melting pot. This consequence was captured well by Alan Dershowitz in a commencement address he gave at Brooklyn College in June 1994 (Dershowitz, 1995):

> Thirty-five years ago, I sat out there like you, surrounded by proud and frightened family members. Proud, because I—like so many in my class and so many in your class—was the first in my immediate family to graduate from college. Frightened, because our family knew that in

order to get the superb education that I was given, I had been asked—subtly to be sure, but asked nonetheless—to make a Faustian pact with a twentieth-century American devil. The bargain was this: in exchange for being taught by some of the finest professors in the world, some of whom are still here today, I was expected to reject my tradition, my ethnicity, my religious background, and my heritage. This was asked not only of me and of my co-religionists, but of my African-American classmates, my Italian-American classmates, my Hispanic-American classmates, my Irish-American classmates, and all the rest of our largely hyphenated class. It was asked of us for the best of motives. Part of the mission of Brooklyn College in those days was to Americanize us, to assimilate us, to homogenize us. It was as if the eleventh commandment and the twenty-fifth amendment read: "Thou Shalt melt into the great melting pot called America and become more like the 'real' Americans who founded this great nation." And many did melt. Names and noses were both shortened. Accents and mannerisms were refined. We learned to wear tweed and we tried to smoke pipes.

Some of us kept our noses and names. Recently, a prominent politician who had read my book *Chutzpah* told me about a situation that was parallel in his life and in mine. He too graduated law school and was turned down by every single law firm to which he applied. He was told by his dean that he'd better change his name. And he went home that night and he made a list of possible names and he finally came up with "Mark Conrad." And then he looked at himself in the mirror and he said "I'm no Mark Conrad. I'm Mario Cuomo, and I'm gonna stay that way!"

The paragraph to which he was referring in my book told about a dream I used to have during my first years of teaching at Harvard. In the dream I was standing in the middle of Harvard Yard, between my mother, who is here today, and Derek Bok, then president of Harvard. Both looked at me and they saw two completely different people. Derek Bok saw in me a shtetl Jew with sidelocks and a prayer shawl; my mother saw in me an assimilated WASP carrying a polo mallet. In many ways it was the worst of all possible worlds. To our parents we had joined the "thems," we were a younger version of our grandparents, still living in the ghettos.

Being discernibly older than Dershowitz, and having joined the Yale faculty in 1945, I can say that what he described when he entered college in 1954 was no less evident in 1945 and that change began during the war years. In any event, the campus had changed; its receptivity to liberal causes was obvious, which is to say that it was no longer a tranquil nonpolitical oasis.

2.   A major contributing factor was the appearance and activities of Senator Joseph McCarthy of Wisconsin who, to say the least, regarded the university as a hotbed of unpatriotic, subversive characters. In his accusations he was incapable of differentiating between a kernel of truth and a field of reckless overgeneralizations. The phenomenon of the "loyalty oath" (federal and state) had three consequences in the university: it further radicalized part of it, it caused divisiveness within the university, and it aroused mistrust of government policies, especially in foreign affairs. The cold war was heating up, the Berlin Blockade raised the specter of another war, and atomic bombs were being tested. Some in the university saw these as manifestations of American imperialism and, therefore, a cause of realistic Soviet fears and paranoia; others attributed the cold war to a historically based Russian imperialism. The Korean

War raised the possibility that the college-age population would be participating in a global war, this but seven years after World War II had ended.

If all this caused divisiveness among faculty, and to a lesser extent among students, the emerging reaction among students was that they lived in a threatening, unsafe, unjust, crazy world. And in that world they included what they saw as an irresponsible, insensitive political system. That conveys too clear a picture. It might be more correct to say that among students there were two contrasting reactions: to engage that world, and to disengage from it. The picture became more clear in 1954.

3.   The 1954 Supreme Court desegregation decision and its almost immediate aftermath had an organizing, galvanizing effect in colleges and universities. The decision gave a strength to the civil rights movement it had never before had. If there was any doubt that the university was no longer an encapsulated part of society, that doubt was dissolved by what was going on elsewhere in society. The outlines of a coalescing of discrete changes could be and was discerned.

Other changes came into the picture of the emerging social change, in popular music, novels, the use of drugs, attitudes toward sexual relationships, and the roles and rights of women. The theme of liberation from stultifying tradition was loud and clear. Later, the assassinations of the two Kennedys and Martin Luther King Jr., plus the most unpopular war in American history, added fuel to the fires of change. And not far from the center of it all, and some would say at the center, were colleges and universities. The coalescence was complete. What had been discrete changes had melded into a social change. Individual change and institutional change came together in what became a social change. It had predictable and unpredictable features. Coincidences played a role; they always do.

When in psychotherapy an individual comes to see the need for personal change, the consequences are almost always a mixture of the intended and the unintended, the positive and the negative, if only because at the end of therapy one should have adapted (or have been helped to adapt) to the brute fact that personal problems are never solved in a once-and-for-all fashion. You learn that there are problems ahead, some from a still-potent present and past, others in an unfolding, inscrutable future. Change is a mixed blessing: you know you cannot remain what you are while choosing from new possibilities for action, and at the same time you sense that solving one problem, taking one course of action, creates new problems. Change's offspring is change.

It is no different in the case of institutional change. Once an institution begins discernibly to change, the desired change has a dynamic character in that it causes other changes the strength and scope of which can be surprising and untoward, especially if the internalized institutional change mirrors changes taking place elsewhere in the society. Dershowitz put it well in his commencement address:

> Then the pendulum suddenly swung: tribalism, separatism, scapegoating, name-calling, claims of superiority became the order of the day. Kahane, Farrakhan, Levin, Jeffries, each preaching not only pride, but prejudice and racial or religious superiority. It was pride run amok.
>
> Calls for censorship, firing, political correctness, political incorrectness, provocations, counter-provocations filled the air. College campuses began to resemble an academic version of Beirut or Sarajevo, where people were no longer judged by the content of their character but rather by the color of their skin, their national origin, their religion, their gender, their sexual preference, and their ethnicity.

If individual and social change teaches us anything, it is that there is no free lunch.

Why try to connect the remarkable increase in the acceptance and use of psychotherapy after World War II and the changes that were occurring at the same time in the university? What needs to be noted is that on a relative basis the number of staff at university centers for psychotherapy and counseling may well have increased as much as or more than in any other part of the university. The very fact that these centers existed, plus the official encouragement of students to use these services, conveyed the message that having personal problems was no stigma but rather reason enough to seek to overcome those problems. And given the dominant psychotherapies (psychoanalytic and Rogerian) of early postwar generations of psychotherapists, it is not wild speculation to say that giving voice in expression and action to one's ideas, longings, and desires was one of the goals of the helping process. The goal was not only to *know thyself* but to *act* consistent with that knowledge. And as one might expect, that knowledge had to do with sexual matters; relations with friends, lovers, and parents; career choice; and not infrequently, resentment toward what people saw as an uncaring or unresponsive or overly controlling, demanding, and constricting faculty and university. What I am suggesting here is that in the university, as outside it, psychotherapy was seen as a means to overcome problems of the self in regard to features of the external world. Psychotherapy was viewed as a way, a process, by which one overcame internal and external barriers to self-expression, "authenticity," and "self-realization." A college education was supposed to liberate one from the acceptance of superstition and myth, and from the consequences of an uncritical acceptance of "conventional wisdom." To be educated meant you should not run with the herd. The unexamined life is not worth living, the self is too precious to be imprisoned by too easily succumbing to internal and external barriers. These messages were not infrequently conveyed to students in classrooms and in the therapist's office. They contain a large kernel of truth, a truth that the postwar generation of students (not all certainly, but many) were primed, so to speak, to hear. But in principle that truth was highly similar to that of which people outside the university were aware. Albeit in different ways, phenomenology, phraseology, and setting, that truth had more than a circumscribed personal meaning for those in and out of the university. And by that I mean that the truth was beginning to be on a collision course with the perception that the great expectations for the post World War II world were not being realized.

What I said earlier about the consequences of the growth of the university added fuel to the fires of resentment in students of the university, and it did not take many years before that resentment generalized to the larger society, culminating in the slogan that "the university is part of the problem, not the solution. The university contains most of the injustices that the society has." The student upheavals, protests, and demonstrations of the sixties bore resemblance to the liberation theology some clerics began to espouse. For two decades after World War II, psychotherapy had its own version of personal liberation.

There is no one word or one explanation or one overarching theory of which I am aware that does justice to the complex origins and course of the post World War II social change. If at the point of a gun I had to say what one theme best describes what psychologically powered the social change it would be: liberation from a personal-social past and resentment of a constraining future. That is oversimple, I know, but it has for me the virtue that it highlights why *today* the antagonisms between proponents and opponents of the social change are (and probably will become) more bitter and divisive. When two worldviews clash and each has a sizeable (but differentiated) constituency, the result is not social noise but social thunder. There are those who will say that I am painting too gloomy a picture. They will also say that I am ahistorical in that I am ignoring that there have always been turbulent times during which prophets of gloom and doom were proved wrong. My answer is in two parts. First, I am not predicting gloom and doom, if only because I believe that the present is pregnant with not one but many futures, that is, contingency is always a variable. Second, I agree with both opponents and proponents of the change that the stakes are very high, so high that it is understandable that they clash with such passion and bitterness. Third, far from being ahistorical, I am very impressed with past turbulent ages that were succeeded by various shades of darkness. To ignore that is to say that history has been on a *continuous* onward and upward course and it will be no different in the future. To hold such a view at the end of the bloodiest century in human history is an incomprehensible indulgence of optimism.

5

Personal Barometers

How do we devise our *personal* barometers of social change? Asking that question can be misleading because it suggests a rational, linear psychological process. It has those properties (somewhat), but in my experience—which is what this essay is about—the barometers I develop are preceded by a reaction of surprise. It is not surprise about what I have thought or done but a reaction to something I have been told or that I have heard about or that I have read. Surprise is a frequent reaction in our lives, but far more often than not it is fleeting in its consequences. It does not cause reverberations in our thinking or actions. So, for example, we may read that a public figure (such as a president) is in his or her private life far less likeable or moral or honest a person than the public has been led to believe. We are surprised by the discrepancy and we are disappointed, but we do not conclude that what caused our surprise is other than another instance of something we have already heard about in our lifetime and in human history. It is put in the "so what else is new?" category; that is, given what "human nature" is, we really should not have been all that surprised.

Why does something cause surprise in one person and not in another? What are the antecedent conditions that, in part at least, explain these individual differences? And what does an *individual's* response of surprise to the perception of a single experience have to do with a conclusion about a possible *social* change? The last question rests on the assumption that some individuals sense social change much earlier than others, although it depends on the particular social change. Unfortunately, that question has, for all practical purposes, not been studied. We know after the fact that some individuals did come to a valid conclusion, but we hardly know how they went from surprise to a conclusion that went far beyond the occasion that caused surprise. We also know that most of the people who had a similar surprise reaction, even to the same event, came to no conclusion or to the wrong one. My starting point is not the validity of the conclusion but rather the antecedents of the surprise and to what they give rise.

There is an interpersonal phenomenon—having nothing to do with social change—that may give us direction. It is the reaction of surprise in a psychotherapist who over a period of time has been listening and reacting to a patient. It is an "aha" reaction for which the therapist was not prepared. It "pops" into his or her awareness and contains an "answer" either to what has previously puzzled the therapist, or it puts into new relationships things the patient had related but to which the therapist had given only passing attention, or both. Psychologically, it is less that the problem *is* solved and more that it had *already* been solved but was waiting, so to speak, to sneak into the therapist's awareness. When that reaction takes place, a reconfiguration of the therapist's thinking and actions follows. It is a reaction about connections heretofore not recognized.

What I am describing is by no means frequent. Indeed, as best as I can determine it is a phenomenon that is familiar to psychoanalysts, but even among them description and discussion are rare. Only one psychoanalyst has systematically described the phenomenon. That was Theodor Reik in what I consider to be two brilliant books: *Surprise and the Psychoanalyst* (1937) and *Listening with the Third Ear* (1983). The phenomenon is real. Patients in psychoanalysis have experienced it, although their numbers are unknown. Let me give a personal example, one that made me read Reik's earlier book. I was relating to my analyst one of my earliest memories.

I could not have been more than four or five years of age. I was standing on the edge of the top of the six-floor apartment house, urinating. As I was relating this it suddenly hit me—that is the way it felt—that what I was relating was blatantly, inescapably, comically wrong, a sheer fantasy. Aside from the fact that the roof of the building had a two-foot parapet, the odds that my mother would have allowed me to be on that roof alone are beyond calculation, even with today's avant-garde computers! Once I got over the surprise reaction, a constellation of thoughts, feelings, and events "appeared" containing *connections* that, to say the least, were illuminatingly explanatory and moving.

What I am describing is sometimes called insight, that is, a sudden reorganization, a repatterning, of thinking about a problem with which one has been struggling. Instances of it have been described in histories of scientific-mathematical discoveries. It is the kind of experience Conan Doyle uses to illuminate one of Sherlock Holmes's ways of solving a mystery. I should hasten to add that I am not suggesting that the substance or content of the phenomenon always in part or in whole is valid or productive. As usual, we are told about the "successes," not the "failures." What I am asserting is that the psychological process is real and, relevant to the purposes of this essay, that it is preceded by an attitude, or set, in regard to a problem—a set compounded of puzzlement, frustration, and a need for clarification. This is most clear in the case of the psychoanalyst, whose basic stance is supposed to be to listen in a way that leaves him or her open to hear and consider the diverse meanings in and connections among what a patient is relating, that is, he or she listens with that "third ear," which, if closed, prevents one from coming up with alternative and more encompassing and productive explanations of the problems a patient is describing and confronting.[1]

---

[1]In a talk Theodor Reik gave at Yale (around 1948) he implied that, despite training and theory, not all analysts could use their third ear. Indeed, it was my impression that Reik believed the number of analysts subject to this criticism was not small.

All of the preceding is prologue to and justification for the use of my personal experience to illustrate how I became aware that a social change had occurred—more correctly, how earlier and disparate events about which I was only somewhat puzzled suddenly took on significances that, for me at least, altered my understanding of my world and its future.

The story begins in 1965 by my reading what I had thought was to be a novel with the title *The Story of O*, by Pauline Reage (1965). The book had originally been published in France in 1954, where, the dust jacket said, it had received critical acclaim and caused controversy. To say that I was not prepared for what I was to read is to indulge understatement. It is a step-by-step account of a woman's willing subjugation to every sexual-physical indignity her lover could imagine and that would give him and her pleasure. As a clinical psychologist I was familiar with the literature on sexual perversions. As someone who had been psychoanalyzed I had lost my innocence about my capacity, past and present, to entertain a not-small gamut of unconventional sexual fantasies; as the clinical jargon would put it: I have an active fantasy life. But my *fantasy* life paled before the *behaviors* detailed in the book. Because you have a fantasy does not justify acting in accord with it. But not in the *Story of O*! It is a small book but packed in it, in escalating, step-by-step fashion, is indulgence of sadomasochistic experience. I admit that I found some of it titillating when it touched on some of my own fantasies. But my overriding reaction was one of revulsion and anger. Revulsion because its contents were calmly described and no explanations given, as if it was the outline of a book on the phenomenology of sadism and masochism. It was pornography pure and simple. My anger, of course, was that I had bought the book. Reading the book occasioned no surprise, although it did indicate that in terms of an active fantasy life I was not in the same league as the author. Not incidentally, I soon found out, the American publisher was known for seeking and publishing books that bordered on the pornographic.

The surprise reaction came several months later when I was leafing through the book review section of the Sunday *New York Times* and my eye was caught by a heading for the review of the book by a professor at Princeton University. That was a surprise, but not of the kind I am discussing in this essay. That kind of surprise came as I began to read the review, which regarded the novel as a strangely moving work of literary art. It was not a long review, but on a rating scale of one through ten, where one is "don't bother to read it" and ten is "go to the phone and order it," the review would have gotten at least a seven.

I could not believe my eyes. I could not believe that two people, full professors from Ivy league colleges to boot, could have such different reactions. I was *surprised*. Was I crazy? Was I really so out of whack about what was worthy literature? Needless to say, I did not change my mind. But in short order I became aware that this was not the first time I was puzzled by a public response in public media to matters sexual. It all connected in my head, whether right or wrong by conventional criteria of logic, appropriateness, or so-called common sense. I say that because they were connections among happenings that on the surface seemed unrelated, sometimes contradictory, but from which I drew conclusions about their role as seeds of a social change. In short, I can be right for the right reasons, right for the wrong reasons, or just plain wrong. The point I am illustrating is that following my surprise reaction to reading the book review, things got connected from past experience that heretofore had been unconnected.

The first of these was not an event but what I shall call an institutional change. Before World War II, psychoanalysis—as theory, research, and therapy—had little standing within the fields of psychiatry and psychology. Students, of course, heard about Freud, were asked to read about him here and there, but in the main, psychoanalysis was not respected; it had little or no points of commonality with mainstream ideas in these fields, it was regarded as unscientific and as egregiously reductionistic in its emphasis on sexuality and in its continuities in development from the earliest days to the adult years. To members of these fields, as to the general public, a major goal of psychoanalytic therapy was to enable the individual to overcome his or her sexual inhibitions and/or crippling guilt about his or her sexual fantasies. The word "catharsis," so frequently a feature in psychoanalytic writing, was taken to mean license to give expression, in words and actions, to the forbidden. If you wanted to learn what psychoanalysis was all about, the university was no place to learn it. Instead, you went to an analytic institute, of which there were very few and all but one were in large urban areas. Psychoanalysis had little or no standing in the social sciences, except for anthropology, and that was because some of Freud's more provocative writings challenged mainstream thinking. Aside from a handful of anthropologists (such as Edward Sapir), Freud's speculations were by no means esteemed, and studies were done that called into question those speculations. As for the professionals in the humanities, Freud was pretty close to being a nonperson.

That picture was true up until we entered World War II in 1941. Within a handful of years after the war ended in the summer of 1945, the picture was obsolete. The academic stage had a new actor, one who had been in the wings, so to speak, and overnight became a star. If being on the analytic couch was somewhat less than a badge of honor, it surely meant that you were fashionable, someone who was keeping up with the times. And if God was on your side and you were admitted to an analytic training institute, *that* was a badge of honor that meant that someday you might be made a training analyst in a secular college of cardinals. All of this took place with startling rapidity.

I know whereof I speak. I was a true believer. It may be that I was the first to teach a graduate course in psychoanalysis in a department of psychology. It was during the second year of teaching the course that my puzzlement began. Initially it concerned the language of psychoanalytic theory: its metaphors, its mechanical-hydraulic-like explanations, and much more. More to the point, I began to wonder why so many people, both in and out of academia, were so attracted to psychoanalytic theory and therapy. I had no doubt then, as I have no doubt now, that Freud gave us kernels of psychological gold. That is the point of the lead essay in my book *Psychoanalysis, General Custer, and the Verdicts of History* (1994). What puzzled me at the time was why so many people thought that psychoanalytic therapy rather than other types of psychotherapy was the answer to their personal problems. What were those problems? I was by no means alone in concluding that a lot of people had sexual hangups. All you had to do was read the clinical psychoanalytic house organs, or attend the meetings, lectures, and conventions of the analytic associations to arrive at the conclusion that all major personal problems were at their roots sexual in nature; some people seeking therapy might not say or believe that their problems were sexual but, just wait, the truth will emerge. Whatever the problem as defined by the patient, he or she far more often than not knew it had a sexual component. And those who did not know it had heard that it would.

My puzzlement was inchoate and fleeting. After all, even if I was slowly losing the attributes of the true believer, I still believed that most people lived lives of quiet desperation, with inhibitions preventing productive self-expression. And psychoanalysis did hold out the prospect of overcoming these conflicts and inhibitions, allowing one to become not only different than one was but nearly a totally new personality. What was not inchoate was my degree of awareness that psychoanalysis had all of the characteristics of a movement quite similar to what I had experienced in radical politics: an idealogy, a messianic quality, a dividing of the world into believers and nonbelievers, the good guys and the bad guys, attacks and counter attacks, and all of this with the passion of zealots and the worshipping of Freud, the founding father. That was true not only for the analytic fraternity but for many of their patients, some of whom seemed to make being in therapy a way of life.

I am not being snide or contemptuous but rather revealing what was in my head in those days. I knew the academic world had radically changed since my graduate days from 1939 to 1942. I also knew that the country had changed, but I did not know what it meant and portended. What I *sensed* was that the change had something to say about what people owed to themselves despite what past conventions said they owed to others. It would be more correct to put it this way: life is too short to spend it within the constraints of traditional American middle-class values about self-expression. Beginning with the end of World War II the divorce rate had begun to rise. I am not aware that anyone has seen it as important to determine the rate of divorce in the period from 1945 to 1950 among patients in psychoanalytic (or other types of) therapy. At the time, my unscientific barometer told me it was higher than in the general population. If true, it is also the case that I sensed but did not know for sure what it might mean.

If the first part of the story was not an event but a kind of institutional change, the second part involves two events occurring less than a year apart. The first event, the publication of the first Kinsey report (1948) on the sexual behavior of males, I have discussed in greater detail elsewhere (Sarason, 1994). Suffice it to say here that the interest and furor aroused by that report—before, on, and after its publication date—was remarkable. It literally was front-page stuff. What would the report on male sexuality reveal? That was the question asked with a degree of interest similar, decades later, to the question "Who shot JR?" on the TV program *Dallas*.

I was not in doubt that people's interest reflected sheer curiosity about a morally loaded activity and about the following concerns: (a) If you were a male, how did you stand in comparison to other males? (b) If you were female, how "normal or abnormal" was your spouse or lover? (c) If you were gay, what was the frequency of such male behavior, when did it begin, and was it absent in the sexual history of apparently "normal" males? (d) What were or should be the criteria of "normality"? What was at issue was whether shame and guilt were justified if one's style of sexual expression was not frequently expressed and/or idiosyncratic. Once when I was discussing the Kinsey report in class, a student said, "In other words, if I see an unidentified flying object land and extraterrestrials start walking out of it, I will think I am nuts. But if some of my neighbors say they also saw what I saw, I will change my diagnosis. I'll stick to what to me was reality." That may not have been the most felicitous of analogies but it was making what to me was the crucial point, that many people desired evidence that a particular style of personal expression was acceptable and, therefore, not to be inhibited. There were, of course, many people who hoped or expected that the report would confirm conventional standards of what was unusual, deviant, and unacceptable.

There were many scientific, methodological, and theoretical aspects of the Kinsey report that were hotly and publicly debated, not the least of which concerned homosexuality and extramarital affairs. Three things puzzled me: I was unprepared for how the report became a media event, the passions it engendered, and what it portended for the future. Would the report be interpreted by some people as justifying continuing what conventional morality deemed unacceptable, and would it embolden some people who had inhibited such activity to engage in that activity? If these questions occurred to and puzzled me, I was not set to pursue the matter, that is, to relate it to other changed features of the society. So, for example, I sensed but did not pursue the possible relationships between what the Kinsey report revealed and engendered and the changes the war years had wrought in the sexual activities of millions of people who had been in the armed services and those who had not.

My puzzlement got somewhat clarified, but only somewhat, by another media event some months later, an event that, again, was on the front pages of the newspapers, including the more august ones. It was about the actress Ingrid Bergman, who had gone to Italy to make a picture with the director Roberto Rossellini, had became pregnant with his child, and was seeking a divorce from her husband with whom she had had two children. To the American public,

Miss Bergman was the epitome of a divinely gifted but secular angel. *Casablanca* was only one of the movies in which her angelic "purity" provided the basis for her widespread acclaim and belovedness.

The reaction to what she did was explosive, immediate, and divided. The Hollywood protectors of American morality pronounced anathema, papal style. She was vilified on the floors of Congress. Some of her adoring public gave voice to their bitter disappointment. But some of that public defended her. There were many public figures who in later years said they did not defend her at the time for fear of meeting her fate of excommunication. And that was the source of my surprise: despite the Hollywood and other public denunciations, I do not think I talked with anyone who condemned her, who thought that she had done something wicked, and who felt that the punishment fit the public crime. You can sum up the reaction of almost everyone I spoke with in this way: Having an affair is no big deal. She had the misfortune to get pregnant. Poor judgment. But the way the media are playing it, as if she deserves to be burned at the stake, is hypocritical.

I had no basis whatsoever for claiming that the people I spoke with were representative of people in general. They were not. But it was my distinct impression—from reading letters to the editor and mass media magazines—that the number of people who thought Ingrid Bergman was being unfairly tarred and feathered was far from minuscule. Also, coming as it did so soon after the Kinsey report, I did make the assumption that a lot of those who greeted the report positively were on Miss Bergman's side. That is to say, they were not recommending that others do what she did, but they certainly were not about to nail her to the cross. American society was losing some of the force of its puritanism. I put it that way because her denunciators unknowingly, in part but only in part, regarded what she had done as a sign of a spreading alteration in the criteria for socially appropriate moral behavior. I was sensing that alteration, but my interests at the time were about clinical matters, not social ones.

Another part of the story was not an event. By the early 1950s, urban juvenile delinquency among minority youth was recognized as a serious problem. Many different factors were given as explanations for why these young people were attracted to criminal activities. Racial unrest, poverty, poor and overcrowded housing conditions, and social disorganization caused by the war were the most frequent explanations. If the problem was serious, it did not lead to federal governmental initiatives. Local governments did not have adequate financial resources, aggravated as their plight was by the war-produced baby boom for whom there were insufficient and very inadequate school buildings as well as not enough school personnel. It was at this time that the newly created Ford Foundation conceived and began to implement its "gray area" projects in five cities, an effort that in a few years was to be very influential in the design of federal interventions.

Urban juvenile delinquency was seen as a racial, political, economic, and moral problem. Those kinds of global explanations, however valid as descriptive labels, did not explain how what they stood for was assimilated by increasing numbers of young people to justify their criminal behavior. Was there more to it than just wanting to get some of the goodies of this world? Or in addition was there the element of a conscious rebellion against a perceived unjust society? Was there a countercultural aim, a rejection of convention?

I was a resident of New Haven, which was one of the Ford Foundation's "gray area" cities. I was aware that something was brewing in this deteriorating, ugly, unsafe, problem-plagued city. But again my barometers of social change were quite insensitive. Yale was in but not of New Haven. What began to open my eyes were the controversies and open conflicts following the 1954 desegregation decision. Yes, juvenile delinquency was a serious problem, but it took on greater significance in light of a pervasive change in the black community as to what was right, natural, and proper. Young people in that community were hearing messages from others in that community. I am not suggesting that they were messages that stimulated and condoned crime, but I am saying that these messages had to be an influence on how young people saw their world and justified criminal activity. It goes without saying that most young black people engaged in no criminal activity; they expressed their rebelliousness in other ways, if they did at all.

What I inchoately sensed became more clear when several years later I became affiliated with the Ford Foundation project in New Haven. It became clear that a social change had already occurred and not only in the black community. The leaders of the project were largely white, and they were no less militant and rebellious about social discrimination than black leaders. In fact, they made no bones, at least in private conversation, about their almost total rejection of the idea that any part of the answer to righting wrongs could come via existing institutions such as schools and the array of public and private social agencies, including, of course, Yale University, which they regarded (realistically) as one of many lost causes. What these leaders intended to do and did do was to create a variety of new agencies in which blacks would play key roles. The social pot was getting hot. The theme of and justification for empowerment were clearly articulated. Even altering or abolishing the *ancien régime* was one of the implications of the messages, and voices that had never before received expression now began to demand expression, attention, and action. These were not messages heard only by young and old in the black community. They were heard in the white community, especially among its youth.

One more step in the story: Jack Kerouac's *On the Road* was published in 1957. It had been written several years before when Kerouac was part of a small group of social rebels at Columbia University who became icons and cult figures in what later was called the counterculture. A dominant theme in the book is not only the importance of self-expression as an axiom for living but the thirst for and strength of the importance of new experience. When I read that book and the critical acclaim it received—a heralding of the wave of the future—I knew that a social change had already occurred and was picking up steam, and I was far from clear about what to make of it all. If it was a new world, I certainly had not been one of its explorers. I was straight, and I did not know if, when, and how to bend, if I were to bend at all. As the sixties started and began to explode, a lot became clearer to me. I shall refrain from giving more examples of how events made my interest in social change so fascinating and perplexing to me.

What has all of this to do with my reading of a review of *The Story of O* in 1965? Why did the review stun me and bring together in my mind what I have related above, as if those past experiences and observations were primed to be brought together, however different they were in time, form, and substance? And by the words "bringing together" I do not mean it was wholly or in large measure the result of a conscious, rational searching. Part of it was the "popping into my head" phenomenon so well described by Reik. Perhaps the best way to explain why these things came together is to state the conclusions I drew from the process.

1. For different reasons for different people in and out of the armed services, World War II increased the preoccupation with self and an uncertain future. The war years were not a hiatus but a disruption, a spur to the making up for "the best years of our lives." The self that had been was one thing, the self that could and should be was a different matter. It was not a break with but a variant of American individualism.

2. Again for different reasons for different people, the frustrations, constraints, and the not-infrequent tragedies experienced in the war years increased the force of the need for self-expression, that is, it was believed that convention could and should be less of an obstacle to the fulfillment of goals, dreams, and fantasies. In an uncertain future governed by fickle fate, one had an obligation to one's self not to rely on the long-term future for personal expression and happiness.

3. In different ways in different *groups* a redefinition of self took the form: no longer will we regard ourselves as others have regarded us in the past; we will no longer be content to suffer lack of recognition or anonymity or injustice or poverty, even if what we seek is opposed by legalisms or conventional standards of morality.

4.   However different these groups were, they had in common the goal of freeing themselves from and changing the status quo. Alone, none of these groups would have had a relatively quick, let alone dramatic, impact but because they were active *at the same time* they came to see kinship with each other—at the least they were in sympathy with each other. That degree of coalescence had a multiplicative effect.

5.   Every call for *social and institutional* change in the two decades after the war—be it from an individual or groups—had its origins in World War II. We are used to hearing that war is a continuation of politics by other means, and implied in that statement is conscious decision making. Even if that statement is universally historically valid, it is also the case that wars, especially total ones, unwittingly provide the context for mammoth, unanticipated social-institutional change.

That was what came together in my head after I read the review of *The Story of O*. I read other reviews all of which were on the favorable side. *Newsweek* wrote, "An ironic fable of unfreedom, a mystic document that transcends the pornographic and even the erotic." We were not told to what it transcended. The daily *Times Book Review* saw the author as "a more dangerous writer than the Marquis de Sade. . . . Art is more persuasive than propaganda. . . . Aiming only to reveal, to clarify, to make real to the reader those dark and repulsive practices and emotions that his better self rejects as improbable or evil, she succeeds in drawing us irresistibly into her perverse world through the magnetism of her own selfless absorption in it." My view was obviously a minority one. Even if I was a dinosaur from an earlier era—which cannot be discounted—I did not have difficulty concluding *in 1965* that the book would be persuasive and irresistible to more than a few people. By 1965, you did not have to be the most astute social analyst to perceive that many people were severing the chains of "unfreedom" they perceived.

I am reminded here of the critical acclaim Marlon Brando received years earlier for his persuasive and irresistible portrayal in

A *Streetcar Named Desire* of male sexuality, physicality, explosiveness, and cruelty. That kind of portrayal had not been seen in the theater. Stanley Kowalski was not bound by the chains of convention. The Brando style, a seething volcano with the most thin of caps, became a "style" in the theater. Brando was tailor-made for the broodings and physical-sexual explosions in the autobiographical plays of Tennessee Williams. I am also reminded of the Elvis Presley phenomenon, and of Frank Sinatra, Bing Crosby, and Perry Como, singers who stood up and sang. Presley's singing came with suggestive bodily movements. The story has it that Ed Sullivan allowed Presley to appear on his TV program if he promised to shake only from the waist up! The reader who wants to understand why Elvis Presley appealed to white *and* black youth should read Peter Guralnik's *Last Train to Memphis* (1994). The Elvis Presley social phenomenon is also well-captured in Stephen Wright's review in the Sunday Book Review section of *The New York Times* for October 30, 1994. Here is an excerpt:

> As Presley's career catches fire, so does the narrative momentum. Mr. Guralnick puts you through the heady, frightening ride to the top that was as startling to Elvis as it was to the rest of the country.
>
> Presley's first record, "That's All Right (Mama)," was released in July 1954. A week and a half later he performed professionally for the first time before a live audience. In a month the record entered the Billboard regional charts. On Oct. 2 Presley sang at the Grand Ole Opry in Nashville. By Oct. 20 he was a regular on the Louisiana Hayride out of Shreveport. Throughout the fall he and his guitarist, Scotty Moore, and his bassist, Bill Black, toured across the South; in the spring of 1955 they went up to Cleveland and to an audition for "Arthur Godfrey's Talent Scouts" in New York. The first riot occurred in May in Jacksonville, Fla., where Presley's

clothes were torn from his back. The touring continued almost nonstop.

In November 1955 RCA bought Presley's contract from Sun for a record-setting amount: $35,000. His network television debut occurred in January 1956 on the Dorsey Brothers' "Stage Show" on CBS, the first of six appearances. In April he sang "Blue Suede Shoes" on "The Milton Berle Show." He played two weeks in Las Vegas, and by the time he appeared on "The Steve Allen Show" in July there was an Elvis Presley record sitting atop each of the three in-store charts: pop, rhythm-and-blues and country. In August he began filming his first motion picture, "Love Me Tender." In September he was seen on "The Ed Sullivan Show," the first of three appearances, and by October he had sold more than 10 million singles for RCA, which represented approximately two-thirds of the label's singles business. He was 21 years old.

That kind of social response is not explained solely by the sound of music.

The Story of O was published in the United States in 1965. It had quite a sale. It would not or could not have been published here in 1954 when it was published in France. If it had been published here in 1954, it would not have received the reviews it did, for the same reason that so many people would not publicly express criticism of the denunciations of Ingrid Bergman. But in 1965 it was another story. It was evident that a social change had not only occurred but was picking up steam, and sexuality was but one of the features of a movement for self-expression and against "unfreedom."[2]

[2]In the August 1, 1994 issue of *The New Yorker*, John de St. Jorre has an article with the title "The Unmasking of O." The subheading reads: "It's been forty years since the publication of "Story of O"—the sexual landmark that became one of the most widely read French novels. But, until now, the author's true identity

The degree and pace of social change were in part determined as they usually are, by adventitious factors—such as assassinations of figures revered by many groups, and the Vietnam War—that galvanized and coalesced different groups with different agendas.

I have said that we do not become aware of social change until after that change has begun to occur. I have indicated in this essay that I did not perceive the change in its early sproutings. If I noted this and that sprouting I certainly did not know what weight to give them or if and how to put them together. Using hindsight, I and others have tried to assign weights and bring the barometers into relationship with each other. There is no general agreement, only agreement on certain factors. Future historians probably will discern patterns we do not or cannot.

But why do we try to explain the changes wrought by World War II? Basic to such attempts is the assumption that we can devise better barometers to catch future changes earlier than we have caught changes in the past. That assumption is not as reasonable as it sounds, because social change is never static. It is not that it gets played out but that it is always *playing* out, its impact, better yet impacts, causing other changes, or at least setting the stage for new changes. As Robert Nisbet has pointed out so well (1969), the present is not pregnant with a future but with many futures. The question becomes not what barometers we need to sense future change but rather how well our barometers are telling us about the present.

---

has been shrouded in a literary mystery." St. Jorre does not say why he considers it a "sexual landmark." He quotes the author, Dominique Aury, as saying that she wrote much of the book in a dreamlike state as an expression of love to her lover, whom she had feared would abandon her. What she wrote was never intended for publication. Her lover, influential in publishing circles, insisted on getting it published. Why she was reluctant to go public (albeit masking her identity) may be gleamed from the final paragraph of the article: "Who am I finally," she once wrote, "if not the long-silent part of someone, the secret and nocturnal part which has never betrayed itself in public by any thought, word, or deed, but communicates through subterranean depths of the imaginary with dreams as old as the world itself." Social change is a *combination* of forces each of which gives expression to dreams, sexual or otherwise, "as old as the world itself."

In a society as large and as complicated as ours, to what among all that we can attend to are we attending?

In the economic sphere we have many barometers some of which are quite sensitive to economic changes and their consequences. So, for example, if starts for new housing rise then we expect that companies manufacturing home furnishings will do well. If interest rates rise, we know that it will affect the rate of building or buying homes, and a lot more. What we do not know is how many people build or buy new homes because they realistically can afford to do so or because, as happened in the mid to late eighties, they believed that their incomes would continue to rise, that their property would appreciate in value, and that the future was unclouded. In those years the construction industry seemed to build on the premise that materials were going out of style. Nor do we know what happens to the outlooks of people in different age groups when they have inadequate housing and no reason to believe they will ever be able to afford better housing. To say they will be unhappy is to explain nothing, because unhappiness means different things and has different consequences in different age groups and social strata.

Today (1995) economic barometers tell us that we have emerged from the recent recession, although people in New England and California find it hard to believe. The economists point, among other things, to a low unemployment rate and to an increase in productivity and the gross national product. What the economist cannot tell us is how those who had worked at well-paying jobs with the expectation that in the future their income would increase and their positions would be of higher status have experienced a change in personal and worldview by virtue of losing their jobs with no prospect of achieving what they had dreamed. We are not talking about a few people but about millions, especially if you include young people whose level of education, skills, and expectations are much higher than is or will be called for in the job market.

Economic barometers are about change, but *not* social change.

The referents of social change are ways of thinking, feeling, and acting that are nontransient alterations of usual norms, and they
become widespread. The alterations are experienced and manifested
differently in different individuals. They may not be experienced as
alterations, but at some point they are recognized as such because
they are recognized by others whose ways of thinking, feeling, and
acting have *not* been altered.

Three things happen at that point: the "altered" individuals are
given a label, those individuals perceive themselves as a group, and
a gulf develops between them and other "nonaltered" segments of
the society. A single perceived alteration does not make for or contribute to social change unless there is a coincidence of different
alterations that play into each other, so to speak. Social change is
the opposite of a fad or fashion. It is a percolating interrelating of
different alterations among different groups. Especially in its earliest phases, social change cannot be discerned by statistical indices
because the manifestations of the alteration, its phenotypic features,
vary widely and are not and cannot be labeled. We are never in the
position of the Federal Center for Disease Control, which on the
basis of very few reported cases, sometimes as little as one, alerts us
to a situation potentially dangerous to people's health. Their barometers give readings for conditions about which a good deal is known,
such as that pneumonias today are not different from those ten or
more years ago. But what happens when their barometers give
unclear or misleading readings? That is what happened in the case
of early reports about a constellation of symptoms later called AIDS.
What did this constellation signify? What was its geographical dis-
tribution? What were the social, psychological, gender, and social
characteristics of those who had the condition? The center was criticized for not picking up earlier the different significances of the disease. That criticism was as justified as the criticism directed to social
analysts for not recognizing that a social change had occurred. It
was unjustified because it was a new medical-social phenomenon
for which no barometer existed; such a barometer had to be devised,

altered, refined. The time it took to devise the barometer was small compared to the time it takes to become aware that a social change has occurred.

Social change always has its proponents and opponents. They see the world in black and white terms; there is no gray. It is also the case that neither recognizes the iron law of unintended consequences. Winners and losers always pay a price for apparently achieving their goals. What that price is becomes clear only with the passage of time and when it does, the seeds of another social change are already germinating.

6

The Changing Ecology of Child Rearing

Social change has unintended consequences in the short and long term. We can know the long-term consequences only in a vague, general way, and that statement can only be made because there have been a few who in the long-ago past wrote about the long-term future in ways that continue to amaze us. For example, Tocqueville's *Democracy in America* (1945/1845) continues to amaze us, more than 150 years after it was written. And although Karl Marx was egregiously wrong about a lot of things, he was right about how the capitalist ethos would increase the sense of rootlessness and decrease the sense of community. And what about the clerics and others in the Age of Enlightenment who said that once religion became generally weak or absent, its secular substitutes (such as nationalism and individualism) would be a bitter cup of tea? Marx and the clerics regarded each other as abominations, but each in his own way saw a future that would be marked by people's inhumanity to other people. Some will say they were right for the wrong reasons. Others will say they were right for the right reasons in that both Marx and the clerics believed that people could not live without some sense of transcendence. The clerics stood for transcendence via a divinity. Marx provided it by portraying a vision of the triumph of the brotherhood of man by abolishing the sources of personal and social degradation. Marx and the clerics assumed that the need for transcendence was real. You may damn both Marx and the clerics, but neither of them would be surprised that the twentieth century has been the bloodiest in human history.

The above is prologue to a question about the long-term future of the social change that has occurred in the post World War II era. It concerns the long-term future of young children who are now growing up. Before stating and discussing the question, it is necessary to trace briefly some of the ways children have been regarded since the end of the war, because how they are regarded has always said something about what present and future generations of children should experience and be. That "something" was not of a piece and, as I shall indicate later, it ignored the implications of the social change that was already occurring in society.

There is no one generalization that sums up people's attitudes towards the future after World War II. However, there is one generalization that captures their attitudes toward coming generations of children: they deserved lives unmarked by war, social unrest, and interruptions in the fulfillment of personal goals. Very soon after the war the Full Employment Act was passed, the purpose of which was to prevent the recurrence and tragedy of economic depressions. It concerned adults. But in the minds of parents of the beginning "baby boom" explosion, most had their own "A Full Life for Children Act" and it was not going to be like the lives of their parents. Children deserved better and parents expected them to be and do better. If it meant different things to different people, it nevertheless confronted parents with the question: what is the best way to help my child be and do better?

That parental objective goes a long way toward explaining why Dr. Spock's (1946) book on baby and child rearing had such meteoric sales. It is probably the case that more parents read *and* used his book than they did the bible. Much of the book concerned bodily symptoms and diseases, but it also said a lot about how to stimulate and support the mind of the developing infant-child. Another example is the reception accorded Skinner's *Walden II* (1948). It is a book about a utopian adult community, but the reader is never left in doubt that Skinner is enunciating psychological principles that he said should inform the rearing of children. When the book was published its sales were modest, but in less than a handful of years it became a best-seller.

No one will dispute the assertion that Jean Piaget, the Swiss psychologist, is one of the two most impactful figures in child development in this century. Although he was known earlier (but not truly appreciated) in relatively narrow circles in academia in the United States, his real impact started to be felt in the late forties and early fifties when the bulk of the corpus of his writings began to appear in English translations, writings describing studies done decades before. It was also at this time that the fields of child psychology and child psychiatry burgeoned as never before, and Piaget, together with Freud, occupied center stage. Piaget was no dispenser of parental advice, but his work on cognitive development from infancy to early adolescence had obvious implications for understanding and supporting the stages of cognitive development. Parents heard about Piaget and more than a few parents tried to read his work, although he is not an easy read.

A more personal example: After the war I wrote a book *Psychological Problems in Mental Deficiency* (1949). I submitted it to Harper & Row; they said it was a good book but who was interested in mentally defective children and their parents? If I was willing to take reduced royalties on the first 2,500 copies, they would publish it. If they had said they could give me no royalties, I would have agreed to such an arrangement. I had absolutely no doubt that the book would sell well (for that kind of a book). Indeed, I predicted then that one of the coming big fields in psychology would center around children, parents, and families. I wish I could say that the prediction was based on my possessing sensitive barometers of social change, but it was not. It was "one of those feelings" that are probably wrong more often than right. The book sold well.

I had come to Yale in 1945 and in that initial postwar cohort of graduate students were Paul Mussen and John Conger, whose major

interest was in child development. Not long after my book was published I learned that they were writing a book on child development. I spoke to the editor at Harper and urged him to sign them
up sight unseen. By that time the editor had somewhat more respect
for my opinion and he did sign them up. The sales of that book
climbed at an ever accelerating rate. It sold hundreds of thousands
of copies. It was truly a sign of the times.

Without question, however, one of the most obvious signs of the
times was that by 1950 psychoanalysis (as theory, therapy, and
research) had been legitimated in the university where before the
war it was, for all practical purposes, unrepresented. *That* was a
change, a remarkable one that had percolating effects, and it happened quickly. To someone like me who was in graduate school from
1939 to 1942, who spent several years as a clinical psychologist in
a state training school for mentally retarded individuals in Connecticut's rural nowhere and then came to Yale in 1945, I was witness to that change in all of the social sciences and in psychiatry, at
Yale and most other universities. To my knowledge, no one has seen
fit to describe those years as a barometer signaling a social change,
as a barometer of an emerging zeitgeist that went far beyond the
university. I would go so far as to say that no future historian will
understand the postwar years—to give due weight to this or that
factor—unless that historian confronts and answers this question:
How and why did this remarkable change come about so quickly
and what did it reflect about other changes that were consequences
of the war? That question was not and could not be asked in those
early postwar years. The participants (including me) had no interest
in devising barometers to detect and make sense of the change. We
knew the seeds of change had begun to sprout but it did not occur
to anyone to relate it to other developments in the societal garden.
As the years go by I see no evidence that anyone is interested in the
significances of the change.

If anything is distinctive about psychoanalysis, it is its emphasis
on the significance of childhood. That focus is too narrow unless

you mean that childhood begins from the day of birth, because that is where analytic theory starts. What happens in those early years is crucial for all else that follows. Oak trees from little acorns grow. To Freud, the way a child develops may cause him or her to be psychologically stunted and barren of the expected fruits of maturity. It does not have to be that way but it frequently is. Childhood is a series of internal and external conflicts never experienced as less than momentous. It is like going down a road mined with explosives, except the child does not know that there is a road and that there are explosives. The aim of therapy is to make sense of that childhood and its relationship to the problems that bring the adult patient to the analytic couch. (Therapy is conducted quite differently in the case of children whose problems are already crippling.)

Today, psychoanalysis is far from the dominant influence it was in the first two decades after the war. However, it is too easy to forget—and for those born after, say, 1970 there is little to remember—that one of Freud's great contributions was to direct attention to infantile sexuality and childhood, to make them a legitimate subject of inquiry as never before. That was one of the allures of psychoanalysis, and those in the immediate postwar decade who had become or would become parents who wanted a different and better world for their children were receptive to new messages. And that is the point: a renewed and expanded interest in childhood meant a renewed and expanded interest in parents and families. When the National Institute of Mental Health was created in 1948, it soon started to support "womb-to-the-tomb" psychoanalytic research on neonates and their families.

Spurred by the influence of psychoanalytic theory, researchers began to carry out numerous studies to determine the relation of specific child rearing practices to later behavior and personality. What were the differential effects of feeding infants by a schedule compared to feeding them when the parent decided the child was hungry? What were the later differences between those who were breast fed and those who were bottle fed? What were the differences between those who were toilet trained when they were "supposed" to be ready and those who were toilet trained much later? What were the differences between infants who were allowed to cry and were not picked up and those who were picked up once they started to cry? Would the neonates who during their hospital stay were in the same room as the mother show a more favorable development than those who remained in the hospital nursery? In regard to these and similar studies, parental attitudinal factors were deemed important, that is, each specific practice said something about parental attitude and personality that was salient for the very young child.

All of this was not lost on mass media magazines, which monthly reported the "latest" advice of child rearing experts. However different the advice, the implicit message was: this or that specific practice or experience could have negative, long-term consequences and parents should know that. Rearing the very young child was a tricky, precarious affair and not one to be handled, as it previously had been, by following the advice of your mother, grandmother, favorite aunt, or close friends—this at a time when the prewar nuclear and extended family was rather quickly becoming dispersed. Young parents felt a need—and the mass media reinforced it—for advice from the new experts almost all of whom, albeit in varying degrees, had been influenced by psychoanalytic thinking. I think it is fair to say that as a group, young postwar parents were insecure about how to rear children who over the long term would not be psychologically-socially impaired. I knew many parents who were wedded to this or that specific practice but who "inside" had all kinds of qualms and anxieties. As one friend said, "I'm going by the book but my mother said I am reading the wrong one, and I sometimes wonder if she is right."

Subsequent research demolished the simpleminded assumption about the correlation between a specific child rearing practice and later personality. Aside from demolishing that assumption, it gave credence to the belief that what was important were parental personality styles, which were reflected in their ways of viewing and handling the child. That is to say, if anything was crucial for the child in the long term it was parental personality style, whether there was or was not a conflict in style between mother and father. Parental style was the one constant between the short and long term.

Social change cannot be accounted for by any single barometer. I am asserting that one of the barometers of the seeds of the social change that was taking root in the decade or so after World War II had to do with a change in parental attitudes in regard to how one viewed the relationship between the short- and long-term consequences of child rearing experiences. What relationships, if any, were there between that barometer and others that could have been devised for what was beginning to happen? For example, the move to suburbia, a rising divorce rate, the increase of women in the work place, the shrinkage of family size, and the emergence, magnetism, and role of TV—were these and other barometers discrete and psychologically unrelated? Were the reaction to atomic tests and the disillusionments with the fruits of victory in World War II encapsulated areas in the minds of parents? Was that also the case for the steady rise and ease of long-distance travel? In asking these questions I am saying that World War II changed the worldview of people, and one of the ingredients of a worldview is the relationship of the short to the long term, that is, how things are; how they should be; what is right, natural and proper; and what people are and what they should be in their relations with one another.

A change in worldview does not take place quickly, except in the case of a world catastrophe, which World War I and II were. And the change is not noted in the way we note a change in a house we have renovated. Nor is it completely lacking in some of the features of the worldview it has supplanted. Worldviews are undergirded, usually silently, by axioms we have no cause to articulate or challenge. Worldviews have not one source but many which over time coalesce and have a truly gestalt quality. We know that in past times people had different worldviews, and historians spend their days ferreting out the sources of those views and the coincidences that brought them into some relationship with each other. Ferreting them out in regard to one's own worldview is in practice extraordinarily difficult and, I would argue, possible only in small degree in its early phases.

What about the emergence and role of TV? TV was a technological achievement, but in its early years it was neither an effect of or an intended cause of social change. Initially, it was a novel medium for entertainment and news, both for children and adults. There were some people who feared that it could become an addiction for children, one that could distract attention away from schoolwork, reading, and sufficient time for play and sleep. The fact is that rather quickly TV became an addiction for most children and adults. That did not constitute a social change, nor was it intended to. Film, plays, cartoons, and news reels had long been standard fare in theaters, but now it was available in quantity without leaving the house, and it was "free," under one's control. Young people *today* may be surprised to learn that for the first decade or so of its existence TV was governed by the same criteria of morality as Hollywood movies, which is to say that the content and language of programs in no way stimulated or advocated social change in regard to what was right, natural, and proper by conventional standards. Contentwise, TV reinforced the status quo. And there were more than a few parents who applauded some of the children's programs for their attempt to be morally and educationally instructive.

Social change has to do with alterations in thinking, feelings, and attitudes about the world as it is. Although TV was not intended to be a vehicle of social change, several things made it a conveyer of information-news that was the stuff of social change. That is to say, TV pictured aspects of the world as it is that aroused in many people, children and adults, questions about whether the world as it is is the world as it should be. What needs to be kept in mind is that for a decade and more there were very few channels, which meant that at any one time millions of people were seeing much the same things, probably to a degree far greater than had been the case for radio. And what did they see and hear? The destructive power of atomic test blasts, civil rights demonstrations, the National Guard at a Little Rock school, the murdered bodies of civil rights activists, the hurling of invectives and rocks at black school children and police in Louisiana parishes, riots in urban areas, the Berlin blockade, the assassination of President Kennedy, and more—all of this side by side with sitcoms of the *Ozzie and Harriet* genre and, of course, the Ed Sullivan show.

Explaining social change became of obsessive interest to me around 1970. Since that time I have had scores of opportunities to question young people who grew up in the 1950s and 1960s about events that stood out in their minds because they stimulated them to see the world differently than their parents. Practically no one failed to recall being riveted to the TV set beginning on the Friday of President Kennedy's assassination until the Tuesday or Wednesday when schools were reopened. But, I would ask, were not their parents also glued to the set with a mixture of horror and sadness? The answers, albeit not always stated clearly, had or implied a common theme: this was a crazy, immoral world out of control, a world that needed a lot of fixing, a world parents seemed not to question in that they regarded the tragedy as reflective of the disordered minds of individuals (Oswald and Ruby). Their answers did not surprise me, although I wondered to what extent the subsequent murders of Martin Luther King and Robert Kennedy colored their thinking.

There was only one other event that was reported with surprising frequency, an event several years before the presidential tragedy and one that I had not seen. I refer to the appearances of Elvis Presley on the Ed Sullivan show. Candor requires that I confess that I still am puzzled not only by the frequency with which his appearance was reported but how movingly it was described. As one person said (paraphrased), "When I went to school the next day, that's all everyone was talking about. It said something to us that is hard to put into words. It was more a feeling that we had seen the wave of the future, and that wave was literally captivating and enthralling. We had never seen anything like that before. Life was never the same again. We could not get enough of Elvis. If you want to understand the impact of the Beatles on us several years later, you have to understand how Elvis hit us. By the time of the Beatles, my parents and I were in different worlds." It is noteworthy that this individual, then as now, loved classical music. But Elvis "spoke" to him in a way that had personal meaning for life as he was experiencing it, a life from which he sought liberation.

I said earlier that the postwar generation of parents was, generally speaking, concerned with employing child rearing practices that would allow their children to become productive and happy adults. And what constituted productive and happy in no way contained the faintest hint of generational conflict. What parents did they did with the best of intentions and the advice of the experts. But, as we now know, these parents were, to indulge understatement, unprepared for what we call the turbulent sixties, when they could not avoid the conclusion that the minds of their children contained thoughts, desires, and feelings of which they were unaware. We are still trying to comprehend what happened and why.

One of the more interesting and provocative attempts is Tom Engelhardt's *The End of Victory Culture*, published in 1995. He has looked seriously at the different messages children were getting from diverse sources. When Salinger's postwar novel *Catcher in the Rye* (1968/1951) became one of the most widely read books of youngsters, no one to my knowledge asked why a book about a boy who lived in a world he deemed crazy and predictable only for its insensitivities should have been so engrossing to its readers and, perhaps, portended something about the future.

Now to the question that stimulated this essay. With each passing year, increasing numbers of children have parents who are divorced. (In an affluent New York suburb somewhat more than half of the students are in that category.) That rate of increase is more than equaled by that of children whose parents both work. We have heard much about latch-key children as well as about those who experience the difficulties of shared custody. It should also be noted that a new phrase has come into wide use. The phrase is "quality time," denoting that part of evening hours or weekend periods when a parent or parents concentrate on being with their child or children. The phrase has several connotations. First, it suggests that the time children of working parents spend with surrogates lacks the intimacy and stimulation characteristic of "quality time." Second, "quality time" can make up for whatever is lacking in the hours the child spends with surrogates. Third, in a world where it is an economic necessity for both parents to work or for the single parent to work, or where it is necessary for both parents to work because it is central to their self-definition and life goals, compromises in regard to child rearing are both justified and inevitable. So, in recent years day care for infants has become quite a business. The number of nursery schools has also increased dramatically. And there is a movement gaining force, often supported by legislation and public funds, for public schools to develop facilities and services for all preschool children from early morning to the evening hours, and similar programs would be available before and after school for school-age children. What is happening is a consequence of a social change reflecting, among other things, changes in the concept and role of women, the tentativeness or instability of marital relationships, the idea of work as necessary for personal and social expression, and the geographical dispersion of the parental and extended family. These are momentous consequences of a momentous social change. To someone like me who grew up in the pre World War II era, it is like comparing an information processor to an old fashioned typewriter, or the modern copier to the unlamented mimeograph machine. The point is that the change has come to be seen not only as normal in a statistical sense but as a barometer of progress. That, of course, is not the way the parents of the parents of the post World War era judged these developments! They deplored these changes and their children deplored their deplorings. What they had in common with the post World War parents was their centering on long-term consequences. One group could only envision long-term negative consequences, the other could only see positive ones.

Now, to the question that interests me and one that assumes that with each passing year infants and children will spend the bulk of their school hours in the care of people other than their parent or parents: on what grounds is it conceivable that such a change will have no long-term consequences? Please note that I am not saying (or implying) that those consequences will be positive or negative. I am just saying that I know of no psychological or social theory that would regard such a widespread change as of no consequence. It is not a change in a single practice like toilet training or others I have previously mentioned. It is a change in the physical, psychological, and social ecology of infants, preschoolers, and school children. To concretize what I mean I shall describe two of my recent experiences.

A church rents out part of its facilities to a local college that has programs for the training of infant and child care workers. One of the rooms, approximately ten by sixteen feet, is for infants from one month to eighteen months of age. It houses six infants who are brought there early in the morning. Some remain there half a day, others a full day that ends around six o'clock. Some children are brought there at noon and spend the rest of the day there. When I was there, all the infants were lying on their backs on soft mattresses. None was crying, they appeared content. There was a large refrigerator, numerous bottle warmers, and diaper disposal containers. One wall was full of sheets of paper, one or two for each child, on which there was information about the child's feeding schedule and habits, other information provided by parents and pediatricians, and a record of liquid intake. There were three workers, all in their late teens or early twenties. There was a supervisor, who was not there in my hour-long visit; she was in another room for older preschoolers.

During my visit there were no more than ten times when a worker approached or picked up a child. With one exception, the children seemed alert as well as responsive to noise, loud speech, and certainly to being picked up. Nevertheless, I could not justify calling the atmosphere psychologically and physically stimulating, especially when I recalled how my wife and I interacted with our infant daughter. And yet, I had to conclude that if we had had to put our infant daughter in a day care center, this was an okay setting. The fee was substantial and there was a waiting list.

In a much larger room down the hall was the nursery school for ambulatory children approximately two to four years of age, not all of whom were fully toilet trained, and who also varied in language development. On the day I visited there were eight children, several being absent because of colds. The children were appropriately active, noisy, either interacting with each other or engaged in playing with toys, building blocks, and the like. There were three staff members in attendance, one of whom was the supervising teacher. The staff members were vigilant but not intrusive. They were not directive except when it came to snack time, when the routine for getting milk and cookies, sitting down, and then disposing of utensils was clearly articulated. The children appeared content and happy except for one boy and one girl who did not appear unhappy but were silent observers of what other children were doing. Children did pretty much what they wanted as long as it was not obviously interfering with someone else's activity. The staff members circulated the room, occasionally asking a child what he or she was doing, saying words of encouragement, offering suggestions, always in a quiet, somewhat tentative way. Toward the end of my visit they played a group game, which the children seemed to enjoy. I left shortly after one of the staff organized the children into a circle and started to read a story. If I had to sum up my impression of the aim of the program, it would be that the children be kept interested, engaged, and content. It was like most other preschool programs I had observed, especially those for children from relatively affluent or middle class or professional families. Most of the children were there from eight in the morning until between five and five-thirty in the evening.

The parents of these children averaged around thirty years of age. With few exceptions both parents worked. I said earlier that I was assuming that what I described would become increasingly the norm, and I would predict that that norm would be reached sooner rather than later. I further assumed that none of the parents whose children I observed spent their first two years of life in a day care setting. Some parents, perhaps most, had been in a nursery school beginning at age three, and it is likely that they were there for a half day. The point is that in contrast to their experience, their children spend about nine plus hours a day away from parents, with other children, in the care of teenagers and/or young adults with whom the forging of close, intimate, sustained, affective relationships cannot be counted on. This, I should hasten to say, does not mean that they will not in some way "bond" with the staff, but rather that there are bonds and there are bonds. The question is, of course, is this a difference that does or will make a difference? I will return to this question shortly. Several other questions have to be asked first. How much agreement is there about the "ideal" size, staff, program of full-time infant and nursery school centers? What should be the preparation of the staff? Who should be selected? What incentives (intellectual, educational, monetary) would create a large-enough pool from which to attract and select staff? What in-service features should exist that make for the sense of challenge, growth, and collegiality? By what explicit criteria should a program be judged to be meeting its objectives? What are *minimal* conditions (aside from the physical safety of children) below which a program should be terminated?

In his recent book, *Headstart and Beyond* (1993, with S. J. Styfco), Edward Zigler, one of the founders of Headstart, makes it perfectly clear that the above questions were glossed over in Headstart because political and time considerations did not permit the "luxury" of thinking through those questions and, even if they had been thought through, there was no way their economic implications would have realistically been confronted, let alone accepted. No one has been more responsible than Zigler for keeping Headstart alive, and no one was more aware than he was, despite all of the hoopla and hype, that Headstart could at best be a very modest success. That is why in his book he pleads that these questions be confronted as we move steadily to programs for infant and preschool care.

Many Headstart programs do not pass muster, but we have no evidence that private programs are of dramatically higher quality on average. By private I include women who for a fee care for several infants and/or preschoolers in their homes; their numbers are by no means small. And I also include families in which both parents work and the children are cared for by a "nanny." The point of all this is that current and future generations of young children will not be reared as their parents were. Some will argue that that is a good thing. Others will argue that it is an ill-advised development. I agree with the basic assumption of both positions: there will be long-term consequences. As I said earlier, it is inconceivable that such a change will have no consequences in the long term.

I wrote these words the day before I had my weekly telephone conversation with my daughter, Julie. She and her husband, Paul, are working parents. My grandson, Nathaniel, is now twenty-two months of age. After he was born Julie stayed home for two months. He was then cared for ten hours a day by a young girl who appeared and turned out to be a responsible, loving person. Needless to say, my wife and I frowned, to say the least, on such an arrangement, so we offered to pay Julie her take-home salary if she stayed home with Nathaniel until he was ready for nursery school. Julie, who knows her own mind, paid us no mind, of course! By all criteria of development, Nathaniel has flourished. He walked and began to talk at one year, as his mother had. (He does not stop talking.)

I started the telephone conversation with some chitchat about my activities. Julie interrupted me, saying, "I have to tell you what happened yesterday. The baby-sitter and I took Nathaniel for a try-out session at a nursery school. When we got there Nathaniel took one look at the other children and made a beeline for them. I told the baby-sitter we had better stick around for fifteen or twenty minutes in case he became aware of our absence. The baby-sitter said that would not be necessary for the Nathaniel she knew. Five minutes later the head teacher came over and said she saw no reason for us to stay. I didn't want to contradict her, so we left. Nathaniel had a ball." The fact is that Nathaniel has never had what is called "stranger anxiety." There are times when a stranger comes to the house and Nathaniel becomes silent and vigilant, but it does not last long, especially if the stranger responds to him in an obviously friendly fashion. To call it anxiety would be misleading. He becomes tentative and vigilant, not anxious. His mother at his age—indeed, beginning at nine months—was a textbook case of stranger anxiety. When she began nursery school, which was in the same building as my Yale office, I spent more time sitting in the nursery school than in my office. That went on for several months. Julie become a somewhat laid back, astute observer of people and situations, very sensitive to the feelings of others, one who finds it hard to toot her own horn. I know that sounds like the words of a proud father but this is not the place to bring independent evidence to buttress my admittedly personal opinion.

So what significances do I draw from this anecdote? I can assure the reader that I am quite aware that drawing conclusions from one anecdote is scandalously impermissible. The fact is that I draw no conclusions but rather raise questions that reflect other observations of children having the same daily experience as my grandson. And I feel justified in doing so because my interest is in long-term consequences and the time to *speculate* is now, that is, when a social change has just begun. It is in the nature of the questions that they cannot be answered now, but if I am right, that there will be long term consequences, I must ask questions now, when I am alive, questions that future researchers and historians may ask.

I have interrogated several preschool teachers and infant care-takers. I put to them this question: how frequently do you encounter in children an obvious stranger anxiety? With no exception they have said it was rarely encountered. I find that remarkable because forty years ago the answer would have been "infrequent but by no means rare." What these teachers told me got connected, in my mind at least, with observations of children like Nathaniel. These were not observations I set out to make; they were unplanned and crept up on me, so to speak, although I cannot dismiss the possibil-ity that I saw what I wanted to see, given my biases. These children, all between the ages of four to six, tended to be outer directed rather than inner directed, and I know I am using terminology developed decades ago to describe adults. But that is the way I saw them: friendly, acquisitive, socially adaptable, seekers of center stage, and their overt behavior struck me as a mite hyperactive. You do not expect children of that age to be exemplars of interpersonal sensi-tivity, but neither do you expect them to be insensitive to interper-sonal boundaries. Perhaps a better way to describe what I thought I saw is to say that they appeared to be and do what they thought oth-ers wanted them to do or be. They were very likeable children who very much wanted to be liked and gratified, and rather quickly so. The sample of children was small and blatantly nonrandom.

Is it possible that there is a relationship between what I thought I observed and the fact that these children had from early infancy spent most of each day (usually six days a week) in the care of peo-ple (and it is plural) other than their parents? Was it unconnected to their developing conception of time, space, and the need to adapt to a variety of caregivers who differed in styles of caregiving? If I do not have answers, that is no basis for dismissing the questions unless, of course, you are of the opinion that generational differences in caregiving are differences that make no difference in the long term. Opinions like that have one unassailable adaptive virtue: you do not have to speculate and think; today is today and there is no point in thinking about long-term tomorrows.

Even if my speculations are right, one has to assume that not all children will manifest their care-receiving experiences in similar ways. Indeed, I would expect many children to appear less extroverted and more inner directed, more overtly passive and less active. Given the fact that at birth there are large differences in temperament, that is reason enough to expect that objectively similar caregiving experiences will be assimilated and manifested in different ways in different children. What they will have in common with those I observed is the experience of the *transience* of relationships both with adults and with other children. By transience I mean having to comprehend and adapt to different people and situations in the course of a day. That, I contend, may be a mixed blessing. At the same time that it may be adaptive it may also set limits on the level of sustained emotionality in relationships.

In offering these speculations I am not suggesting that what happens in those early years determines the course of later development in social relationships, as if experience subsequent to those years plays little or no role. That simpleminded way of judging the later effects of a particular child rearing practice (such as toilet training and style of feeding) has long been discredited. *The social change that is taking place is not about discrete practices but about a changed, total, physical, social ecology remarkably different from that of only several decades ago, and in which all practices and a lot more are experienced.* It is a change that is related to other changes in the post World War II period and the long-term consequences will be influenced by how present and future changes get played out and interwoven, a predictable fact in line with the caveat that the present is not pregnant with a future but with many futures. I did not justify my speculations on a "forewarned or forearmed" basis but rather as a way of paying respect to two related laws of human history: there are always unintended consequences, and there is no free lunch. We know those laws from our individual lives; we have great difficulty applying that knowledge to issues of social change.

The problem I have posed and the speculations I have made

were in all respects illustrated in the advent of television. TV was greeted as warmly, indeed as enthusiastically, as any technological feat in human history. With very few exceptions the positive wonders and possibilities of TV were seen as limited only by one's imagination—more correctly, the "you have not seen anything yet" visions of the scientific-technological communities. Few were in doubt that TV would make for social change. Those few were the parents who in some inchoate way intuited that TV could be for their children a distraction from reading, studying, and thinking as well as an unwelcome intruder in social-family life. But they were a small minority.

It did not take long before most people began to see that for children TV was a kind of addiction with which few other activities could compete. Children spent (and spend) many hours each day glued to the TV screen. Even parents who had resisted buying a set gave up the struggle. The unintended consequences of the technological feat were apparent. TV began to be blamed for major problems in schools, especially in regard to drops in school achievement, intellectual passivity, shortened attention span, and more. Beginning in the late fifties the amount of violence children saw on TV became a matter of public controversy and policy. The most ambitious, indeed heroic, study on the relationship between aggressive behavior and the amount of viewing of TV violence was initiated forty years ago by Leonard Eron. The longitudinal study is a continuing one. Here is part of Eron's testimony before a senate subcommittee on June 18, 1992 (Congressional Record, S8538):

> There can no longer be any doubt that heavy exposure to televised violence is one of the causes of aggressive behavior, crime and violence in society. The evidence comes from both the laboratory and real-life studies. Television violence affects youngsters of all ages, of both genders, at all socio-economic levels and all levels of intelligence. The effect is not limited to children who

are already disposed to being aggressive and is not restricted to this country. The fact that we get this same finding of a relation between television violence and aggression in children in study after study, in one country after another, cannot be ignored. The causal effect of television violence on aggression, even though it is not very large, exists. It cannot be denied or explained away. We have demonstrated this causal effect outside the laboratory in real-life among many different children. We have come to believe that a vicious cycle exists in which television violence makes children more aggressive and these more aggressive children turn to watching more violence to justify their own behaviors. Statistically this means that the effect is bidirectional. Practically it means that if media violence is reduced, the level of interpersonal aggression in our society will be reduced eventually.

Over 30 years ago, when I started to do research on how children learn to be aggressive, I had no idea how important TV was as a determinant of aggressive behavior. I thought it was no more influential than the Saturday afternoon serial westerns that I used to attend, or the fairy stories my parents used to read to me before I went to bed or the comic books I pored over instead of doing my lessons. These, certainly, were very violent. But I grew up OK, I didn't enter a life of crime. I was not very violent. So I was skeptical about the effects of television violence. And I think most people come to this subject matter with this same sort of set, unconvinced that television can have such deleterious effects. However, in 1960, we completed a survey of all third grade school children in a semi-rural county in New York State. We interviewed 875 boys and girls in school and did separate interviews with 80 percent of their parents. We were interested in how aggressive behavior, as it is manifested in school, is related to the kinds of childrearing practices parents use. An unexpected finding was that for boys there seemed to be a direct positive relation between the violence of the TV programs they preferred and how aggressive they were in school. Since this was not more than a contemporaneous relation we didn't have too much confidence in the finding by itself. You couldn't tell by these data alone whether aggressive boys liked violent television programs or whether the violent programs made boys aggressive—or whether aggression and watching violent television were both due to some other third variable. However, because these findings fit in well with certain theories about learning by imitation, a cause and effect relation was certainly plausible.

Ten years later, however, in 1970, we were fortunate in being able to reinterview over half of our original sample. Our most striking finding now was the positive relation between viewing of violent television at age eight and aggression at age 19 in the male subjects. Actually the relation was even stronger than it was when both variables were measured at age eight. . . .

Then twelve years after that when the subjects were 30 years old, we interviewed them again and consulted archival data such as criminal justice records and found that the more frequently our subjects watched television at age 8 the more serious were the crimes for which they were convicted by age 30; the more aggressive was their behavior while under the influence of alcohol; and, the harsher was the punishment they administered to their own children. There was a strong correlation between a variety of television viewing behaviors at age 8 and a composite of aggressive behavior at age 30. These relations held up even when the subjects' initial aggressiveness, social class and IQ were controlled. Further, measurements of the subjects' own children, who were now the same age as the subjects when we first saw them, showed that the subjects' aggressiveness and violence viewing at age 8 related to their children's aggressiveness and their children's preferences for violence viewing 22 years later, when the subjects themselves were 30 years old. What one learns about life from the television screen seems to be transmitted even to the next generation!

. . . As I pointed out earlier, this finding of a causal link between the watching of violent television and subsequent aggressive behavior is not an isolated finding among a unique or nonrepresentative population in one area of the U.S., at a particular time. Seventeen years after our original data collection, we studied another large group of youngsters in a different geographical section of the U.S., a heterogeneous suburb of Chicago, following them for three years, and we obtained essentially the same results. . . . Further, this three year follow up was replicated in four other countries, Australia, Finland, Israel, and Poland (Huesmann & Eron, 1986). The data from all five countries investigated in the study clearly indicate that more aggressive children watch more television, prefer more violent programs, identify more with TV characters, and perceive violence as more like real life than do less aggressive children. Further, it became clear that the relation between TV habits and aggression was not limited to boys as we had found in our original study. Girls, too, are affected. And generally the causal relation was bidirectional, with aggressive children watching more violent television and the violent television making them more aggressive.

Some people have quarreled with this or that aspect of Eron's research, but to my knowledge, no one has denied that TV has had long-term consequences for children (and adults!). They were unintended consequences that could not be recognized because its "obvious" positive potential made the few naysayers look like modern-day Luddites intent on stopping the march of science and technology. They were put into the same category as those who many decades ago warned about the negative, unintended consequences of the intended consequence of pleasure from smoking.

The official and unofficial policy to make full-time infant day care and preschool programs more widespread is being promulgated as necessary for children and working parents. From the standpoint of working parents, some of whom *want* to work and some of whom *must* work, it clearly is necessary. The world has changed in converging ways so as to make such a policy necessary. The social clock cannot be rolled back. That is not the issue. The issue, as I see it, is the inability of proponents to own up to the iron law of unintended consequences. I am not being an alarmist or a naysayer. Although I have speculated about possible unintended consequences, it was not because I felt secure about them—I certainly do not—but rather to point to the obvious: social change always has intended and unintended consequences, and we are entranced by the former with a passion that makes thinking about the latter next to impossible. It was Lady Luck, so to speak, that accounted for Eron beginning his study a decade or so after TV became a living room fixture. I am aware that few see fit to study the issues I have raised in this essay about the daily care of very young children by people other than parents.

I am quite far from being anything resembling a semiexpert on British history and literature. With that statement of fact, I can say that over the years I have been struck by what appeared to have been a British custom among its elitist upper classes and nobility to give their infants and very young children to the care of hirelings (or impecunious relatives) who not infrequently lived elsewhere. When I have queried scholars in British history and literature, they have assured me that what had struck me may not have been the norm but it was not far from it. Knowing that I was a psychologist, they volunteered the caveat that it would be an egregious mistake either to explain British history or the personality characteristics of those in its elite social classes by that mode of rearing their young. I quite agreed with the caveat. But, I asked, was it their opinion that the consequences of the custom were nowhere in the picture, that it was just one of those things that played no role whatsoever in what may be called the style, tone, or strength of interpersonal relationships in that social stratum? None of these scholars would go that far. As one of them said, "It's probably in the picture somewhere. The custom certainly is described *in passing* [her emphasis] in novels of those days and in biographies of notables of past days. But that is about all you could say." No argument from me on that score. But that in no way has bearing on the hypothesis (better yet, a belief) that a dramatic change in the ecology of child rearing will have no long-term consequences, or if it does that they will only be positive in nature as "positive" will be judged by posterity. That, to me, is inconceivable, just as it was inconceivable—to its developers and the public generally—that television may be far from a boon to human welfare. As Eron indicated, his research program initially had nothing to do with television and its possible negative impacts. He had the good sense to see that television, embedded as it was in a particular society in a particular era, may not be the best thing since sliced bread.

7

· ·

The Abortion Issue

The awareness of social change explicitly assumes a knowledge and sense of the past. Every biologically intact individual has a sense of the past, however rudimentary it may be. When an infant responds differentially to a parent, we may say it is conditioning or recognition or some other term. We shy away from saying that an infant has a sense of the past because that suggests a cognitive state and process of which the infant is not yet capable. However, in ways we do not understand we assume that a sense of the past does not just happen; rather, it develops from converging experiences, for instance, "It *was* here, it *is* not here *now*"; "Mommy *was* here, she *is* not here *now*"; "The light *was* on, it *is* not on *now*." As the child grows we see signs of a sense of the past, the near past, which parents not only recognize in a reinforcing way but attempt to enlarge. Being quintessential question-asking characters, preschool children provide us with countless opportunities to help them sharpen the distinctions between what is and what was, between "what I am and what I was," between "where I have been and where I am now." When parents come home from the hospital with their second newborn, their first child—who may be three or four or five years of age or perhaps younger—is capable of putting the new situation in terms of what is and what was (and a lot more!). And when a young child wants to know when, where, and how babies are created, he or she grapples with distinctions between past and present (and, again, with a lot more).

The child's sense of the past is personal and self-centered. It is also social in a very circumscribed interpersonal way, that is, it is limited to those in the circumscribed spaces he or she occupies. It is *not* social in the sense we mean when we say "social change." When we say that someone is aware of social change, we imply and ordinarily clearly mean, that changes are taking place in a larger society comprised of groups, most of whom we have had little or no contact with and know little about, and with whom we share a national identity and some common interests, values, activities, and obligations. However many and different the groups—religiously, ethnically, agewise, politically, regionally—we know that they and we are Americans and not Bulgarians, Iraqis, Japanese, and so forth. If we know it, so do they, which is why many countries resist and resent the Americanization of the world. It is not a negative stance to a particular American behavior or attitude but to many characteristics lumped under the heading of "American." Some people in other countries will reject anything that smacks of America; others will accept only that which can be assimilated into their traditions, their sense of the past, their sense of what is right, natural, and proper.

That is also precisely the case among groups *within* a country as large and diverse as ours. Granted that the similarities among groups are many, the differences can be striking in regard to the awareness and response to the perception of a social change. Nowhere is this more true than in the case of religion, especially in regard to the relationships between religious children's sense of the past and their later response to a perceived social change, that is, how the development of a personal sense of the past can affect outlooks toward social change, or more correctly, how that sense of a circumscribed personal past slowly and seamlessly gets interwoven with views about the larger social world, an interweaving in which there are no boundaries between the circumscribed personal and the truly social.

There can be no doubt that in America, as in most western countries, religion plays less of a role in the psyches of people than it did in earlier times. Having said that, the fact remains that today as in the past, serious (read sincere) religious affiliation has always been a feature in controversies about social change. The latest example, of course, concerns the social change, embodied in law and judicial decisions, about abortion. To people who are pro-choice, the strength and militancy of their opponents are troublesome and mystifying. The controversy is far more than about abortion, as the opposing sides well know but rarely articulate in public. Generally speaking, the proponents of choice see the other side as wanting to turn the clock back in regard to the role of women in the family and the work arena, the definition of the family, the absence of prayer in the schools, attitudes toward homosexual relationships and premarital sex, and the complete secularization of morals (relativism). I have met very few opponents of abortion who do not accept most of these attributions. Both sides know that a social change has occurred and both know that more is at stake than abortion rights. To opponents, abortion is but one part of a constellation of changed attitudes and expectations that has put society on the slippery road to disaster.

What is mystifying to many proponents is the depth of passion and the degree of militant activism of the opponents. The illegal and even murderous actions of a few opponents lead proponents to conclude that, generally speaking, opponents are fanatics, or possessed of authoritarian or antidemocratic dispositions, or they are socially insensitive and obtuse, or unhappy and frustrated people who are unable or unwilling to adapt to the modern world (the King Canute stance), or they are people who are obsessed with a single principle or action that makes them unable to see the forest for the trees. Or all of the above. At least as I conclude from talking with proponents and reading their arguments, their criticisms are about *individuals* and their cognitive and emotional limitations. It is usually only when pressed that some will say that what is at issue are two very contradictory views about what the world is and should be, and why. And central to the worldview of opponents is the belief that God's revelations and instructions to men and women should govern human relationships because only in that way can the evils of which people are capable be kept in check, and the modern world has displayed those evils as never before in human history.

I should hasten to say that not all who are pro-choice are without religious beliefs. But if that is far from the case, it is also the case that religious pro-choicers have affiliations with churches and synagogues that became what they are because of the perceived need and obligation to adapt to a changing world. For them the issue of abortion is a current instance of a long conflict between orthodoxy and modernism, between fundamentalism and an ever changing secularism.

The significance of the abortion controversy is that it is about more than abortion. It is also more than a conflict between religion and secularism. And its significance cannot be grasped by riveting on those who are its articulate opponents and proponents, because its larger significance is an active concern to most people. Its significance inheres in the perception that the social change ushered in by World War II had as a central feature an emphasis on individualism and individual rights that was not intended to but did weaken the sense of community. That is to say, individuals increasingly sought to chart and control their destinies in the ways they saw fit, unfettered by past traditions. Indeed, in myriads of ways they were told and encouraged to do so. The implicit social message was: "You can do and be many things in life, there are many experiences you can and should enjoy, your goal should be to get as much out of life as possible before you die." The word "you" refers to individuals and their obligations to themselves. Messages about obligations to family, community, and state are infrequent and muted.

One of the media events of the post World War II period was the documentary on the Loud family of California. For ten successive Sundays, millions of people watched the ongoing, unrehearsed activities and interactions of two parents and their children. The words community and mutuality did not come to mind when you watched the program. As in Pirandello's classic "Six Characters in Search of an Author," each member of the Loud family seemed in search of identity and purpose, openly or passively resentful of their assigned roles. When near the end of the series Mr. Loud tells his wife he wants a divorce, we are surprised but not shocked. What is portrayed in the series is the polar opposite of what was portrayed in the Ozzie and Harriet series, where at the end of each program mishaps and misunderstandings were overcome and sweetness and light suffused everyone. It was not happenstance that during the sixties and even today, the Ozzie and Harriet show was referred to as an illustration of the use of pernicious myth to mask a reality in which individuals led unhappy, fractured lives mired in an unwanted privacy. And it was not happenstance that in the sixties and part of the seventies young people sought freedom from the constraints of the past to "do your own thing" at the same time they sought a sense of belongingness and community of which Woodstock was an unusually clear example, as were the many attempts to create communes in rural areas. Nor was it happenstance during those years that Far Eastern philosophies became fashionable as ways by which an individual could find a new self, become a new individual, freed from the usual constraints and pressures of a misguided, unfulfilling society.

In the Arts and Leisure section of *The New York Times* for Sunday, January 29, 1995, on the front page Verlyn Klinkenborg has an article titled "The Ideal Family on Film," the subtitle being "Three Documentaries Challenge the Shallowness of the Political Myth." Here are his opening paragraphs:

> If you listen long enough to the conservative ode to family values—in the Quayle or Limbaugh or Gingrich

version—you realize that it celebrates not the shape of the family but the restraint of the individual. In fact, the ideal conservative family is the smallest state, a paternal state strong enough to withstand the anarchic pressures that every family member puts upon it.

To conservatives, the family is a hierarchy—father, mother and cadets—and the conservative dream is a life-time within the crystalline bosom of a perfect family, where individual liberty (always a disruptive force) has been sacrificed to familial coherence. It goes without saying that in a nation of perfectly ordered families, small government is a sure thing.

But perfectly ordered families belong to the world of political myth, which is where political discourse takes place. The realities of family life are always more diverse, more chaotic than politicians seem to remember. This year, among the documentaries eligible for Academy Award nominations, three films challenge this repressive fantasy of family life.

Mr. Klinkenborg leaves us in no doubt that he regards individual liberty as an overarching goal not to be impinged upon or constrained by family or, by implication, any other group of which the individual is a part. Invoking as he does the names of Quayle, Limbaugh, and Gingrich he makes it clear that differing attitudes toward "family values" are correlated with differing stances in regard to a lot more than the family. The word "abortion" does not appear in the article, but one runs no risk in assuming that he is pro-choice.

The abortion controversy is about more than abortion and that "more" is what an individual owes to a collectivity. More concretely, by what criteria should an individual judge his or her obligations to adherence to the criteria of a collectivity? That question, I would argue, is at the root of almost every major social issue in the welter of issues comprising the social change that was and is the aftermath of World War II. I would go so far as to say that social change, anytime, anywhere, catapults that question into public awareness. Social change is never about only one type of behavior or practice or expectation, but about many types, each of which in some way involves the individual-collectivity relationship. However, far more often than not attention is not drawn to the general factor but to this or that single issue, as if the general factor is not in the picture. But if that appears to be the case in public debate, it frequently is otherwise in private discussion when it is recognized that the different manifestations of the social change have a common core: the constraints, if any, that a collectivity should put on individual freedom of action. Put another way: what does the individual "owe" the collectivity? And that is my point: an issue like abortion gets publicly posed as a discrete issue whereas phenomenologically it is seen as but one of many related issues. I am not suggesting that such a public discussion of a discrete issue is unproductive. Far from it. What I am suggesting is that such a focus on one issue is like riveting on a battle while a war is going on. That may not be (I am sure it is not) the most felicitous of analogies but it is my way of saying that discussions about abortion are not discussions about social change. In some ultimate sense our future will be determined less by how the abortion issue gets played out and more by the degree to which the underlying core driving a social change gets clearly posed and discussed, and generalizes.

For the past year I have asked people this question: "Of all the inaugural addresses you heard or read about in the post World War II period, what utterance, if any, has stayed with you?" Within five seconds everyone gave the same answer, following which was silence: they could remember content or problem areas a president highlighted, but with one exception no sentence remained in memory. The exception was President Kennedy's "Ask not what your country can do for you but what you can do for your country." Wrapped up in that utterance is the individual-collectivity relationship. What requires explanation is why it reverberated and still reverberates in the minds of people.

Recall that in the 1960 presidential campaign the controversial issues had been religion, abortion, civil rights, civil disobedience, race, violence, poverty, women's rights, state rights, and more. Rights: not only rights to give expression to individual strivings, styles, and goals, but also the rights of groups that saw themselves as burdened and oppressed by stultifying tradition and legislation. It was a time when the country could be seen as comprised of askers, and what they were asking required action in Washington. Some were asking to be left alone to live life as they saw fit, others asked for opportunity and support not to live as they had but as they wanted and deserved to. President Kennedy did not say what he wanted people to do for their country, or how the different askers should discharge their obligation to the country in order to reinforce the sense of a national community rather than to contribute to social instability, or how trying to satisfy everyone meant that no one would be satisfied. Regardless of what he had in mind concretely, his utterance struck a responsive chord in people because they were already aware—it was more feeling than cognitive awareness—that the individual-collectivity relationship had become very problematic in diverse arenas: family, church, work, gender, community, and region. None of this was new, but all of it was at an unprecedented strength, and everything seemed to be changing at the same time. But the responsive chord is not explained only by the words of the utterance or by the social context of the times. It was an utterance by a youthful, articulate, charismatic president who convinced many people why they should not let religious prejudice be a reason not to vote for a Catholic; why, despite his young and affluent-patrician background he could be trusted to keep the country together; and why his obligations to his country—not to his father, church, or class—should be those that everyone should feel. For a brief time, doing something for your country (such as joining the Peace Corps) was "good"; doing for others was in the national interest. It did not last long. For the remainder of the six-ties, individual and group concerns drowned out the idea of oblig-ations to country (except in the case of young people willing to devote a year or more of their lives in programs like the Urban Corp and the Teacher Corp).

In labeling individuals and groups as askers I was not passing judgment on their positions. What I was emphasizing was the dilu-tion of the sense of community, of belongingness to a group, small or large, from family to nation, to which one willingly had and dis-charged obligations even though they involved a degree of self-restraint and sacrifice, that is, you gave without asking in return. That is, of course, what happens when a tragedy occurs in the lives of individuals we know and to whom we feel an obligation to seek to be helpful. We may not act that way as often as we should, at which times we may feel guilt because we know what we owe to others. The clearest examples on a larger scale are wars, floods, and earthquakes, when many people interrupt their lives to discharge a felt obligation to people they do not know or to a cause beyond the confines of individual living. Precisely because social change is a percolating, widespread phenomenon and by its nature gives rise to conflicts, the danger inheres not in the challenge to an overarch-ing sense of community but in blotting out that sense. And that is what began to happen in the post World War II era.

Why did that happen to a far lesser degree when the Great Depression hit this country like the proverbial ton of bricks, with its attendant convulsive social change? The answer or answers are very complicated and I am not prepared to discuss them. Having lived through the Great Depression I can point to one ingredient of any answer historians have provided or will provide. And that aspect is in the difference between Herbert Hoover and Franklin Delano Roosevelt.

For many people the word "patriot" has come into disrepute, an indication of what I have tried to say in this essay. I can assure the reader that I know all of the ways the shibboleth patriotism has been used in destructive ways. But that is no warrant for ignoring the fact that patriotism—although it can be the first and last refuge of scoundrels—implies a mutuality of interests and obligations without which the society becomes a Tower of Babel where no one can and no one seeks to understand others, let alone seeks a piece of common ground. It's like the Loud family I discussed earlier, where no one seemed to understand each other; there was little or no sense of family. In any event, Herbert Hoover and Franklin Roosevelt were patriots, each wholeheartedly concerned with keeping the social and economic fabric together, to engender in people the feeling that the storm would be weathered. Desires and goals aside, Hoover's style and personality did not instill in people the feeling that he was saying those things and would take those actions that would allow people to hope that their disrupted lives would return to "normal." Bear in mind that in the 1932 presidential campaign the economic platforms of both parties were startlingly similar. Roosevelt, in fact, called for a reduced budget! It was not until he got into office that he saw the dimensions of the catastrophe. No, the people were responding far less to any of the candidates' economic differences than to Roosevelt's capacity to engender a sense of national family. His "fireside chats" on the radio were eagerly listened to because he made it possible for most people to believe that the mutuality of obligation between government and people was not empty rhetoric.

As the Great Depression continued and deepened, with all kinds of conflicts and controversies, people continued to believe that the government was trying its best for its people. People heard and believed. Today, people hear but do not believe. As poll after poll tell us, a large number of people see the country as governed by individuals and groups intent on feathering their own nests and unable to comprehend why people's sense of national purpose is so weak. As a friend of mine said, "You're damn right I am for myself, because they [in Washington] are sure as hell not for me."

My argument has been in several parts. First, social change is manifested and experienced in different ways in different groups. Second, many of these groups and these different ways do not on the surface appear to be related or interconnected, at least not initially. Third, publicly at least, proponents of a particular aspect of social change see the world in terms of that aspect, and that aspect alone. Fourth, because social change has many aspects, giving it a crazy-quilt character, and because each aspect has its passionate proponents and opponents, what happens and tends to go unnoticed (or unarticulated) is the weakening of a sense of community or national purpose in individual, group, and social living, that is, people are infinitely more aware of what divides one individual or group from the others than they are of a need to submerge in any way and to any degree their passionate devotion to any overarching communal purpose or value—indeed, the possibility of the need for such a submergence, in any way and to any degree, is a thought that cannot even be entertained, and to some people anathema is pronounced on such a thought.

Proponents and opponents of a particular social change confirm two maxims. The first is Mencken's quip that for any complex problem there is a simple answer that is wrong. The second is that in winning a battle you might lose the war. In regard to the second maxim it is obvious that I believe that in the post World War II era many battles have been conducted and won (or lost) in ways that have contributed to the dilution of a need to feel part of a larger society that, despite its many fault lines, has virtues and benefits in which most people can take pride. Most people do not like to live in a moral jungle, which is where too many people feel they now live, a jungle in which power and winning and modes of individual expression have unprecedented precedence, contributing to a sense of unwanted privacy.

What I am saying has a long history in this country, and I am not one enamored by the mythical "good old days." But neither am I one who believes that history repeats itself other than that genotypically identical problems recur in phenotypically different contexts and their destabilizing and destructive consequences are similar. That argument will not sit well with Bosnians, Armenians, the Jews of Nazi Germany, African-Americans, Native Americans, and the scores of millions murdered by Stalin, Mao, and their Cambodian kin. There have always been civil wars, but relative to the percentage of the population that died, the American Civil War is judged to have been among the most costly in terms of human lives. I refer to these events only to make the point that what I have said about our country in the post World War II period is a recurrence of old problems, but with the difference that they are associated with a deterioration in the sense of communal living, something our founding fathers feared about the excesses of narrow partisanship. If they feared it then, we have more reason to fear it today.

What makes the comprehension of social change difficult and almost always belated is, as I have said, that the words "social change" do not have referents the way words like "rock" and "chair" have. Social change has many referents not all of which appear at the same time and with the same clarity or visibility. Because they appear to be discrete, and in a literal or overt sense they are, it is both difficult and risky to see what they may have in common. Is what they have in common a particular effect they produce, such as a diluted sense of community or an increase in self-centered individualism? Or is it as much cause as it is effect? Or both?

The concept of social change is similar to the concept of personality. Two things have long puzzled (and plagued) personality theorists and researchers. The first is that personality is a complex, multifaceted organization of characteristics, styles, and behaviors, and more. All theorists assume that personality is not a randomly developed and organized individual "system" but rather that it is a dynamic system in that it is always in action and always changing in small or large ways. How does one do justice to that dynamic system, which can appear so different in different situations? That question alone goes a long way toward explaining why personality researchers rivet on one aspect of personality, such as introversion, extroversion, self-regard and self-esteem, motivations, reactions to frustration, inner- or outer-directed response styles, dependence, and so on. Their hope is that if they get a handle on one aspect of personality, they have a basis for exploring how it is related to other aspects. It is like a jigsaw puzzle, where you know what the final product should look like but you have to determine with which of the scores of pieces you should start in order to facilitate connecting one piece with another. Jigsaw puzzles are a piece of cake compared to making organized sense of what we call personality.

The second problem is one that very few psychologists have the courage or arrogance to face: what are those relatively few "forces"—needs, motivations, relationships, goals—with which one can make sense of a bewildering overt array of behaviors and actions of a personality? Freud, Jung, Adler, Maslow, Rogers, Allport, Murray, Bowlby and a few others come to mind. They are all dead. No one in the current scene has anything like the degree of impact these figures had. As I have discussed elsewhere (1994) the field of psychology has become, like the larger society, a dramatically differentiated field compromised of scores of "parts" that are isolated from each other and that show little need or interest in how the parts go together. There is no overarching conceptualization, little or no basis on which to begin to approach the jigsaw puzzle of personality.

In the case of social change, we have very few barometers to tell us that this or that social phenomenon may be a harbinger of social change, nor do we have a basis for discerning what these barometers have in common until, so to speak, it hits us in the face, that is, when surface diversity no longer masks a covert commonality. Even then, there is the danger of either unwarranted generalization or an equally unwarranted reductionism in which all manifestations of social change are explained by a few factors. Some readers may have already concluded that I have indulged those dangers by emphasizing the dilution of the sense of community and the increasing elevation of the priority given to individual and group purposes. My defense to such a criticism is in four parts. The first may be viewed by some as an assumption but I consider it a fact: there is and has always been *in every collectivity* in recorded history tensions between the individual and the collectivity. Whether those tensions fluctuate in strength within narrow limits and do not produce open conflict or social change depends on a number of factors, one and only one of which is a felt obligation to be constrained by a willing adherence to the perceived purposes of the collectivity. Second, and again depending on circumstances, the weakening of that adherence *may* be a major cause of social change. World War II mightily increased the sense of community but it also set the stage for weakening that sense after the war. Third, however weakened the sense of community becomes, and however intense and divisive the conflicts within the collectivity may be, in most people's phenomenology is an unfulfilled need for belonging, while at the same time it may play no role in how they advocate for or against a particular aspect of social change. Fourth, the course of social change depends on, among other things, how well leaders sincerely and effectively speak *and* act in accord with that need, that is, social living should not be experienced as a zero-sum game.

Let me now return to where I began: the abortion issue. Proponents of abortion present one or more or all of these arguments: people have a legal and moral right to determine for themselves what happens to their bodies; to bring an unwanted child into this world, whatever the reason, is harmful and unfair to child and mother; the historical record has been that when abortion was illegal, it fostered illegal abortions, which frequently were carried out under conditions causing illness, injury, misery, and death; getting an illegal abortion under medically sound conditions could be obtained in this or a foreign country but only by those with financial means to do so, that is, there was economic discrimination.

The opponents of abortion fall into several groups. The largest comprises those who regard abortion as a violation of divine law. A second group does not invoke religious teaching but on purely moral grounds is against terminating life even if that life is still in utero. A third group consists of those who are not against abortion in principle but only after the fetus can be considered to look like and possess human characteristics, at which time abortion is the unjustified termination of a life.

Far more than the proponents, the opponents (generally speaking) are crystal clear that what is at stake is the basis of the relationship between the individual and the collectivity—more concretely, the mutual obligations each should have to the other. In other words, there should be definite limits to what an individual can do and those limits should be determined by the collectivity of which the individual is a willing member. Put in still another way, the agreed upon values of the collectivity are *the* governing moral imperatives even if they present problems, conflicts, and hardships for individuals.

The proponents hold, at least on the surface, that the right to abortion is largely or purely a matter of individual rights that the collectivity should not in any way restrict. I say "on the surface" because they know—and make that most clear in private conversation—that the bulk of their opponents are not only opposed to abortions but also to the civil-legal legitimation of homosexuality, to sex education and the provisions of condoms to school children, to non–legally sanctioned "living together" and premarital sex, to the absence of prayer in schools, to government programs that foster dependence and irresponsibility, a too permissive criminal justice system, and to whatever contributes to the weakening of the integrity of the traditional nuclear family. Some proponents acknowledge that not all opponents hold all of these positions, but in the main they see them as a relatively homogeneous group consisting of religious Christians, Jews, and Muslims, in addition to many public officials whose continuation in public life requires that they not alienate their constituents who are opposed to abortion, although some of these officials oppose abortion because they agree with those constituents.

Two things are missing in my characterization of the two sides.

The first is that for proponents the issue is not social change in the sense that social change manifests itself in a variety of ways that despite their variety tend to have an underlying common theme or themes. For most proponents, abortion is a constitutional issue centering on individual rights, an old issue in modern garb, an important issue about individual liberty. For opponents, however, it is an issue of social change in that it is but one of many instances of a widespread social change of a "slippery slope" nature, that is, in combination these instances describe and herald a deterioration of the social fabric. What proponents view as progressive, opponents view as regressive and anarchic.

The second thing that was missing in my characterizations is that many people who favor abortion as an individual right note and negatively judge the social change but do not see the abortion issue as a reflection of that change. Aside from that issue, they see the social change in ways similar to but not identical with the judgment of the opponents of abortion. Independent of my own personal experience, I have no basis for estimating the percentage of proponents who separate the abortion issue from their negative view of the social change. My personal experience suggests that the percentage is not small. This raises the general question: by what criteria does or should a collectivity decide to place constraints on freedom of individual action?

That question goes back a long way in our national history; it has always been the root question in our democracy. It is a question that gets asked and settled (if it gets settled at all) after events force the collectivity to confront the question. So, for example, those whom we call the "robber barons" of the nineteenth and early twentieth centuries engaged in activities that were not only largely legal but consistent with the ethos of entrepreneurial capitalism and its rugged individualism. Constraints were imposed when the nation, the largest collectivity, decided that allowing such freedom of action would no longer be permitted because it was inimical to that collectivity's welfare. Similarly, it was not many years ago that owners

of companies could dispose of waste where they pleased, use whatever materials and chemicals they wanted, construct buildings
pretty much where it was convenient for them, and so on. Such
freedom of action, it was decided, could no longer be permitted if
the welfare of the larger collectivity was to be safeguarded. The
requirement for an "environmental impact report" well captures the
point that there are times when a collectivity has the right and
obligation to restrict individual freedom of action. With this, of
course, the opponents of abortion are in full agreement and on two
highly related grounds: it is a violation of divine law and it contributes to a pernicious "anything goes" individualism that is
destroying the social fabric, that is, it accelerates the pace of an
unwanted social change.

Many who support the right to abort do not invoke "the environmental impact" rationale. For them it is an absolute right the
collectivity should not restrain in any way, unlike free speech, free
press, and free travel abroad, on each of which there are some
restraints. This absolutism is matched by that of some opponents
who are against abortion under any or all conditions.

There is only one instance where there is some overlap between
opponents and *some* proponents, an overlap based on the environmental impact rationale. It has to do with governmental financing
of welfare mothers who continue to have children. Some proponents acknowledge that such a policy not only may sustain social
irresponsibility but it also places a financial burden on the collectivity that is unfair and wasteful of limited resources, that is, the
money could be used in more socially productive ways. If they do
not oppose the policy, it is because they feel that the collectivity
has an overriding obligation to protect the unwanted children, that
is, to avoid punishing innocent children. That argument assumes
that over their lifetimes these unwanted children and the contexts
in which they will live will have a relatively small negative impact
on the larger society, an assumption that has to be regarded as a
dubious one.

Before stating my own position on abortion let me relate an anecdote that brought the underlying issue to me as never before. It was not about abortion but very much about the perplexities of the individual-collectivity relationship. Back in the mid sixties my late wife, Esther, a clinical psychologist, was a consultant to a worker in that part of a community action agency that served un-wed, very young mothers with very young children. The worker was, to put it mildly, frustrated and overwhelmed both by the number of cases and the irresponsible ways many of these young women spent their welfare and Aid to Dependent Children checks. After several such meetings Esther said that it was unfair to the children for these women to be allowed to spend the money only as they saw fit, and that these women should be told about and helped to understand the whys and wherefores of responsible budgeting. Esther said that that should be a condition for receiving financial help. Esther was white and the worker was an African-American minister. His reaction to what Esther said was both polemical and clear: white, mid-dle-class America had no right to foist its values on black women whose plight was caused by the larger white society; if the actions of many of these young women were irresponsible, that was the price white society would have to pay for a history of subjugation; besides, if that society was so solicitous of the welfare of the chil-dren, it should substantially increase the size of payments. When Esther replied that her position was no less applicable to white teenagers on welfare, his reply was that they, like their black coun-terparts, were not only entitled to support but also entitled to be left alone to decide how they would conduct their individual lives on precisely the same basis that nonwelfare people were left alone. To him the rights of the individual were paramount, if not absolute. When Esther related the interaction to me I criticized her for artic-ulating her position, those being the days when that position was neither fashionable or discussable; it was seen as a racist position, another example of a paternalistic trampling on individual rights. It took me a while to see that we were in an era when "doing your own thing" was a right that took precedence over the right of the collectivity to constrain individual actions. The response of the minister was completely understandable to Esther and me. But to say that it was understandable is not to say that the principle on which his argument rested was justified. His history was justified, his principle was not. (Memory being the sometime thing it is, I do not remember whether I apologized to Esther.)

Now to my position. I agree with that aspect of the antiabortion argument that sees the abortion issue as reflective of a social change manifested in a variety of ways each of which centers on the individual-collectivity relationships. I agree that if you are for abortion you must, at the least, acknowledge that such assent is not without consequences for how that relationship will be posed and argued, and what its impact may be upon other manifestations of the social change. I believe that to the extent that increasing emphasis on individual rights dilutes the sense of community, of belonging to a larger collectivity, the collectivity will take on more of the features of a jungle where individual purpose is the norm and rootlessness and disconnectedness are destabilizing features in people's lives.

I hope the following will not be viewed as an irrelevance or digression. I write these words on the day when President Clinton is meeting in the White House with representatives of major league baseball owners and the players' union in an effort to end a strike that terminated the previous season, there was no World Series, and in countless ways the strike will adversely affect coming seasons. Up until a decade or so ago, baseball players for all practical purposes had little or no control over where they worked and for what compensation. They were indentured servants. The owners were like robber barons, but legally sanctioned ones because Congress had decades earlier exempted baseball from the provisions of the anti-trust laws. The players' union fought and changed the old balance of power, one consequence of which was a fantastic increase in the average player's salary, and in the case of "stars," fantastic is somewhat of an understatement. The consequence of that increase was that players no longer had strong loyalty to their teams and were prepared to move to any other team that would pay them a higher salary and for a longer time. Needless to say, the owners fought these changes, kicking and screaming and sometimes illegally while at the same time they played the game of "market forces." Complaining that too many teams were losing money, the owners put a cap on what players could earn, and that brought on the strike. The argument that too many teams were losing money was literally accepted by no one, including those who regarded the players as no less greedy than the owners. As someone said, "The ruling principle of players and owners is greed, get as much for yourself as you can, and to hell with everyone else." And who is everyone else? It is millions of baseball fans who feel unheard, unrecognized, let alone unrepresented.

I am a sports fan, although baseball is one of my lesser interests ever since the Brooklyn Dodgers were removed by their owners to Los Angeles. That removal represented to me the triumph of individual interest (read greed) over a sense of community I felt with thousands of people in metropolitan New York and beyond. (I never felt alone walking on a sunny summer day down a Brooklyn street and hearing the voice of the play-by-play announcer come clearly through the open windows of homes and apartment houses—those being pre-TV days.) It so happens that there is a radio station in New York, WFAN, which for twenty hours each day is devoted to call-in programs about sports. Hardly a day goes by when I do not tune in to listen to the conversations. Well, ever since the strike began, and before, the main topic of conversation has been how angry fans are about how their interests are being disregarded. One listener summed up what practically all callers have said before and since, "The fans are the ones who pay for and support baseball, we are the ones those greedy individualists say they play for, without us they would have to apply for food stamps, but in fact they don't give a damn about us. Their national pastime is making as much money as each can make, even to the point where players charge people, including kids, for giving them their autographs." On the one hand, I find it monotonous to hear each caller vent his (sometimes her) spleen; on the other hand, I am fascinated by the anger at feeling alienated from an activity that had given them a sense of belonging to something larger and beyond the social confines of their individual lives. It is noteworthy that in recent years coaches and knowledgeable observers have criticized a fair number of professional basketball players who in their quest for astronomical salaries have prized their individual accomplishments over team play. That is what I meant when I said earlier that the emphasis on individualism comes with a price.

Back to abortion. I agree with proponents that a woman has the right to decide whether to abort or not. In the case of very young girls there should be the opportunity to discuss the possible biological and psychological consequences, on the same basis that I want my physician or surgeon to inform me about the pros and cons of any medication or surgical procedures he or she recommends from the universe of alternatives appropriate to my condition. I expect him or her to give me an opinion, but it is my right to decide my own course of action. I know that the physician is not a computer, that is, I cannot press a button and be given on the display window in the most impersonal style all of the information I need. The physician is not without opinions and personal values, but I expect the physician to respect his or her obligation to provide me with the pros and cons of each alternative in the universe of alternatives. I say this because physicians, generally speaking, do an inadequate job of providing information in a helpful way about almost anything, and as an unpublished study by one of my students indicated, that is clearly the case when the disparity between the educational level and status of doctor and patient is great. So, when I say that a very young pregnant girl should have the opportunity, not a mandate, to discuss with someone whether to abort or not, I do not intend to gloss over the ways the potentials of that opportunity can be wittingly or unwittingly subverted. There is a difference between being helpful and being an enthusiastic partisan, pro or con.

I admit that I am very ambivalent about whether public money should be used to support abortion, and for the major reason that I have been at pains to elaborate on in this essay. Does such support strengthen an individualism that is so much a feature of the social change, at the expense of further weakening the sense of obligation to a larger collectivity? Is such a question off limits because the right to abortion is an absolute one not to be abrogated by economic considerations? Is such support without *any* adverse consequences for the larger society? Are those adverse consequences so minimal as to make my question not worthy of thought and study? Is it possible that if such support were nonexistent, the adverse consequences might be greater than those I believe *may* be the consequences of the present policy of support? The thrust of these questions is that we do not live in a world, human or otherwise, in which there is a single cause for a single effect. We live in a world of contexts (and contingencies) in which any aspect we try to explain does not exist in a vacuum but in a gestalt of aspects interrelated in varying degrees and strengths over time, so that when you try to influence and change one aspect you inevitably change others with which it is related in intended and unintended ways. I am not saying that in regard to any one aspect that we should or can take all aspects of the gestalt into account. But that is no excuse for looking at an aspect with tunnel vision. If we do not know all that we need to know, it is no excuse for not trying to learn more than we do. And it certainly is no excuse for allowing passionate convictions to picture aspects of our world in simple, either-or terms.

Let me give one more example of the major point I have been trying to make. On Monday, February 6, 1995, on a national network there was a movie version of Colonel Greta Cammermeyer's expulsion from the armed services, in which she functioned for well over two decades in a distinguished way. In the course of the process of promotion to an even higher level requiring top level clearance, the investigating officer asked her scads of personal questions one of which was whether she had engaged in any immoral activity that would disqualify her. One of those activities was homosexuality.

Colonel Cammermeyer, the mother of four grown children, said she was a lesbian. Not only did that disqualify her but according to regulations she was discharged (with an honorable discharge). Why did she not say earlier in her career that she was a lesbian? Since no one knew she was a lesbian—nothing in the movie suggests that she had engaged in lesbian activity but rather that she had always known she was a lesbian—why did she not lie? Her answer was that no one had ever asked her but, having been asked, she felt obliged to give the truth.

The Colonel was dedicated to and loved (not too strong a word) the army, its tradition, and her country. No one who worked or had ever worked with her, and no officer who was part of the investigation and hearing, felt that discharging her was fair, right, and necessary. But the regulations were unambiguous and had to be followed. I think it is fair to assume that the moral values embodied in those regulations are those of a majority of the citizenry, that is, that homosexuality is a physical affliction and/or immoral and that therefore collectivities (such as the army, schools, private sector organizations, and public agencies like the FBI and CIA) have a basis on which to deny them status, recognition, and rights enjoyed by other people. This is a classic case of the problematics of the individual-collectivity relationship, and one of many problems characterizing the social change in the post World War II era. Indeed, the emphasis in the social change on individual and group rights in large part accounts for legal and attitudinal changes in regard to the rights of homosexuals, alterations that have been, still are, and will be sources of social conflict and divisiveness.

In the minds of most people, how do organizations justify denying to homosexuals the rights accorded to other people? I shall not repeat the religious arguments people give. What all answers have in common is that homosexuality is an unfortunate, abnormal condition and lifestyle; its acceptance and spread would have a baleful effect on the society, especially on younger people; if it is so viewed, the collectivity has the obligation in no way to encourage it. To adopt a "live and let live" stance is to open wider the flood gates of license to act only in accord with individual norms, a kind of "falling domino effect." The counter arguments are that homosexuality is not an abnormal condition; that sexual preference and style are private, individual matters that are not to be the objects of discrimination; and that discriminating actions are at their roots powered by fear, ignorance, and myth, and those roots are precisely the ones historically used to justify prejudicial actions toward individuals and groups who are seen as strange and who do not conform to criteria of socially acceptable behavior.

What about Colonel Cammermeyer? Here is a person no one denies has led a socially acceptable and productive life. Why should she be denied the right to continue what she was doing? I doubt that most of those who view homosexuality negatively and prejudicially and saw the film were not in conflict about her expulsion. She harmed no one, except that she was a lesbian she was as morally "straight" as people might wish.

I asked several people who saw the film if they thought it had changed people's minds. One person said, "The very fact that it was shown in prime time, and sponsored by Hallmark cards to boot, in itself indicates that people are changing their minds." Another person said, "For people who cannot abide homosexuality, they will say that for every Cammermeyer there are many more who are off the wall, and they will tell you about parading transvestites, the death rate from AIDS among homosexuals, and the financial burden that has placed on society." Another person replied, "It may have changed some people's minds for the moment, but I am willing to bet that if at that moment you asked them if they were in favor of legalizing homosexual marriage, permitting these couples to have children through adoption or other means, or including what some would call an enlightened view in school textbooks, their changed minds would change back to where they were."

The conflicts and divisiveness that accompany social change are never, and I mean never, about one aspect of the change. They are always about how one aspect is related to or will impact upon other aspects that bring into question the status of individual-collectivity relationships. You do not have to be much of a historian to know that when collectivities trample on individual rights, injustice will follow. But you also do not have to be much of a historian to know that when a collectivity's ties that bind begin to be frayed or loosened, it can be destabilizing and destructive both for individuals and the collectivity. Either way, there is no free lunch, a law that opponents and proponents ignore. Each side rivets on intended consequences as if each of the different aspects of the social change operates in a social vacuum, or if those aspects are seen as interrelated, they are opposed or supported as if all consequences will be positive or negative, there is no in between zone of comfort.

Has our country ever felt justified in denying rights to individuals (or groups to which they belong) that are accorded to others as a matter of course in law? Can one justify the founding fathers' legitimation of slavery in the constitution? Some people have argued that the verdict of history is loud and clear: it was wrong and unjust and we are still paying a high price. That it was unjust goes without saying and there were people in 1787 who so considered it. But it also has been argued that it was not wrong in the sense that the overriding goal at the constitutional convention was the forging of a *united* states and there was no way that could be accomplished if the opponents of slavery insisted that it be abolished. There would have been no United States of America. If that had been the case, would U.S. and world history have been more to our liking? There is, of course, no way to answer the question. What we can say is that the judgments and decisions of a collectivity are determined as much by what it seeks to avoid as by what it intends to accomplish, and to expect otherwise is illusory. By "seeking to avoid" I mean countenancing injustice or denial of rights to individuals and groups because not to do so will negatively alter the basis of social life, that is, if they are not denied, the effect will not be specific but general. That assumption has frequently been wrong, powered by scenarios of futures in which the last act takes place in hell. When it is so powered the proponents cannot entertain the possibility that what they see and conduct as a life and death struggle may, in unintended ways, be counterproductive to their interests. And that holds for their opponents. For both sides it is a zero-sum game. Each side denies the maxim that it is hard to be completely wrong. Each sees the other as completely wrong, each sees itself as completely right. The verdicts of history say otherwise.

Decades ago Congress passed legislation that denied rights to a group that were accorded to other citizens, rights that were bedrock to the ethos of American individualism. They were not allowed to seek similar employment elsewhere unless their employers agreed. If they felt their salaries were unfair, that was too bad, they had no recourse; their employers possessed the combined powers of executives, legislators, and judges. Employers could literally "sell" their employees. Why was there no hue and cry about such a flagrant denial of rights? Why did the national collectivity, with few exceptions, go along with this state of affairs? Why were there no barricades and no one to storm them? I am talking (again), of course, about the business of baseball and the strike by the players. It is far beyond my purpose to discuss the history of the issues. But there are several aspects of the story that are relevant to the purposes of this essay. The first is that the issue of individual rights of players came to the fore at the same time that the issue became pivotal in diverse ways in the post World War II social change. It was not happenstance that the first successful legal challenge came from an African-American player (Curt Flood). Second, the owners resisted *any* change because any change would set the stage for other changes that would alter the character of the game. The owners were right, albeit their reasons were self-serving and shortsighted in the extreme. Third, as the individual rights of players were enlarged, and as the average salary mammothly escalated and that of many individual players became astronomical, individual goals began to take precedence over loyalty to team and fans. The players, of course, denied and still deny that their position has any untoward consequences, just as the owners denied that any change could have a positive effect.[1]

I write these words several weeks before the opening of the 1995 season, a season that may not take place. Regardless of what happens, both sides have contributed to a situation in which they are victims of the unintended consequences of their positions and actions. And those consequences will be of a long-term nature.

But for my purposes here the most important and instructive question is: why did the country for decades go along with the denial of rights accorded other citizens? If the answer is a complex one, there is one part of it that I consider the most important: *In denying certain individual rights to players, the collectivity saw no danger that such denial would have percolating and interactive effects elsewhere in the society.* Baseball was seen as an entertainment, not as a business. It was not seen as a denial of rights but as a protection of a game, "the national pastime." It represented no danger to the status quo. It had nothing to do with social change. If we see it differently today, it is because we are living at a time when individual rights—be they for the single individual or for the members of a group—have gained such force as to weaken the sense of community people have had in the small or large collectivities of which they are a part.

I close this essay with some brief comments on a factor the presence or absence of which plays a role in the pace and playing out of social change. I refer to the style, courage, and vision of national leaders. The specific example I will use concerns what happened in Little Rock when Governor Faubus defied court order to desegregate schools, which in that instance involved a small number of black students seeking admission to an all white high school. The encounter was seen by millions on TV. It was no secret that President Eisenhower had a lot of reservations about the 1954 desegregation decision. He sent troops to Little Rock less because

[1]For an elaboration of this point I refer the reader to an article by Murray Chass in the sports section of *The New York Times* for Sunday, February 19, 1995.

he wanted to and more because he was obligated to do so. The president was a much beloved individual. He had demonstrated remarkable leadership qualities in World War II, responsible as he was for welding and presiding over generals from different countries who varied mightily in ambition, egocentricity, and likability. He muted those differences and got the best out of his military colleagues. He used his charm, sincerity, and persuasiveness to good effect. But Little Rock was not an interpersonal affair. It was both a legal and a moral affair centering around the individual-collectivity relationship, that is, the mutuality of obligations. The fact is that Little Rock (and before that, the 1954 decision) was an opportunity for the president to use his influence and moral power, both of which were enormous, to persuade the people why the court's decision was overdue and necessary, albeit one that would present problems. Instead, he took a passive, purely legal position, uttered clichés and generalities, and disabused few of the impression that the court's decision was regrettable. I also have no doubt that he well knew that the decision would cause turmoil and divisiveness. But it is precisely in that kind of an instance that persistent, courageous, and unambiguous moral leadership is called for. The president did not pass that test. I do assume that if he had passed the test, he would have made *some* kind of difference. I am not one who believes that the forces of history and social change are so inexorable, so basically impersonal, as to be impervious to any degree to leaders who seek to lead, to be proactive rather than reactive.

Too many people today think of President Lyndon Johnson only in relation to the Vietnam War. I suggest that they read his first address to Congress, which he gave after President Kennedy's assassination. A southerner, a master of the uses of power, he delivered an address that left no doubt about where he stood and where the citizenry should stand about the overriding moral issue of the times. And he put more legislative flesh on the bones of his words than anyone before or after him. If Lincoln had not been assassinated, I have no doubt that I would have to amend that assessment. But that is the point: leaders can make a difference.

8

Recollected Sexual Memories

The further we get from our early adulthood the more we are likely to become aware not only that we have changed but also that the world around us has changed. That world literally looks different than it once did to us or, leaving the visual side, we are aware that people younger than we are seem to think and act differently than we do now or than we did when we were their age. It is more than a perception of difference, it is almost always accompanied, clearly or vaguely, by the conclusion that a change external to us has occurred.

That conclusion may be fleeting and unimpactful; it may be no cause for thought or reflection, let alone explanation. Or it may be enormously impactful. For example, a colleague tells me in the strictest confidence, and with tears in his eyes, that his grown daughter is accusing him of molesting her when she was a young child. To say that his world came apart is a gross understatement. To him it was a personal disaster. To seek help for how to handle the situation he went to a psychotherapist who told him that he was not the first parent who had reported to him such an accusation. Indeed, the psychotherapist said that he and some of his colleagues had been meeting to discuss why they were seeing an increase in such accusations. That prompted my colleague to spend a fair amount of time and money collecting newspaper and magazine accounts of such accusations for three years prior to our talk. And

he began to read books on the subject. He was not prepared for
what he found: what he had experienced was by no means infrequent, indeed it had not only increased in frequency but had
become the center of a raging controversy in psychological, legal,
and judicial circles. Even so, my colleague defined the problem in
narrow psychological terms, that is, as a series of cases in which the
minds of young people, mostly female, had become unaccountably
unhinged, or had been influenced by the suggestions of psychotherapists too eager to see molestation where it was unwarranted.
One experience led him to see different facets of "the problem." He
told his closest friend what he had told me and he was flabbergasted
to hear that his friend's daughter—they lived in different states and
his friend's daughter was in her mid teens—had similarly accused
her father.

When in a subsequent meeting my colleague related that conversation to me, he hardly said a word about his personal plight.
What he did say can best be subsumed under several headings—
really, questions. What is happening to our country? How do you
make sense out of all of this? Why is it happening now? Where are
we heading? What does it signify? Where will it and we end up? My
colleague, who is no social scientist, raised these questions in a
stunned and impotent way. But even if he had been a social scientist, answers would not have been forthcoming. Yes, there is abun-
dant evidence that in the post World War II era there has been a
dramatic change in attitudes towards matters sexual. You do not
have to be a social scientist to arrive at that conclusion. *That* my
colleague knew, albeit in a detached, impersonal way. What he was
asking was how his experience and those of other parents were illuminated and explained by those changes. He was not in doubt that
his experience had significance beyond the personal and the present, that is, what was "going on" would continue to go on and the
consequences would be, to put it mildly, negative. It is as if he considered what had happened to him as a barometer of a social change
that had a past and a future, a barometer reflecting forces he could

not comprehend, let alone control. His comprehension never got beyond the most general cause and effect explanation: in unexplained ways a sexual revolution had caused his daughter to think and act as she did.

I do not relate this anecdote only as an example of how a personal experience can lead us to conclude that a social change has taken (or is taking) place, a change we had vaguely noted but never expected to be a factor in our lives. That kind of conclusion can come about in many ways. The significance of the anecdote for me was that it reinforced my interest in two related questions: Why is the tendency to view the future as a carbon copy of the present so strong at the same time that we know we live in a society that in the past has witnessed numerous social changes? How do we become more sensitive to current social phenomena that *may* signal a social change? There really was a third question of longstanding interest to me: Is it likely, as I believe, that no extant theory of individual development (behavioral, psychoanalytic, or otherwise) has much, if anything, to contribute to an understanding of social change? That is to say, in riveting on the wonders, complexities, and puzzlements of the human mind, we have learned little about how, when, and why the individual perceives or does not perceive, reacts to or acts on, passively accepts or actively transforms, the meanings of social phenomena he or she hears about or is given. We have learned many things about the mind and the most important is that it is a vehicle that transforms what it takes in and experiences. It never was and never is an empty vessel. If the neonate does not come into the world with a worldview, it does not take long for one to begin to evolve, which is to say that what evolves are explanations of how the world works, and about what is right, natural, and proper. There was a time—before movies, radios and TV— when the family was the major site in which the ingredients of a worldview were transmitted, absorbed, and organized. Those days are, of course, over. Today, evolving worldviews are literally about the world and the universe: messages and their meanings come continuously and from all over, more often than not they make a virtue of change, as if change is to be equated with progress.

A friend of mine said to me, "You are interested in the barometers of social change. Fine, be my guest. I hope you will not do what so many in your fraternity do: you start counting this or that, you end up with numbers on this or that and you intercorrelate them, and then your imagination takes over and, presto, you have a theory but not one about how people have changed or are changing. If you asked for my advice, which you haven't, I would say that you start with the question: why do so many people no longer know what they should think or believe about their worlds? If I am right about that, it signifies a change from the past that is remarkable, and suggests that the future is something to worry about."

That was said to me long before I started this book. He did not have to tell me what I should avoid doing because temperamentally and conceptually I had no intention of counting this or that. But his words came back to me after my colleague had told me about his daughter's accusation, his scouring of the mass media, the books that were being published on the issues, and after I began to read the psychological–social science literature, which to say the least was escalating in numbers and polemical tone. How should I think about it? What were the "lessons to be learned?" What, if anything, did it suggest about barometers of social change?

Predictably, the most obvious feature of what I read was the question: were the accusations valid? No writer took the position that all reported cases were figments of imagination. Where writers disagreed was about the number of valid accusations. Some claimed the number was small, that the bulk of accusers had confused fantasy with reality. Others saw it in the reverse. This was no simple difference of opinion in which each side used a different theory to explain the phenomenon. It was war, the no holds barred variety. The nonbelievers resorted to logic, or the results of research, or the requirements of scientific criteria for admissible evidence, or *ad hominems*, or all of these. The believers used the compellingness of clinical material, or the startling clarity of the details of the molestations, or what these encounters confirmed about the sexual derogation and subjugation of females by males, or they would ask why in an era in which physical child abuse was daily fare should nonbelievers find accusations of molestation by parents so hard to accept? The believers were peers of nonbelievers when it came to ad hominems.

Strangely, the controversy hardly concerns the frequency of molestation, real or imagined. I expected that the believers more than the nonbelievers would make an issue of frequency and indicate the thorny problems that obtaining even a semirespectable estimate of frequency would have to overcome. It seemed as if the nonbelievers accepted the possibility that imagined molestation may not be minuscule but that in a number of cases the fantasy was not one from childhood but one that biased psychotherapists had "planted" by suggestion, that is, they had started with a bias and proceeded in the ways of the self-fulfilling prophecy to prove their point. The believers, of course, will have none of that and counter with the criticism that the nonbelievers—hiding under the cloak of rationality and science, unable or unwilling to face up to present and past sexual exploitation of females, uncomfortable with the sordid and the perverted—were victims of their own socialization into a society in which females were second class citizens.

What significance, if any, does this ongoing controversy have as a barometer of social change? Should we regard it as an interesting and important professional-scientific-technical controversy that will, so to speak, get played out in narrow circles, having no percolating effects elsewhere? Does this controversy have roots in the societal past that we may have noted but the significance of which we did not grasp? If that is the case, what does the controversy portend for social change? Are we dealing with an ocean ripple subsiding into a beach's sands at low tide or a wave that tells us to move back on the beach? Should we be indifferent to whether it is a ripple or a wave?

Let me start with a conclusion that surprised me. Although it would be wrong to regard each side as homogeneous in outlook and substance of criticism, both sides have very different conceptions or explanations for how our society has been and is organized and what the adverse consequences have been for relations between boys and girls, men and women. The nonbelievers do not quarrel with that view of adverse consequences—it is a glimpse of the obvious—but they imply (it is rarely said explicitly) that whatever drives the different manifestations of sexual exploitation and abuse of females is more generally recognized than ever before, and corrective actions (legislation, education) are being taken, although no one holds that such manifestations will disappear. What the nonbelievers dispute is the contention that there is a pervasive, raging hot war between the sexes centering around power in general and sex in particular, a war in which a fair number of the combatants do not know they are combatants, that is, they have been so thoroughly socialized in their sexual, working, social roles that they have been rendered incapable of recognizing their role as perpetrator or victim. To explain sexual molestation of children by parents as symptomatic of a widespread conflict is, to say the least, scientifically untenable and borders on a paranoia akin to the Salem witch persecutions (and others in history) or the antics of a Senator McCarthy. To the nonbelievers, the believers are not interested in understanding real (or imagined for that matter) molestation but in pushing a social agenda that is more than radical, it is revolutionary.

The believers deeply resent the impugning of their therapeutic motivations, conduct, and social perspective. Indeed, they use such criticisms as evidence of how strong and effective are the barriers to the recognition by males (and many females) of the protean ways by which males exercise power over females in our society. Pornography, portrayal of women as sex objects in advertisements, sexual harassment, discrimination in regard to salary and promotion, prostitution, derogation of assertive women, differential teacher response to boys and girls, men and women in classrooms—these and more, the believers contend, are sufficient basis for regarding sexual molestation by a parent as indicative of more than personality dynamics, that is, as isolated instances unrelated to the messages absorbed by people growing up in such a society. Not only are these instances to be given credence, but it is likely that the frequency of such occurrences is greater than we know because the victims are reluctant to speak out.

Why was I surprised that the two sides saw the problem from such different perspectives? And by "problem" I do not refer to the scientific-technical-therapeutic issues involved in determining the validity of the accusations but rather to the significances, if any, of why these accusations seem to have become more frequent *now* and have engendered such public controversy. Whether the accusations are real or imagined is less crucial than the apparent fact that there are young people, therapists, and others in the general population who believe that the accusations are probably valid. Even the nonbelievers seem not to dispute the possibility that the number of accusers *today* who confuse fantasy with reality is greater than ever before, but the nonbelievers give no explanation for why this is so *now* more than before, that is, why are accusers *today* so willing to believe a therapist's suggestion that they have been molested by parents? Is this explainable only in terms of suggestibility and personality dynamics? Is it unrelated to perceptions of, messages from, and reading about our quotidian world? Is it a clinical phenomenon to be studied and judged only by careful, controlled research? Or should we also see it as an indicator of a social change that has already taken place and that will have social consequences in the future?

My surprise stemmed from one belief and one assumption which I regard as axiomatic. The belief is that by scientific criteria of evidence *some* of these instances of parental molestation are *not* valid replicas of lived experience. The assumption is that social behavior is always a reflection—in one or another way, large or small, obvious or subtle—of the culture. John Dollard said it well in his *Criteria for the Life History* (1935, pp. 4–5):

The taking of a life history is here viewed as a problem of the student of culture; it can, of course, be done by persons who do not formally acknowledge that they are students of social life, but this does not change the essence of the matter; they are students of culture by definition if they attempt to deal with acculturated individuals. What particular "ist" they wear at the end of their field designation is merely traditionally determined and unimportant. . . . The formal view of culture provides an indispensable backdrop for individual studies but via it we do not arrive at theories of meaningful action. As soon as we take the post of observer on the cultural level the individual is lost in a crowd and our concepts never lead us back to him. After we have "gone cultural" we experience the person as a fragment of a (derived) culture pattern, as a marionette dancing on the strings of (reified) culture forms. A culture-personality problem can be identified in every case by observing whether the person is "there" in full emotional reality; if he is not there, then we are dealing with a straight cultural or institutional study. If he is there and we can ask how he feels, then we have a culture-personality problem. It is stressed emphatically that there are no personality problems alone. Personality problems are always culture-personality problems.

Dollard not only said it well but illustrated the point by using case material from Adler, Freud, Jung, Thomas and Zaniecki, Clifford Shaw, and H.G. Wells. For Dollard, whatever the ostensible goals of the clinical interaction, the substance of that interaction always contained and reflected a culture-personality problem even though patient and therapist were unaware of it, as Dollard made clear in his analysis of the published case material of the above writers.

Someone said that it is hard to be completely wrong, and that is how I feel about the believers and nonbelievers. Some believers assume that what accusers have told them is valid, period. They cannot entertain the significance of the possibility that they and their clients have lived in and been shaped by the same culture at a particular time, not in 1950, or 1940, or earlier. There has been obvious social-cultural change, and neither accuser or hearer are unmarked by that change. Awareness of that should be warning enough that what the accuser says *and* what the hearer says and believes bear in some way the imprimatur of the social-cultural change, of place and era. That does not necessarily invalidate what is said and believed but it does suggest that what is said and believed cannot be explained only by the personality dynamics given us by extant theories of personalities. The disposition to believe or not to believe is in large part cultural. I do not expect a therapist to discuss the culture-personality problems with a client! But when a believer presents to a professional audience or to the reading public his or her beliefs and does not at least suggest that the culture-personality problem *may* have bearing on the validity of those beliefs, I consider it at best the hallmark of the "true believer" and at worst irresponsible. The fantasy of molestation is, so to speak, in the head, but it is a head that has been bombarded with all kinds of related messages from diverse sources. And that is also true in the case of the hearer.

But what about the believers who place these accusations in a truly wide social-cultural conflict about male-female relationships? From my standpoint, that is the context in which the accusations (real or imagined) should be seen and placed. But placing them there does not explain them, that is, it does not in any single case tell us how these related cultural phenomena impinged upon, were absorbed by, and were or were not transformed by the accusers. Nor do they tell us why the number of accusers is apparently increasing, a fair number of whom feel compelled to confront the parent who molested them. It could be argued, as believers have, that the frequency of molestation by parents has not increased but that today people are more willing to acknowledge that they have been victimized. Assuming that is true, what does that mean for how we explain the social-cultural change that makes people more "willing" and what might that mean for the future course of the ongoing social change?

In regard to the nonbelievers, as well as those who suspend judgment, I start with two articles in *The National Psychologist*, a publication that contains news and information for practitioners, most of the readers being clinical psychologists. The issue came to me the day before the previous two paragraphs were written. Here is the first article (APA Working Group, 1994, p. 7):

> The key points of agreement among members of the Working Group on Investigation of Childhood Abuse, after reviewing current research literature on trauma and memories, were:
>
> Controversies regarding adult recollections should not be allowed to obscure the fact that sexual abuse is a complex and pervasive problem in America which has historically gone unacknowledged.
>
> Most people who were sexually abused as children remember all or part of what happened to them.
>
> It is possible for memories or abuse that have been forgotten for a long time to be remembered. The mechanism(s) by which such delayed recall occur(s) is/are not currently well understood.
>
> It is also possible to construct convincing pseudomemories for events that never occurred. The mechanism(s) by which these pseudomemories occur(s) is/are not currently well understood.
>
> There are gaps in knowledge about the processes that lead to accurate and inaccurate recollections of childhood abuse.

According to APA, the working group will identify specific gaps in knowledge and suggest research directions that may lead to better understanding of mechanisms associated with accurate or inaccurate recollections. APA said the working group would address research questions raised by clinical experience as well as the application of clinical process research and treatment outcome validity studies to clinical practice issues.

The final report in February is to explore ways current data may add to legal testimony, forensic evaluations, therapeutic strategies and professional training.

Nothing in what I shall say should be interpreted as a criticism of this interim report. Indeed, it is a reasonable statement with which believers and nonbelievers alike would probably not quarrel. No sane professional would assert that we do not need "better understanding of mechanisms associated with accurate or inaccurate recollections." But to someone like me who views the controversy from the standpoint of whether it is a barometer of an ongoing social change, the report is disappointing. As best as I can determine, the members of this working group, a highly respectable one, tend to be nonbelievers, some of them passionately so. And that is my point: not a few nonbelievers regard the believers as not being interested *primarily* in the scientific status of recollected memories but in promoting a social diagnosis centering around male-female relationships, a diagnosis that indicts male power and dominance as well as female passivity to such subjugation. Put another way, the believers do not see child sexual abuse as the primary problem but as a social symptom of pervasive unjust power relationships that must be altered. I am not aware that any nonbeliever has ever accused believer clinicians of not wanting to be helpful to a victim of child abuse. They criticize them on two counts. First, in addition to an individual diagnosis they have a social one. Second, partisanship to the social diagnosis causes them to see sexual abuse where such an individual diagnosis is frequently unwarranted, with untoward effects on everyone concerned. As someone said, "They are not scientists and they are not interested in the rules of evidence. They are activists, pure and simple."

The interim report is right in saying that establishing the validity of recollected memories is tricky business and we know less than we need to know about it. But is the significance of the validity of recollected issue the only important feature of the controversy? Let us, for the sake of argument, make three assumptions. First, most of the recollected memories are fantasy; second, there are too many therapists who uncritically believe what they are told; and third, some of these therapists are predisposed to accept accusations as valid, and even when no accusation is being given they suggest to the client that he or she has or may have been a victim of sexual abuse. How do we explain how these therapists came to believe what they do? Nonbelievers have said that the answer is their poor professional preparation. But what if these therapists absorbed their point of view from faculty or others who supervised them? Or from best selling books? On what basis can we assume that among the teachers of these people there are not a few, perhaps even more, who are true believers? Since when are university faculty homogeneous in social outlook or on any important social issue? Is it happenstance that this controversy has erupted during a time when, more than ever before, the number of women entering the field (psychology, psychiatry, clinical social work, counselling) has dramatically increased, as has the number of women on the relevant faculties? And are there not male therapists and faculty who are also true believers?

I asked earlier why some young people are "willing" to believe that they are victims of child abuse. That is precisely the question I am asking about therapists and others who are believers. I am *not* asking if they are right or not in their clinical outlook. I am suggesting that a significant fraction of the population, probably most of whom are women, some of whom are in influential positions, have no difficulty accepting accusations of child abuse as probably valid. If that is the case, as I think it is, it is unlikely that such acceptance is unrelated or even uncaused by beliefs about how the society has changed and is changing. So, for example, the militant feminists (and they are not only women) do not see sexual victimization as an isolated phenomenon but as one instance of how the combination of the puritan ethos and male dominance has had pervasive, untoward effects on different individuals and groups, such as women in general, men (although they may not be aware of their victimhood), lesbians, gays, and those who have "unconventional" lifestyles. And they also see that in the case of relationships between black men and women that the combination of puritan ethics and male dominance is mightily fueled by the origins and dynamics of racial discrimination. Although not all believers are militant feminists, others may not be feminists at all; when they view the social scene they are not surprised at accounts of recollected memories of sexual abuse. As not a few (nonfeminists) have remarked, "I have heard everything. I am no longer surprised at anything. I almost believe everything bad I hear or read about." The point is that the frequent accounts of child abuse are seen in some unspecified way as an indication of a sea-swell social change that has taken place and is continuing. When you see the world that way, the "will to believe" gains strength, and that is true for nonvictims as well as for victims whose accusations may be real or imagined. I have no doubt that *some* clinicians unwarrantedly suggest the occurrence of abuse, but the willingness to accept the suggestion is not explained solely by invoking the concept of suggestibility. The content of recollected memories, real or imagined, is in an individual's head, but it is a head that has been shaped in a society containing myriads of possibilities about sexual matters.

As Dollard said, "Every personality problem is a culture-personality problem." That point is made almost in passing by the APA's Working Group. "Controversies regarding adult recollections should not be allowed to obscure the fact that child sexual abuse is a complex and pervasive problem in America which has historically gone unacknowledged".[1] Believers would agree with that statement if "unacknowledgement" and "complex" meant that child sexual abuse was only one symptom of a society based on male dominance, power, and an unwillingness or inability to change. And furthermore, they would argue that what was historically unacknowledged still largely is, and they use the passion of the nonbelievers as proof of their defense of a narrow and invalid social diagnosis. The believers are making Dollard's point, which is not to say that their defense of the validity of recollected memories in individual cases is justified, or that their conceptualization of the "culture problem" is not without serious flaws. *But, to repeat, the believers are less subject to Dollard's criticisms of an individual psychology, of an acultural psychology, than the nonbelievers.*

In the same issue of *The National Psychologist* that contained the report on the report of the working group is a letter to the editor. The letter (p. 4) was stimulated by a longstanding controversy in the American Psychological Association: what professional or credentialing recognition should be given to psychologists who "only" have a master's degree, no doctorate?

---

[1]It is not strictly true that it went unacknowledged. The longest-running play in the New York theaters was *Tobacco Road*, in which molestation was a prominent feature. What was not acknowledged as a possibility was that molestation may occur other than in poor, southern, rural families. It is also worthy of note that with the legitimation of psychoanalysis in the university soon after World War II, generations of students were made familiar with the role of the *incest fantasy* in childhood, a role that although it exculpated parents may have had *some* personal meaning for *some* people. Also noteworthy is that the "explosion" in reported cases coincided with—or perhaps came somewhat after—the controversy (professional, public, legal) about when and why Freud changed his mind and theory about the validity of patients' accounts of parental molestation. *That* was a controversey the reading public ate up, so to speak, and I have no doubt that it was more than newsworthy to segments of the mental health community and to feminist groups, from which I do not exclude some men, both inside and outside the therapeutic community. Anyone who interprets what I say as a criticism of psychoanalysis, a blaming of it, is totally off base. My criticisms of psychoanalysis are of a very different nature.

MA narrates her trials

Editor:

I have two masters degrees. After a B.S. in home economics from Purdue University in the early 1930s, my psychology professor inspired me to continue with graduate study. That brought me the M.S. degree in psychology and education at Purdue. An invitation was given me to study in Human Growth and Development at the University of Chicago. I completed a plan for the Ph.D. When I refused to go to bed with my major professor, he withdrew from my doctoral committee, and refused to sign for me to obtain a student loan for my second year. The late Carl Rogers, Ph.D., a member of my committee, advised me not to transfer to psychology: they were not approving of women obtaining the Ph.D. I stayed on a second year, then returned to my teaching position at Western Illinois State Teachers College.

Two years later, I applied and was accepted in the Family Life Doctoral Program at Teachers College in New York City. A woman professor was assigned as my major professor. She was having trouble with graduate students, therefore, I was not permitted to make a choice. Under the then prevailing circumstances, I was left without an advisor.

The next year, I was asked to teach at Pratt Institute in Brooklyn. Somehow, my path touched the path of Emily Mudd, owner/director of Marriage Council of Philadelphia. My application for a year of marriage counseling training was accepted. I was asked to stay a second year to help with research. Then, she suggested I apply for a second masters degree in view of two tries for the Ph.D. without success. My application for the M.A. in

Social Work was accepted by Indiana University. I was granted the degree after two years.

Positions to teach in college were offered. Later, I came to Cleveland, met the administrative judge who asked me to work at the Domestic Relations Court. I was the first mental health consultant there to judges, referees, families they referred. A man was hired, crowded me out. I opened my own office for private practice in July 1982.

How many women and men are awarded the doctorate because their major professor sees them through for personal/sexual reasons?

Esther Langlois, M.S., M.A.
Psychologist and Marriage Counselor
Licensed Independent Social Worker

Ms. Langlois's account of gender discrimination in the 1930s can be matched by hundreds, perhaps thousands, of women seeking the doctorate in psychology and other fields. That would also be the case for what she recounts about job discrimination. What I find especially significant is her last, short paragraph about the situation *now*. Ms. Langlois is today a senior citizen (like me) and she sees the conflict between the sexes as not having changed much, if at all. I do not think I am putting words in her mouth when I say that she does not see gender relationships in the university as an isolated phenomenon unrelated to social phenomena elsewhere. Just as child sexual abuse is not explainable only by the personalities of victimizer and victim, I assume that Ms. Langlois does not see gender discrimination in academia as explainable only in terms of the personality of graduate students and faculty. Not incidentally, in my fifty years in academia the question she asks in the last paragraph is one I heard scores of times from colleagues around the country. Being a "straight," conventional person, I reacted in my earlier years to the stories as if they were malicious gossip. I had to change my mind because of accounts told to me personally by participants in such goings on, and those accounts were not only from victims. If I changed my mind, it did not mean that I accepted all such stories I heard as valid. But I have to say that there was a part of me *willing* to believe they were valid. And that is the point: my willingness to believe was related to my perception of a lot more going on that I once regarded as strange and dismaying but which I no longer could so regard. My world had changed, and given my longstanding acceptance of John Dollard's thinking (he was a colleague) I had to conclude that these goings on, which on the surface appeared discrete and unrelated, were a personality and culture problem, they were not culturally uncorrelated.

Nonbelievers do not grasp this point because they are seeing the current controversy only as a scientific-technical-professional problem, not as a *possible* barometer of an ongoing social change. If it is such a barometer, it is likely that research riveted on the validity or invalidity of recollected memories will have little or no impact on what believers say, do, and report.

The point nonbelievers make is that believers start with a social-cultural diagnosis that causes them to distort their judgments about the validity of recollected memories. They may be right about distortion (in an undetermined number of cases, probably more than a few), but are they wrong in assuming that the phenomena of sexual abuse are unrelated to other phenomena that are manifestations of a society distinctively organized on the basis of axioms about what is right, natural, and proper? Are they wrong in suggesting that the willingness of people today to believe and report experience of child abuse is a barometer of an ongoing social change, that it is not only a personality problem of the victimizer and victim? You can say they are not wrong, but that does not mean they are right for the right reasons. Karl Marx was surely right in directing attention to the significances of the economic factor, but he was surely wrong in using that factor as an explanation for almost everything. Freud was surely right in his emphasis on the sexual, but he was surely wrong in seeming to invoke the dynamics of the sexual everywhere. They were both right in principle, that is, the tendency to look at discrete social phenomena as unrelated, to subsume each under a different rubric (psychological, sexual, economic, political) is a culturally learned way to avoid coming to grips with the task of flushing out the unverbalized axioms that would permit us to see relationships where heretofore we could not because we did not want to see those relationships. In my opinion the more extreme articulate believers are right in principle but like Freud and Marx they have cast their conceptual net so wide that they end up having simple answers for everything.

Again for the sake of argument, let us assume that the believer's social diagnosis is largely correct. Does that exempt them from the obligation to attempt to demonstrate *in the individual case* how the abstractions "culture" or "society," which are what the social diagnosis purports to explain, became transmitted, absorbed, transformed, and part of the personality? The answer is no, and I suggest that the reader who is a believer read Dollard's book. The fact is that the clinical enterprise as it now is structured cannot be used by believers to confirm their social diagnosis, and it cannot be used by nonbelievers to rebut the believer's social diagnosis.

I regard the controversy about recollected memories to be a barometer of social change, and for several reasons. The first is the heat it has engendered both in and out of circumscribed professional circles. More seems to be at stake for the combatants than recollected memories. What that more is is somewhat clearer among believers than among nonbelievers, who publicly tend to stay within the confines of "this is a scientific controversy."

Second, many people on either side see the controversy as a confirming instance of something wrong and disturbing about society. The nonbelievers see it as an unjustified willingness to explain it as part and parcel of a society that has oppressed and continues to oppress diverse groups because of their gender, sexual lifestyle, race, or economic status; or that has, as in the case of rape, blamed the victim. Some believers say the willingness is justified. Others who are not able to go that far nevertheless feel, as they survey the social scene, that the society has changed in untoward ways and that *this is likely to continue*. They, like most nonbelievers, look to the future with foreboding. They, again like some nonbelievers, are uncomfortable with the perception that too many people seem to act as if "anything is permissible, anything goes."

Third and unrelated to the second, and perhaps most significant of all: many people (especially those over forty years of age) react to the controversy, and other phenomena I have mentioned, with the feeling that their accustomed beliefs and values (what is right and wrong, what is the nature of the society) *perhaps* should be changed. At the very least, they do not hold those beliefs and values with the conviction they once did. Something has happened in and to the society and they do not know how to think about it. Whether recollected memories are real or imagined is almost beside the point; it is another example to them that the world they thought they knew is not the world they now live in.

On public television a couple of years ago there was a program on the sexual attitudes and practices of senior citizens (in Florida, of course). Two themes were dominant in the program. One theme was that too many aging people had accepted the conventional societal view that they were sexless, or nearly so, and that if they were not, something was amiss in their psyche about which they should be ashamed. The second and related theme was that they should liberate themselves from such a view and seek sexual pleasures with a partner in whatever ways were available to them. I agreed with both themes. When I expressed my agreement to a colleague far younger than I, she said (paraphrased), "Well, I suppose I should not be surprised that another group is being told to come out of the closet in which society told them to stay. This is really the age of empowerment, isn't it? I wonder how many old people are sorry, maybe angry, that they did not get the message earlier." What my young colleague said was significant to me not because of

the substance of her remarks but because she, probably unknowingly, was illustrating a very important aspect of people's perception
of social change: judgments about whether a particular issue is a
barometer of social change depend, or certainly are mammothly
influenced by, how it is seen in relation to other social issues that
on the surface may appear to have nothing to do with the particular issue. And that is what I have argued here in regard to the controversy about recollected memories. That all these issues may in
some way be interrelated is an assumption that its proponents are
obliged to buttress with more than rhetoric, just as opponents
should be obliged to avoid rhetoric as argument. A variant of that
argument is that when a particular issue strikes a person as perhaps
signaling a social change, one should not only try to determine
where the participants are coming from, so to speak, but one should
also ask what other signals from other controversies one has used as
a barometer of social change.

One reaction I had to the TV program stuck with me because,
in ways not clear to me then, it was troubling. It was hard for me to
watch the program and avoid concluding that one of its clear and
yet unverbalized messages was that individuals should feel a responsibility to themselves to resist conventional attitudes that require
the inhibition of the expression of strong personal longings. In the
abstract I could only agree. Concretely, in regard to old people and
sexual activity, I also could take no exception to the message. But
that program was being watched by a lot of people who were not
old, each one of whom, I assumed, had at least one strong, personal
longing which if given expression would be frowned on by society.
How were these people interpreting the message? Was that a message infrequently heard by them? If it was a frequent message coming from diverse sources, would some viewers think of acting on it
in regard to their longings? The more I thought about it the more I
realized that, prior to and independent of the program, I had been
bothered by the frequency of the message about the primary importance of self-expression in a conventional society that was anti-

thetical to such expression. Having lived through the sixties and its postscripts, my conclusion was no great feat of insight. The TV program, I came to conclude, was one of those postscripts, although I am sure that neither the senior citizen participants or the producers and writers of the program saw it that way.

I kept asking myself why the frequency of that message bothered me. I cannot adduce evidence for my answer and I am sure it will not sit well with many readers. Pitting the individual against society the way this frequent message does can have one or all of several consequences: the individual may become more absorbed in the self; action may become more salient and compelling; resentment towards society and its different representatives may be fueled; and the individual may be caused to see in a more favorable light others who are struggling against an oppressive society. The obligations to self have priority over perceived conventions of the society. My difficulty here is that it is hard to say these things without being seen as an old fogey on the barricades against social change, as someone insensitive to the injustices in the society. So, in defense let me say two things:

1. Social change is probably never an unalloyed blessing, at least the way I read the history. Whether or not its positive effects will have more social impact than the negative ones is hard to predict while the change is occurring.

2. When one lives at a time when social change is occurring, one inevitably, and I do mean inevitably, is not neutral toward what one perceives may be one more of its manifestations. Socialized as we have been into this society, there will be individual differences in the degree to which we are blind or sensitive to what I have called the barometers of social change.

So, in saying that the message conveyed so frequently and from so many sources may have certain consequences, I in no way meant to imply that they would be uniformly baleful. What I did mean was that the influence of that message had to be a mixed one. And in using the words "*pitting* the individual against society" I was trying to identify one of the troublesome consequences: that in emphasizing, indeed overemphasizing, the rights of *individuals* and their primacy over the requirements for a cohesive *society*, what may continue to erode is the psychological sense of community, a sense and need that grow more insistent as we traverse the lifespan, and without which all other needs and goals wither into relative insignificance. I have never met a sane middle-aged person who disagreed with my assertion that the absence of the sense of community robbed their other achievements of their expected satisfactions. That is no argument for conformity, for stopping the social clock, or anything of that kind. It is an argument that we should take seriously, that somewhere in the process of passing judgment on what we perceive as barometers of social change, we should pause and ask ourselves whether our judgment has taken into account possible alterations in the status and power of an indisputably individual and social need, because when we ask that we are asking what the reciprocal relationships between individual and society should be, which is not the same as pitting one against the other. There is no way that a society can avoid causing discontent in its people, just as there is no way a group can avoid resentment among its members towards other members, or of one or more of its members toward the group as a whole. Should one not ask if the fires fueling resentment may weaken or destroy what one later may regret? Mencken said that for every complex problem there is a simple answer that is wrong. The wisdom in that quip has been lost on many proponents of social change, now and in our long human history.

I used to envy the historian because he or she studied a period about which a good deal was already known and, more importantly, some of its distinctive features were contained in labels, such as, prebellum and postbellum South, the Renaissance, Periclean Athens, America in the Great Depression. No historian begins investigation in order to regurgitate what is already known. The historian has respect for what already has been uncovered, while at the same time he or she has questions about, for example, the weight given to this or that factor, or the adequacy of generally accepted explanations, or the possibility that archival material was inadequately mined, or it may be that new theories or new data justify further study and reevaluation. A person who reads widely but is not a historian or a social scientist is very likely aware how Marxism, psychoanalysis, and the women's movement have stimulated historians to look at the past in a new light.

The basis for my envy was twofold. The historian already knows how the period that is of interest and concern underwent change. And the historian has the luxury of time: he or she literally can take years seeking answers to questions about the past. And, of course, the historian has distance from the past, making it more likely that dispassion can be sustained. In brief, the historian does not have the problem that someone (like me) has trying to make ordered sense out of the times into which he or she was born and in which he or she was reared, times that in countless ways he or she reacted to and acted upon, none of this in a calm, uninvolved way. For that person to assume or believe that he or she can adopt a detached, let alone an Olympian, view of self and society is sheer fantasy. You do your best, knowing that at best your failures may have significance for the historian who will come along after you have departed.

But the more I have thought about it, and the more I have talked to historians, the more I have concluded that my envy was justified only in part. For one thing, for any one historical era or problem, historians may differ dramatically on the status of what is regarded as factual or, if the status is not in question, in how the factual is to be interpreted, and that frequently means deducing the world view and mind-set of the people in that past. The process of deduction is one in which the historian plays the psychologist, going from the ostensible, the factual, to the psychological. Let me excerpt and paraphrase what one historian said in a rather long, rambling discussion with me on my questions about discerning barometers of social change in society today.

Of course what you are trying to think through is, to say the least, messy. In my work I suffer from the defects of my virtue. My virtue is that I did not live in the past I study; I was not caught up in the happenings of those days; I would not have been able if I lived then to see and understand other than a piece of a social jigsaw puzzle, and if I thought that I saw and understood what was going on around me, it may have been from an atypical standpoint. That is why the historian tries, he should at least try, to uncover what the perceptions of differently placed people were in order to conclude which standpoints were most likely to explain more about the event, era, or person you are riveted on. My virtue is distance from the past. But the defect of that virtue is that precisely because I did not live in that past, I am never secure in feeling that I really know how different individuals and groups saw or interpreted their world. You also suffer from the defects of your virtue. You know what you think, what other people think, what is on the surface and underneath it. You pass judgment and you know you may be wrong. The fact is that whether you are right or wrong, and why, is what the historians in the future will want to know, but from the vantage point of a society that has changed dramatically in the intervening decades, and that the historian will know only partially and probably distortedly.

Let me give you an example of what I am trying to say. You know about Socrates and how and why he was given hemlock to die. He was seen by Athenians as a corrupter of youth. Historians and philosophers may disagree about one or another aspect of what happened and why, but it is fair to say that, generally speaking, they pretty much are in agreement. About ten years ago along comes I. F. Stone with a truly radical and ingenious interpretation. Stone was no professional historian; he spent his life in journalism, but he did immerse himself in what had been written about Athens of that day, even becoming proficient in Greek. [I told him I had read the book.] So you know that Stone essentially claimed that the conflict between Socrates and the ruling politicos did not stem from moral considerations but political ones, that is, Socrates, Stone said, was an arch conservative elitist, antidemocratic character who had to be gotten out of the way. Stone did not make this up out of whole cloth. What he did was to reinterpret available knowledge, weigh this or that factor differently than others had done, and he comes up with a new picture of Socrates' "mind" in the context of an ongoing social-political struggle. Stone caught hell from the different academic fraternities, some of them saying that given Stone's life-long liberal-leftist leanings his analysis and interpretation led him to make egregious mistakes, that is, the picture he painted, the pattern of relationships he thought he saw, the deductions of a psychological and social nature he made were unjustified. The fact is that Stone was doing what all historians more or less do and what you are doing: is there a pattern of relationships that is different from or a challenge to the so-called conventional wisdom? Is it possible that the conventional view is weighting factors wrongly or that it is overlooking or even ignoring some important factors? I can't give you an answer or judgment. The Greeks are far from my specialty. We probably will never really know unless something like the Dead Sea scrolls are found which sheds some light on the validity of Stone's argument. If something like the scrolls are found, you can bet your bottom dollar that arguments

about interpretation, about psychology in relation to
social phenomena will start all over again.

I found what my historian colleague said semitherapeutic because it spurred me to stay with the question: what relationships, if
any, would future historians see between recollected memories and
related social problems? Would they say I had asked the right question about the right phenomena? The right question about the
wrong phenomena? Or what? At least I understand an aspect of the
attractiveness of the fantasy of life after death!

9

Working and Loving

It was Freud who said that the two major tasks in life are loving and working. It is fair to say that he devoted a lifetime to describing loving—explaining its origins, biological substrate, developmental vicissitudes, personal and interpersonal dynamics, and the host of factors that make the giving and getting of love problematic and sometimes impossible. More than that, he asserted that cultures were incomprehensible when considered apart from the ways they have developed over time, reacting to and restricting the more volcano-like, percolating, threatening aspects of libidinal phenomena, ways that go back to the dawn of history (or prehistory). Freud was not surprised that the world did not roll out the welcome mat and accept his clinical observations, conclusions, and theory. Like Copernicus and Darwin, he said, psychoanalysis presented a view of human beings, a worldview, that was too discrepant with the conventional view. It is hard to read Freud's post World War II writings and avoid the impression that he had concluded that civilization as we know it so subverts the capacity to give and get love as to suggest a most gloomy future. The rise of Hitler's Germany, and Freud's fleeing Vienna, was unwelcome confirmation.

About work Freud said virtually nothing. That is strange, and for several reasons. For one thing, Europe in the latter part of the eighteenth century and almost all of the nineteenth century had

171
. . . . .

experienced class warfare in which, of course, the opportunity to
work, to challenge the control of the workplace, to demand remuneration that would avoid degrading poverty, and to close and even
abolish the gap between the haves and the have nots were controversial, socially divisive issues. Marx and other socialist leaders and
writers described the just society as one that would allow its people
to become all they could potentially be, and that meant working
and not laboring. Laboring meant the expenditure of energy to produce an outcome, some kind of a product, that in no way reflected
anything about its maker. Regardless of the maker, the product did
not change. In work the outcome bore the imprimatur of the maker:
his or her needs, imagery, and purposes. Work and its contexts were
live, social-political issues. Freud knew that. It is safe to assume that
he also knew that a person's sense of identity was very much tied to
how that person and others regarded the person's competence and
worth as a worker. Freud wrote a good deal about the origins and
force of the sense of personal identity, but that never led him to ask
in what way the personal identity of A and B is different because A
is a street cleaner and B is a professor. And of course it never led
him to ask why the sense of personal identity differed in men and
women because women worked in only one place and men worked
in scores of elsewheres.

Freud used his own life (events, imagery, dreams, conflicts, and
so on) to illustrate his theories. But he never pursued the significance of what *he* expected work to provide *him*, and what he did
expect were outlets for his curiosity, stimulating and enlarging experiences, intellectual challenge, the sense of personal growth, and
recognition not only of his ambitious goals but of his accomplishments. Freud knew that about himself; it was as much a part of his
sense of personal identity as was the fact that he was a Jew, a physician, a Viennese, a father, and a husband. Yet, despite the fact that
Freud saw his contributions as a basis for making society more just
and humane, less likely to be torn apart by humanity's potential for

savagery, he said nothing about one of the two major problems he considered to be of overarching importance in living. It is not surprising that in his clinical writings, and in those of his colleagues and followers, the clinical case material says little or nothing about working.

I offer the hypothesis that Freud's neglect of work and its contexts has to be seen in light of the fact that he, his colleagues, and his patients, as well as the audience he sought to reach, were largely highly educated, professional people from the middle and upper social classes. I am not aware of statistics bearing on the emergence and increase of professionals (of all kinds) in Europe at the turn of the century. It is my impression that the increase was already remarkable, especially in Europe's major cities. In part it was stimulated by what can be termed a kind of explosion of knowledge and inquiry in a wide variety of fields and, related to that, an opening up of the European university system to groups who previously had been discriminated against for economic and religious reasons. For example, Jews, like Freud, could now go to the university in unprecedented numbers—almost the polar opposite of what was the case in American colleges and universities. (Prejudice did not decrease, of course, but official discrimination in access to higher education did.) The rise of professionalism, the emergence of new fields of inquiry and practice, and the pressure for specialization were apparent, that is, they were harbingers of what became distinctive features of the twentieth century. They were aspects of a social change in that they signaled not only the rise and growth of what may be called a professional social-economic-intellectual class but also the widening of a gulf between that class and the rest of society. By that I mean that the rest of society became increasingly dependent on the new professions at the same time that the understanding that society and the professions had of each other was at best superficial. It was the beginning of a relatively silent social change that would later have noisy consequences. Put another way, the silent social change inhered in a changed conception of who was entitled to do what for whom.[1]

It is a feature of all new professions that they clearly set boundaries to distinguish themselves from existing professions or others that are emerging. This need for a distinctive identity has two consequences that are at odds with each other, although they are not recognized. On the one hand, the new profession makes a point of the potential it has to make a unique contribution to knowledge and practice; on the other hand, in order to substantiate its uniqueness it gives a place of honor, so to speak, to some problems over others, thus narrowing considerably its conceptual reach and range of inquiry. So, biology was biology, chemistry was chemistry. Each defined itself in very distinctive ways, and it took decades for the parochialism of each to be overcome and for the discipline of biochemistry to emerge. (The appearance in recent years of "neuroscience" as a distinctive discipline, a congeries of different disciplines, is another clear example.) This does not occur only because of new knowledge, although that is the powering force. It occurs after a struggle, an institutional power struggle, to breech the walls of parochialism. And in that struggle the seeds of a new, unrecognized parochialism are sown. This, I think, explains in part why Freud said little about work even though he regarded it as one of the two major *psychological* tasks in life. He wanted to insure that psychoanalysis would not be confused with the extant psychiatry and psychology; indeed, his dream was that psychoanalysis would supplant both. Theorizing about the role of work in life was not a route to take to achieve such a role.

My comments on Freud's assertion were not for the purpose of suggesting that if he had expanded on the assertion he would have been illuminating. Instead, my purpose was twofold. The first pur-

---

[1] If this aspect was a silent social change, its historical roots were not. The French Revolution of 1789, the Age of Enlightenment, suffused the entire social, political, and intellectual atmosphere of the nineteenth century, about which Freud was very knowledgeable.

pose was to express the opinion that he was absolutely on target in saying what he did. Not only are loving and working crucial in living but they are phenomenologically, indissolubly related, so related that any description or explanation of a person that compartmentalizes work and loving is at best a distortion and at worst a fiction. Ironically, Freud makes that perfectly clear countless times when he tells the reader that doing psychoanalytic work could be unbearably demanding and frustrating, that it contained the seeds of personal and moral corruption, and that by the criterion of positive and sustained therapeutic outcomes such work was frequently not very rewarding. Deserving of emphasis here is that toward the end of his life Freud, having his analytic colleagues in mind as well as his own experience as an analyst, recommended that for the psychological protection of the analyst and his or her patients, analysts themselves should be reanalyzed every five years, a suggestion that had all of the ballast of a lead balloon. But Freud's work (in the conventional sense) went beyond the therapeutic relationship. The more important work for him was the institutionalization and promotion of his theories and their applications to therapeutic practice and diverse areas of human activity. Countless books and articles have now been written, leaving his own accounts aside, about how the work of creating an institution and fathering a movement suffused every part of his life, including his loving. It is not what you would call a happy, uplifting story, containing as it does disappointments, rivalries, hostility, broken friendships, turmoil, and more. When Freud said what he did about working he knew what he was talking about, but he never made it a part of his conceptualizations. He compartmentalized working, even though, I have to assume, he knew better, much better.

The second purpose of my beginning with comments about Freud's assertion was to lead to a point that is as subtle as it is significant: the historical emergence and steady growth of professions and professionalism—and in the twentieth century the growth has been startling—make it extraordinarily difficult for a professional to speak openly and candidly. To put it another way: the reasons one enters a profession are transforming ones, and the training-educational-indoctrination process whereby one becomes a professional is a transforming one, in which frequently but not inevitably a marked difference develops between the professional's private view of what his or her work means for and does (or has done) to his or her life and what that person will say or acknowledge publicly. The significance of that difference inheres in several things. The first is that ours is a society in which the label "professional" is so highly honorific and so frequently used to describe people in such diverse activities as to render the label unrevealing at best and meaningless at worst. It was not always that way, and that is indicative of how important that label has become as a sign of self-respect and the respect expected from others. Electricians, plumbers, athletes, airplane pilots and flight attendants, police officers, auto mechanics, and so forth do not want to be seen only as highly skilled and valued workers but also as "professionals" possessing knowledge, experience, and responsibilities that set them apart from others. At the very least, the loose use of the label is indicative of how much the sense of personal identity is seen to depend on judgments of one's work by self and others. The increase of the loose use of the label, I would suggest, reflects the strength of the need to be seen as a worker, not a laborer, as a self-directed, autonomous person, not a drone, as a person fulfilled by his or her activity, not a person directed or controlled by others. The assumption, of course, is that those who for so long have been regarded as professionals (such as professors, scientists, physicians, clerics, lawyers—the "real" professionals, so to speak) are engaged in autonomous, fulfilling, challenging, and materially rewarding work.

I shall have more to say about this later when I discuss how the post World War II social change has called into question this elevated view of highly educated, traditional professionals, a social change that confronts them with the specter of reduced respect, autonomy, and fulfillment. But first I must direct my remarks to the

pre World War II era when the phenomenology of the professional—his or her expectations and experience of a career—was not
much or at all discordant with social, economic, institutional realities or with conventional attitudes and conceptions about why a
professional career was and should be a source of fulfillment and satisfaction over the lifetime. The professional was a fortunate person
who had chosen a career that was honorific and materially rewarding, that was relatively insulated from economic disaster, and that
served a public good; that good fortune insured a sustained stimulating, personally and intellectually, enriching life. The professional
was one of a fortunate few who, unlike most people, could count on
a good life.

These views were undergirded by two axioms. I call them axioms
because they were, so to speak, so self-evident as not to require
articulation— "that is the way things are and that is the way they
should be, period." They were axioms about how lives should be
lived. The first axiom was what I have called the one life–one career
imperative (Sarason, 1977). In countless ways beginning very early
in their lives, young people hear this message: "You can be several,
indeed many, things in life. You can be A or B or C but you cannot
be A *and* B or A *and* C, and so forth. There is a smorgasbord of types
of work and you have to decide the one line of work that will
engage you over your lifetime." It has always been the case, of
course, that socioeconomic status mightily determines the range of
possibilities the young person can consider. Even so, at some point
the young person has to choose, aware that the path chosen realistically rules out ever traversing other ones.

For many young people of modest or no means, the phenomenology of choosing a path was not what you would call a pleasant
prospect, but because the human animal is capable of dreams about
happy futures, the restriction of choices was not totally lacking in
anticipations of personal and material satisfactions, such as love,
marriage, and family. Indeed, for these young people, working and
loving tended to have immediacy and cogency, that is, the path

chosen was largely instrumental to personal happiness that would be experienced elsewhere. If they did not have great expectations from and in their work days—if they knew they were expendable and replaceable, if they did not regard themselves as among the worthies of this world—they saw themselves otherwise in the families they would create. Needless to say, if it turned out, as it frequently did, that the satisfactions from loving did not meet expectations and that the satisfactions from work were painfully few, the good life, however defined, went the way of most dreams. Working and loving were a phenomenologically and truly seamless web of experience, a web in which the person was "caught." There was no way out; that is the way the person had "chosen" in the card game of life, and the person had not chosen well. The game was to be played out with resignation. The one life–one career imperative left little or no room for second chances. In those pre World War II days, divorce laws carried a similar message about changing marriage partners. From the standpoint of society, "You made your bed, now lie in it."

For the young person able to contemplate a career in a profession, the situation was both similar and different. It was similar in that the individual had to choose one profession that would occupy him or her over the lifetime. Also, that choice was part of fantasies about lifestyle: marriage, family, the home one would be able to have, the resources that could be provided to children, material possessions, and money and time for recreational pursuits. Because the professions required an extended period of education and supervised experience, marriage frequently had to be postponed, unless of course parental wealth made that unnecessary, or one found a mate whose level of employment and income made it unnecessary. It is obvious, but often overlooked, that the experience of giving and getting love antedates the point at which a career has to be chosen. Indeed, giving and getting love is so much a part of the early years that their relationship to work is inevitable.

Where the situation was different it was because of a second axiom: a professional career would be intrinsically interesting and challenging, it would gave you status and respect, and you would possess a degree of autonomy permitting you to expand the scope of your knowledge, competence, and responsibility. A professional had something to "profess," which others who sought his or her services would acknowledge and respect because what was "professed" was based on years of education, special knowledge, and experience. A professional was the quintessential worker whose work had his or her distinctive imprimatur. Compared to others, especially laborers, the professional had it made.

My comments about the pre World War II era have to be seen in the context of a cultural characteristic that was, so to speak, built into the American ethos from its earliest days, when the newly discovered continent was described as the second Garden of Eden. I refer to great expectations, seemingly so based in reality and so persuasive and explicit that they brought scores of millions of immigrants to our shores. They did not come here for adventure. They came to forge a life for themselves and their children, unlike their life in the "old world," where they were poor, uneducated, oppressed ciphers whose future predictably contained taxes, disappointments, tragedy, and an early death. The message of great expectations was for them a siren call with unheralded meaning and force. If they came "to be free," it was to be free "to make something of one's self" and to experience something of the pleasures of getting and giving love in the context of family. No one needed to tell them that loving and working were interrelated. And they did not need to be told that it was their obligation to help their children do better than they had. The idea that each generation *should* do better than the previous one took hold in this country as in no other. But if their dreams too frequently foundered on social and economic realities, great expectations were far from extinguished.

The point I have been stressing has long been obvious. Within the past hundred years, slowly but with ever-increasing frequency and strength, workers have resented and resisted the conception that they were *only* workers, that is, that their worth inhered only in what they did and produced, and that everything else they might need, want, and hope for from their work were irrelevant personal weaknesses or indulgences, if not flagrant examples of declining moral fiber—or sheer hubris. A shorter-than-twelve-hour day? Rest periods from monotonous, repetitive, bodily debilitating tasks? The right to discuss a variety of issues (pay, pension, vacation, grievances) with supervisors or employers? To ask, if not require, the boss to be more polite, understanding, and sensitive? The right to feel secure through a union of peers? To the modern ear these questions may sound comically antique, but they make clear that what was at issue were two very different conceptions of how work was or should be experienced. It would be an oversimplification to say that these different conceptions were merely a consequence of conflicting economic interests, because that does not explain why in earlier times the different views were not all that different. Nor does it explain why once the divergence appeared, it took so long for it to spread throughout society. To explain the divergence in exclusively economic terms is no less a caricature of reality than it is to say that work, and its concomitant mental operations, is what people do.

What the worker was saying to the employer was: I am more than you think I am. There is a lot more going on in my head and heart while I am doing my work for you. I have feelings, hopes, expectations, and needs. I am not you, I cannot be you, but I am not and do not want to remain what you think I am. I am far more than the doer you see. Although you and I may agree that I am a good worker in your terms, you cannot understand why I am not a satisfied worker. And when I tell you I am dissatisfied, you tell me either that I *should* not feel that way, or that what I experience cannot be your concern. Should not feel that way? It is like commanding the ocean waves to stop. And if what I experience in my work cannot be your concern, are you at least saying, perhaps, that you concede that I experience far more in my work than you ordinarily recognize?

The more benevolent employer might have replied: You have

been a good worker and I have paid you for your work. But you have changed. You no longer are satisfied with doing your job well, with taking pride in the quantity and quality of your output. You have new expectations, new wants you not only wish me to recognize but also to pay for. Of course, I am bothered by the fact that what you want will cost me more money, but that truly bothers me less than the fact that you do not see the radical implications of your thinking. Once I concede, even in the slightest, that you have a right to experience more from your work than you do now, where will it end? It would not be long before you would be telling *me* how *I* should experience my work.

What the worker was saying, and the employer correctly perceiving, was that the relationship between expectations and the traditional conception of work was being called into question. They were not new expectations in the sense that they had never been part of a worker's experience; they were simply now being articulated and pursued. The conflict was out in the open, and it is one that is far from over. Strangely, the semantics of the issue have not changed much. Work is still what a person does, as distinguished from working *conditions*. Although this distinction can be rationalized in terms of economic factors and collective bargaining negotiations, from a psychological standpoint it is another distorted fractionation of the work experience. As long as one stays within the economic framework in which profits, pay, and efficiency are major issues and goals, one is a hopeless prisoner of a perspective that automatically rules out the following questions: What is the meaning of work? How is it experienced? Within such a framework, these questions are irrelevant.

When one considers how the work scene has changed in a century, how work and its conditions have changed and presumably "improved," why is it that so many people are unhappy about their work experience? No one would want to go back to the "good old days," yet many people today talk as if those days are not over. Our benevolent employer of a century ago would, if he could, say: "I told you so. Once you start giving in to what people want and expect, there is no end to it. Today they expect this, tomorrow that, and the pit of expectations is bottomless." Our prophet is right, for the wrong reasons. He is right in suggesting that if you look at work in other than a narrowly technical way and begin to consider seriously how much of an individual's experience is wrapped up in work, and how that experience is indissolubly a part of other "nonwork" experiences, the nature of work will undergo pervasive change. He is wrong in seeing the issue only in terms of individuals, as if they do not exist in a society that has characteristics and dynamics of its own. Expectations exist in individuals, but rarely if ever do they fail to reflect what has happened in the larger society. If our benevolent employer had acceded even in part to what the workers wanted, he probably would have had no more difficulty with them, given the combination of the times and the demand. Having satisfied his workers, however, it did not follow that societal changes affecting those workers were thereby stopped and altered. Precisely because these were societal changes—the perceptible outcroppings of invisible system characteristics and dynamics resting on values and cultural history—one could have predicted that the expectations of the next generation would be different. So, when our benevolent employer sees human nature as inherently greedy, requiring the most strenuous internal and external control lest its self-feeding and self-destructive dynamics be stimulated and reinforced—a view permitting him to say "I told you so"—he is quite wrong. But his view of certain aspects of his society is fairly correct, that is, it has long been a generator of new and more expectations.

It is hard to overestimate what a catastrophe the Great Depression was to most people. It caused personal turmoil, disappointment, and disillusionment from which many in the older segments of our society still carry scars. One must bear in mind that, from the beginning of the Depression in 1929 until a year or so after Roosevelt's inauguration in 1933, being out of work or hungry was an individual catastrophe and not a governmental object for action. And even when the federal government assumed responsibility, the programs were of the Band-Aid variety, leaving millions of citizens, young as well as old, dependent, anxious, and bewildered. And yet, throughout this period of social upheaval, the bulk of the people held to the belief that the situation would change for the better. They still nurtured hope and great expectations that in the not-too-distant future the land of opportunity would again be fertile.

As I have emphasized in earlier essays, World War II changed everything and everyone. For the purposes of this essay, several features of the war years are crucial. The first is that the armed forces faced a staggering manpower shortage, not only in terms of sheer numbers but in the types of occupations they needed. It is fair to say that the military became an educational institution by devising its own training programs and subsidizing college and university programs for physicians, rehabilitation specialists, nurses, engineers, linguists, personnel specialists, scientists of all sorts, and a lot more. As never before in their lives, many recruits became aware of the spectrum of work possibilities and, no less important, had a degree of choice among such possibilities—a spectrum, choice, and opportunity they had not previously envisaged. Also, the manpower shortage was so great in some fields that people were placed in work barely (or not at all) related to their previous experience; for some that was a disappointment, for others it was an intriguing, productive eye-opener in regard to career.[2] The point is that people's

---

[2] I am not aware of systematic studies of how war experience redirected people's careers or pointed them toward lines of work they had never considered, or altered in degree and substance their expectations for life generally and work specifically. Bear in mind that during the war years approximately 10 percent of the population spent time in the armed services. I was a civilian during the war years, and for at least two decades after the war I worked with or taught veterans. If my experience (clinical, pedagogical, and collegial) is only partly typical, the war forever impacted on veterans' conceptions of, attitudes toward, and expectations from work. The war initiated a transformation process in individuals, which means it set the stage for a social transformation. Not incidentally, with a large fraction of the population entering the military, many civilians experienced a similar transforming process, especially women.

conceptions of and attitudes toward the role and status of work in their postwar lives (assuming they survived!) underwent change, and for many that meant a future desirably different from what they had been doing in their prewar civilian life. Expectations not only changed, they became stronger and more salient to conclusions about life's meaning.

Wars are societal catastrophes, but ironically and dialectically they have historically spawned changes that posterity values highly. That is certainly the case in regard to scientific and technological advances. One could similarly argue that World War II opened up new vistas of work opportunity that allowed people to discover and exploit interests and talents to which they heretofore had been denied access by tradition and socioeconomic realities. I say that only in regard to the United States, and for three reasons: it was victorious; in the immediate postwar period it had the resources for and it legislated programs supportive of those new vistas; and all of this was consistent with the American theme of great expectations. I am not saying, of course, that in the case of World War II there were no negative social consequences or that the playing out of scientific-technologic advances was uniformly societally benign. I am saying that the war had both intended and unintended consequences because of the times, the scope, the ideology, and the country. It was not a goal of the war to alter the status of blacks, but it started the process. It was not a goal of the war to alter the status of women, but it did. It was not a goal of the war to cause a baby boom, a population explosion that contributed mightily to social and institutional change, but it did. And it was not a goal of the war to change the map and substance of the arena of work, but it did.

Another crucial aspect of the war years had to do with loving. Before World War II it used to be said and believed—it was more than rhetoric—that when one got married, it was forever—and if not forever, it *should* have been! Religion supported such a view, and civil laws made the obtaining of a divorce a career in itself. But at the same time, there were divorces, extramarital affairs, desertions, and other indications that there was a discrepancy between what people said and what they did, and between what they did and what they would like to have done. If one went by marriage and divorce statistics, let alone the pronouncements of civic and religious leaders, one might have concluded that the traditional institution of marriage had a solid foundation capable of resisting change. However, if one went beyond the conventional statistics and took seriously how people experienced marriage, how they sought, successfully and unsuccessfully, both to maintain and circumvent its spirit and form, one might have felt less secure in viewing the marriage of the future as a carbon copy of the present.[3] This is not to say that one could have predicted when and under what specific circumstances the institution of marriage would change discernibly, as it has. But one could have taken more seriously and validly the indications that in regard to marriage there was a discrepancy between appearance and reality, and one could have grappled with the kinds of societal events and changes that could have unleashed existing antimarriage forces, such as a world war. At the very least, one would have avoided writing scenarios of the future that looked too much like the present.

The problem with statistical projections is that they are based on two types of data: those from the near or far past, which are *now* seen as significant for the shape of the present and presumed to be significant for the future; and current data, usually of an aggregate

---

[3]If you go back to the novels, plays, films, and radio soap operas of the thirties, it becomes obvious how wide the discrepancy was between the public rhetoric about marriage and its realities. The discrepancy had existed for a long time, but with the growth of the mass media, particularly radio and film, the discrepancy became glaring. When the "dream" marriage between movie stars Mary Pickford and Douglas Fairbanks came to an end, it was front-page news, testifying to how much people wanted to believe in the irrevocable ties of marriage, while at the same time they knew how fragile the ties of marriage had become. Hollywood as a cultural phenomenon and product-producing center contained, in people's minds, all of the ingredients of the war between virtue and sin, that is, Hollywood was one big soap opera. From the vantage point of several decades, one could describe the current scene as another example of reality imitating "art."

or global nature, which are presumed to be better indicators of what the future will be. These types of projections (such as demographic or ecological) can be valuable, but more often than not they founder because their assessment of the present either assumes a relatively stable set of forces and events or there is a misweighing or ignorance of emerging and inchoate changes in values and outlooks that do not have the characteristics of social forces and movements but that (together with societal events the timing, strength, and scope of which we can only poorly predict) nevertheless will give shape to the future. It is these events that surface and articulate what previously had seemed atypical outcroppings of antitraditional values and behavior, that is, a view of the self and the world at variance with what is customary.

The war years—and let us remember that it was a long war—occasioned numerous dynamics: hasty or premature marriages; promises of marriage when loved ones returned after the war ended and faithfulness in the interim; women at home who were lonely and frustrated by the lack of heterosexual satisfaction and intimacy; women for whom the war created new work opportunities, taking them out of the home into settings where "normal" sexual attractions and temptations were plentiful; women who sensed (rightly or wrongly) that their men in the war had changed in ways that negatively altered, or that would or might alter, their marriage or promises of faithfulness and marriage; women who were unable or unwilling to forego sexual relationships "for the duration" although they still felt committed to lovers and husbands in the war; and women, and the public generally, who were aware that in the culture of the military, outlets for sexual expression were limited but not frowned upon, that army camps in this or foreign lands contained women who would be attracted and available to soldiers. It was in World War II that women entered the armed services, a break with tradition. The implications of this were not lost on women at home, and the effects on the incidence of sexual affairs in the military were not insignificant.

What I have said about women could be said about men both in and out of the military. Men not in the military, single or not, were quite aware that there were many lonely, presumably sexually frustrated women who were "easy catches," so to speak, whether they were single or not. If the women were married to someone in the armed services, or promised to one, it eliminated some of the obvious complications of sexual affairs. This was also true, of course, in the case of single women. As for the men in the military, it is an old story. Sexual satisfaction, frustration, outlets, prowess, and gossip are more than topics of conversation, and obsessively so. Thoughts of death and injury—or thoughts about the frustration of a prolonged sexual abstinence and loss of a sense of intimacy—are not conducive to delay of gratification, especially if one is located on a base or in a camp where outlets are available and the pangs of guilt are not subject to exposure to a loved one at home. You can indulge with impunity, so to speak, putting aside any pangs of guilt. But it is also the case that many soldiers read letters from home to discern whether a loved one's constancy and faithfulness contradicted the bromide that absence makes the heart grow fonder. It is also the case that not a few soldiers experienced their sexual encounters with a degree of abandon and satisfaction they had not previously enjoyed. I was not in the armed services but if the confessions (they had that quality) of veterans I saw in my clinical work are only half valid, their sexual encounters and affairs had features of "peak experiences" that could not be matched by their prewar and postwar experiences. This was especially true for their relationships with women in foreign lands, women whose countries were threatened or being defeated, whose economic subsistence was precarious, substandard or worse, whose lives and families had been catastrophically disrupted. As one returning veteran put it, "I felt like a lord whose woman would do *anything* [emphasis his] to satisfy any of my needs or whims. They were not like American women."

About none of the above do we have "data," the kinds of numbers that would allow us to say that the war changed sexual attitudes or practices or reinforced and made more manifest the discrepancy between the rhetoric and reality of the prewar years. But if we do not have "hard data," we do have an abundance of novels, plays, and films illustrating the points I have made. (These are points the ancient Greek playwrights and storytellers depicted so well.) Given our cultural history, what has long been known about the force of sexual drives, how prolonged wars disrupt and alter the frequency and contexts in which those drives can be expressed, and other considerations, it is not unreasonable to say that the World War II years saw an increase in the fragility and problems of culturally sanctioned sexual relationships. What would occasion surprise would be if it were otherwise.

The first two decades after the war exposed what on the surface appeared to be two separate phenomena but were not. The first was the beginning of a steady rise in the number of divorces, many of which involved marriages entered before and during the war. What had begun to be challenged, as reflected in less-constraining divorce laws, was the one life–one marriage axiom. There was no one reason powering the challenge, just as there is no one reason that explains why partners seek to go their own ways. Divorce proceedings do not contain anything about the one life–one marriage axiom. Their substance is about incompatibilities, agreements broken, disappointments. But what had begun to enter the psychological picture, especially for veterans (but not for them alone), can be put this way: "Life is short. The war took years out of my life. I can never make them up. I have changed, my partner has changed, the world has changed. I know what delayed gratification means. I know it in spades. I want my share of happiness and I will not get it from my partner. Why should I stay in a marriage that will not give me what I have a right to expect? Life is too short." The message may never have been articulated precisely in the way I have put it but it conveys a sense or a theme, an emerging attitude, that became clear as the postwar years rolled on. That attitude was supported (or interpreted as supported) by the rising acceptance and influence of a psychoanalytic psychology that emphasized the overcoming of inhibitions and frustrations, the importance of recognizing and giving expression to one's deeply felt needs and life goals, and the potential-destroying, misery-producing consequences of undue shame and guilt. It was not happenstance that in the two decades after the war, psychoanalysis and its implicit ideology about living became more than an arena of theory and therapy; it also took on some of the features of a movement. It contained messages that a significant fraction of society—a society that looked to a new future with great expectations both in world affairs and for the lives of its individual members—wanted to hear. No one desired or expected that the country would revert to what it had been; the meaning of convention and tradition was subtly changing. It took the sixties for this aspect of the emerging social change to come to full bloom.

In regard to work, the story is basically similar to that of loving, that is, the one life–one career imperative was mightily challenged. Several things have to be kept in mind.

1.   During the war years, many people, especially the millions who had been in service, found themselves in work that was different from what they previously had been doing. For some that was a source of frustration, but for many others it broadened their knowledge of the variety of work and careers they found interesting and attractive. That was the case, for example, for many physicians who were given responsibilities for which they were little prepared by previous experience. Generally speaking, that was true for all professionals, who were required to adapt to the needs of the military.

2.   War is the one time when a society dramatically alters or lowers educational-training-experiential criteria for choosing who will do what kind of work. The country was unprepared for World War II. It was obvious that the war would be long; for two years the possibility of victory was low. The need for manpower of all types was staggering; it was no time to adhere to customary criteria of who was entitled to do what kind of work. During the war years, people

found themselves in lines of work that inevitably changed in some way what they would do (or not do) when the war ended—more correctly, what they would *like* to do or not do when the war was over. What was true for highly educated professionals was no less true for nonprofessionals, many of whom over the course of the war enjoyed (I use that word advisedly) an elevated work status, responsibility, and rank far above those they had held (or even dreamed of) before the war; understandably, they were not set to see their future as a replica of their prewar past.

3.   If anything became unavoidably clear to those in the armed services, it was the practical, life-determining consequences of the correlation between education and the "goodies" of life. That in large part explains why millions of veterans eagerly took advantage of the GI Bill of Rights. They wanted to be more than their prewar past had led them to expect they could be. The GI Bill conveyed a message: "Because of our gratitude for your service to your country, we give you an opportunity to become what you think you are able to become, regardless of what you have previously been or done."[4]

Just as in the case of loving we have no hard data to substantiate the conclusion that the war years set the stage for the challenge to the one woman (or man)–one life imperative, there are no data for the conclusion that the war years contained the challenge to the one life–one career imperative. Having lived through those years, having talked with countless others who did, and having worked as a teacher and a clinician with hundreds (perhaps thousands) of veterans—and being a reader of novels and a viewer of plays and films—I have been driven to the conclusion that, among other important consequences, World War II exposed how interrelated

---

[4]I have long felt and said that nothing is more revealing of blind spots in the social sciences than their failure to study the role of the GI Bill from several standpoints: how it impacted and unintendedly supported emerging challenges to the one career–one mate imperative, how it coalesced those challenges to a heightened degree, and how it later led to the general post World War II social change. It was a glimpse of the obvious that World War II changed everything and everyone, that the barometers of social change were and could not be static.

psychologically the arenas of loving and working were. More than that, the challenge inhered in the emerging attitude that life was too short to be spent in activities and relationships that were constraining, boring, or unfulfilling. Again, what I am saying is encapsulated in the previously mentioned slogan of my late travel agent, "See the world before you leave it." Applied to loving and working, the slogan would be, "You can be more than one thing in life, and you do not want, nor should you be expected, to be one thing and one thing only. You do not want, nor should you be expected, to live a life of intimacy with only one other person whom you once loved but who now does not satisfy your changed needs. You know you will grow old but that does not mean you must not seek new experience that will be rejuvenating, that will allow you to feel the excitement and enthusiasm of youth, so that your tomorrows will be more interesting than today." That is not a slogan but an attempt on my part to articulate attitudes to two spheres of life, attitudes that were sensed or felt, thoughts and feelings rarely put publicly into words, and this in a context of public acceptance of the stance of great expectations: the old world is dead, should be interred, and we should look forward to a new world. I have called the two decades after the war the "age of psychology" or the "age of mental health." Call it what you will, it was an age of heightened self-scrutiny, a recasting of perspectives toward past and future that inevitably involved loving and working.

In the remaining pages of this essay I shall focus on one profession (medical physicians) that allows me to illustrate and bring together some of the issues I have raised. What I shall say is based on experiences and studies conducted in the early 1970s and discussed in my book *Work, Aging, and Social Change*, published in 1977. For what are purely tactical reasons, what I will initially present reflects the conclusions I came to twenty years ago. As I trust will become clear in my later remarks, those conclusions have been dramatically confirmed by what has happened since. And what has happened in the medical community is representative of what has

happened in many of the older professions as well as in the many
newer ones spawned by World War II. It is a story of great expectations, appearance versus reality, and how institutional and social
change has affected those in the professional groups that grew in
size in the post World War II era. So, permit me now to put the
problem the way I saw it in the early seventies; since then, the scene
for physicians has become explicable as physicians have had to overcome strong internal resistance in order to make public how social
and institutional change has forever changed their expectations.

Over the years there have been scores of studies demonstrating
a substantial positive correlation between level of education and
work satisfaction. Among those groups with the highest levels of
education and professional training there is some variation as to
which report the most satisfaction; doctors, lawyers, and college professors, for example, usually report high levels of satisfaction. In
almost all of these studies, the data were obtained by asking one or
more questions (via questionnaires, telephone public opinion
polling, and occasionally informal discussions and interviews).
These types of studies can be faulted on several grounds, but their
agreement on the correlation between education and reported work
satisfaction forces one to accept the fact that when these types of
methods are employed, the responses will have a predictable order
with a surface plausibility. The question I raise is not whether the
correlation is meaningful or reliable, but whether the methods by
which it is obtained are appropriate to the possibility that the experience of work has become more problematic for highly educated
people.

For example, if we were to employ the usual methodologies with
one hundred physicians and an equal number of garbage collectors,
is there anyone who would not predict that physicians would report
a higher level of work satisfaction than garbage collectors? And if
the members of each group were asked if they would rather be members of the other group, the outcome would not be in doubt. But
what if we asked the same questions of different kinds of physicians,

such as pediatricians, internists, or ophthalmologists? We would not
expect the different groups to report the same high level of satisfaction, although the largest difference between any two groups
would not even approximate the size of the difference between
garbage collectors and physicians. If we were then to ask each member of the different medical groups whether they would rather be a
member of another group, what might we expect? Would similar
numbers of general practitioners and neurologists, for example, opt
for internal medicine? Would similar numbers of orthopedic sur-
geons and pediatricians choose psychiatry? I am not aware of studies that have focused on these questions among physicians, but I
have spent years in and around medical centers and unless my experience is grossly atypical, physician groups would differ markedly in
the degree to which they would remain in their present groups. This
conclusion does not stem from my asking physicians about the level
of their satisfaction or their desire to shift to another specialty. If as
an outsider I had asked them these questions, I have no doubt they
would have reported the usual high level of satisfaction, and few
would have said they would prefer another kind of medical work.
Let me give three examples of some of the conditions in which
physicians voiced views of themselves in relation to their work and
career that ordinarily are not articulated by them in response to
direct questions by "investigators."

   1.   I had just been examined by a locally well-known and
highly-respected surgeon to whom I went whenever I wrenched my
vulnerable knee. He conducted his examination and prescribed a
course of treatment. I started to leave his office and in a perfuncto-
rily courteous manner I asked, "How has life been?" To my surprise
he did not respond "routinely" but sighed and said: "I do not know
why I allow myself to be so busy." His tone of voice suggested that
he wanted to talk, so we did, in the course of which I told him about
my current interests in the increasing frequency with which people
seem to be changing careers. He then said to me: "Surgery *is* interesting. For a period of years it did fascinate me. I *am* a good surgeon.

In fact, I'm a damn good one. So I'm good, so what? What I really want to do is to get into the history of medicine." He went on to relate how so many of his days were filled with uninteresting problems (like my knee), and only occasionally was he faced with a challenge that made his day.

2.   In the course of a social evening there was discussion of the mixed consequences of technical and scientific advances, the so-called knowledge explosion. Three of the five people in the group were physicians, and they were the most articulate in describing the depth of their feelings about knowing less and less about more and more, or as one of them put it, "that mixed feeling of anger and futility that you will never escape from your ever-deepening despair that you are a scholarly fraud. The more my patients treat me as a god, the more hypocritical I feel." Given the opening, I indulged my own interests by saying "You guys don't sound terribly fulfilled in your work." There was an embarrassing silence of several seconds during which I felt remorse at having asked the question. The silence was broken by all three physicians talking at once. Paraphrased, they said: "How can you say that? I get a lot of satisfaction in treating and helping people, although I do not pretend that I help as much as I would like, nor would I say that my work is always interesting either personally or intellectually." To which I replied: "I in no way meant that you did not get satisfaction in your work. It seemed to me that what you were saying was that you no longer felt the excitement of growth and learning, and this was getting you down as you realized that that is the way it was always going to be." Their response was: "But isn't this true in every or most professions? Maybe it is worse in the practice of medicine because the demands for our service make it extremely difficult to give high priority to *our* needs." The possibility that the situation may be similar or worse elsewhere (the grass was browner elsewhere) allowed these physicians to admit, albeit indirectly, that there was an aspect to their work that was deeply troublesome to them. The significance of the conversation lies not only in the degree of poignancy these physi-

cians (all in their mid forties) experienced about a source of dissatisfaction, but also in the suggestion that responses to questions
about work or career satisfaction almost always reflect a relative
judgment, which is rarely articulated.

3.   In any fair-sized community, particularly one in which there
is a medical school, there are a few internists to whom other physicians gravitate as patients, that is, a doctor's doctor. I knew who
some of these physicians were in New Haven, and through the good
offices of my own physician I was able to interview one such doctor, the understanding being, of course, that nothing personal or
identifying would be discussed. I explained to this physician that I
was interested in pursuing some "intuitions" reflected in two questions: What are the rarely articulated work and career problems of
physicians? To what extent are they serious problems? Approximately forty percent of his practice were physicians from all specialties, the modal age being between forty-five and fifty-five years.
(In a large number of instances, wives were also patients of this doctor.) I began the interview with this question: is there any dominant impression you have about these physicians? His answer was:
"In the last five years, 90 percent of what I deal with is depression."
He was not using the term depression in any technical sense, but
rather to convey a very noticeable and articulated sense of unhappiness or frustration, a puzzlement that life was not working out as
they had expected. "In some instances their children are causing
them all kinds of worry, and it really affects the satisfactions they
get from their work. Or there are marital problems which they feel
are destroying them. It is as if they find themselves asking: Is it all
worthwhile? Was it all worthwhile? Where this fits in with what I
think you are after is that it exacerbates their feeling that medicine
is like being on a treadmill, but you can't stop it, and you don't
know who is at the controls. Some doctors don't mind the treadmill because they are being paid rather well to perform on it. But
they are a minority for whom being a physician was probably always a means to other ends, such as a nice house, big cars, frequent

vacations, and a lot of status. I call them the businessmen. But the majority wanted to be healers, not only to understand how the body works, but to contribute to that understanding in some way. In my own case, medicine was a 'calling' in which you took on the obligation to learn, to do your best regardless of what it took out of you, to put the interests of patients at the top of the priority list. But that is maladaptive today because of scads of patients, more and more specialization, and most important of all, the economics of becoming a doctor and becoming a prisoner of a high standard of living. Medicine has become a business and business has become the tail that wags the dog."

I told him that although I understood what he was saying, I somehow felt that something was missing, that is, that there was a disproportion between the degree of frustration he was describing and the factors he was listing to explain it. He replied: "Let me put it to you this way. The public sees us as masters of our fate and captains of our soul, in addition to being their lifesavers. The fact is that we are not only not lifesavers, but we know that we cannot practice medicine by the highest standards. Inside us we judge ourselves much more negatively than the public does. We know, like no one else knows, what a jungle the practice of medicine has become. And we know one other thing: as individuals we have surprisingly little control over how we practice medicine. We are being hemmed in and challenged on all sides, and it will be worse in the future. What the public doesn't understand is that in the current downgrading of physicians they have touched an open nerve, but how can we say that out loud?"

Towards the end of the interview, I asked: "You have said in a number of ways that these midcareer physicians are quite aware of their dissatisfaction, and they cannot talk about it openly. That's a rough feeling to deal with, especially if you see yourself as having that feeling for the rest of your life. How do they cope with it?" His reply: "Psychoanalysis, alcohol, women, and sometimes drugs."

These anecdotes, which can be multiplied, run the risk of conveying a distorted impression in which the "inside story" is really the exact opposite of that conveyed in public rhetoric. For all I know, that may not be far off the mark, but I think that such a sweeping conclusion too easily discounts the strength of the satisfactions, intrinsic and extrinsic, that physicians report. I have presented these anecdotes primarily to indicate that work or career satisfaction is no easy matter for professionals to talk about candidly, *especially if the profession is seen by others as an endlessly fascinating and rewarding line of endeavor.* To proclaim one's dissatisfactions or doubts is tantamount to questioning the significance of one's life and future, to appear to others as "deviant," and to raise questions in their minds about one's personal stability. How can you say that you are frequently bored in or that you frequently feel inadequate about or unchallenged by your work when the rest of the world sees you as meeting and overcoming one challenge after another, as a fount of ever-increasing knowledge and wisdom, as a person obviously entranced with his or her career? It is not made easier when to proclaim such feelings to one's colleagues is perceived as sensible as Macy's telling Gimbels its problems.

Now let us listen to a surgeon who has become a well-known essayist and short story writer. In a short piece in *Harpers*, Richard Selzer (1975, p. 30) asks: why should a surgeon write?

> All through literature the doctor is portrayed as a figure of fun. Shaw was splenetic about him; Molière delighted in pricking his pompous medicine men, and well they deserved it. The doctor is ripe for caricature. But I believe that the truly great writing about doctors has not yet been done. I think it must be done by a doctor, one who is through with the love affair with his technique, who recognizes that he has played Narcissus, raining kisses on a mirror, and who now, out of the impacted masses of his guilt, has expanded into self-doubt and finally into the high state of wonderment. Perhaps he

will be a nonbeliever who, after a lifetime of grand ges-
tures and mighty deeds, comes upon the knowledge that
he has done no more than meddle in the lives of his fellows, and that he has done at least as much harm as
good. Yet he may continue to pretend, at least, that there
is nothing to fear, that death will not come, so long as
people ask it of him. Later, after his patients have left,
he may closet himself in his darkened office, sweating
and afraid.

This is unvarnished candor, the substance of which few physicians allow themselves to voice in public. It is not the voice of a
physician derogating all that he and his peers have done or denying the validity or sincerity of those occasions in which he has had
an experience, that is, the sense that all that he is has in some way
made commerce with the world outside of him. But these experiences are not always positive; they may be those soul-riddling experiences of failure or despair that bring one down to size and that are
reminders of one's puniness and mortality.

No, it is not the surgeon who is God's darling. He is the
victim of vanity. It is the poet who heals with his words,
stanches the flow of blood, stills the rattling breath,
applies poultice to the scalded flesh.
     Did you ask me why a surgeon writes? I think it is
because I wish to be a doctor [p. 34].

This is a revealing ending to Selzer's essay, because it underlines
the unrecognized strength of the need to feel that one is making a
(healing) difference, a *permanent* difference, unimpeded or conta-
minated by people and society's unseemly qualities. It is an ending
that seems to be denying that there are or should be endings. One
should and need not find oneself closeted "in his darkened office,
sweating and afraid." There is "work" that is more creative, more

transcendental, with more staying power than surgery, and that is the work of the poet. The grass is indeed greener elsewhere! Poets will applaud Selzer, but if they were as candid as he, we might find them saying much the same things about their stock-in-trade, except, of course, some of them would draw from a deep well of bitterness filled with the ingredients of lack of income and recognition, as well as the resistance and inadequacy of language to the poet's need to translate ideas and imagery into an external form— or, more frequently, the searing knowledge of the poet's inability to bend language to his purposes. It is one thing to say that every line of work has its obstacles, frustrations, and drawbacks (just as it is probably true that every line of work has some occasional satisfactions). It is quite another thing, however, when the frustration is festering and continuous and centers around one's sense of personal purpose and change, that sense that alone allows one to meet the future and not to avoid it. When Selzer asserts that the surgeon is not "God's darling, he is the victim of vanity," he is failing to recognize how the desire to be God's darling has been built into our society, particularly among those of us, the most highly educated, who have been encouraged to discover God's ways and works, so to speak, and thereby gain something of God's immortality. And so, when we find out that we are not God's darlings, it is a narcissistic wound we are loathe to talk about—unless like Selzer we think we have found a new and better poultice to cure the wound!

Every physician I have described or alluded to thus far was in midlife. This was not fortuitous selection on my part. Work or career satisfaction varies as a consequence of a number of factors and time is certainly a major one, not because of time per se, obviously, but because we use the passage of time as a criterion by which to judge the success of our plans and the fulfillment of our hopes. When a person enters a professional field, his endless future has markers denoting in an approximate way what he would like to or feels he should accomplish at those points. That road to the future also has markers that we distinguish from the professional ones by calling them personal or social or familial: marriage, children and their schooling and careers, and so forth. This distinction may fit the needs of theoreticians and specialists, who understandably are loathe to deal with messy totalities, but we should not take the distinction too seriously. As more than one of my informants indicated (especially the doctors' doctor), the personal and professional are constantly interacting in terms of satisfaction, that is, the experience of each inevitably contains and affects the other. For example, how do we explain a physician (or anybody else) whose satisfaction in his work evaporates following the death of one of his children? Or a physician who says his world is falling apart following the arrest of his child for possession of hard drugs? Or the one who cannot concentrate on his practice because his child has just informed the family she does not wish to go to college? And what about the physician who is seen as sacrificing his work as he gives increasing attention to the practice of love? These are not isolated instances nor, obviously, are they peculiar to one group of people. We work for a number of purposes, but not all of them are contained in the structure of work (narrowly defined), and the outcomes of our plans and hopes in our work and personal lives are not insulated from each other. If we are ordinarily not aware of their interrelationships, it is not because they are nonexistent but because of good fortune or stupidity. There is no doubt that different levels of satisfaction in different areas of experience can compensate for each other or multiplicatively and adversely exacerbate each other.

What I learned about these midcareer physicians, and it is by no means peculiar to them, is that midlife is a confrontation between myth and reality. It is more like a war in which many battles or skirmishes are being fought. Death starts to take away parents, colleagues, friends, and loved ones. Marriage may become an imprisonment. Children may not "turn out well," or they will leave for distant places, leaving emotional vacuums. And of course one begins to reevaluate whether one wants the future of one's career to be a continuation of its past, and in that battle is the question: what are my alternatives? *I mention this here in order to emphasize that for the professional person, midlife, like the beginning of adolescence, is experienced as an eruption of internal stirrings that had best not be articulated.* To say them out loud, to communicate them candidly to others is not made easy for us in our culture. Indeed, we are made to feel gauche or strange if we admit publicly to the strength of these stirrings and their anxious and painful contents. They are viewed and experienced as private problems. So private that they can only be voiced to one's physician or psychotherapist?

But one could ask, is what you are saying about midlife any less true for the lesser-educated segments of society? Are their problems in social living, working, and aging qualitatively different? I assume they are, if only because this group is more economically vulnerable in the marketplace and less protected, again economically, against the ravage of illness and aging. Like everybody else, however, they cannot escape questions about the meaning of their lives, the fate of their hopes, and their worth as they and others judge it. But I am assuming that there is one important difference: in contrast to the lesser educated, the highly educated professional now in midlife came to his career with greater expectations that he was embarking on a quest in which all of his capacities and curiosities would be exploited, the vibrant sense of challenge, growth, and achievement sustained, and his sense of personal worth and importance strengthened; the material rewards he would obtain would be as icing on a delicious cake. He may have harbored some doubts about the size of the cake and the healthfulness of the icing, or about the amplitude of his abilities or talent for and luck in a competitive society, but these doubts were stilled by what he wished to believe and by what he was encouraged by his education to believe. To start the race with these expectations makes one especially vulnerable to whatever suggests that they may have been unrealistic, and so when in midlife these suggestions become varyingly insistent, the resultant dissatisfaction is not easy to take. It is not easy to think about and it is less easy to talk about. Selzer can allude to it because, I presume, his second and concurrent career holds out for him all the great expectations he once had about surgery. But how many who are in midlife can substitute one set of great expectations for another?

Often with controlled anger mixed with resignation, all of the midlife physicians with whom I have talked have echoed these dysphoric themes. When they entered medicine after World War II, they pictured a future of autonomy, healing, and satisfaction, whether in the medical center or the private office. In a chart of occupations, shaped like a pyramid, they were at the apex. They put themselves there, and they saw society as gladly having them. But today they see themselves dethroned as armies of new professionals have taken over and subordinate fields like nursing have asserted their independence of traditional authority. And the paperwork, the ever-increasing and changing governmental regulations, and the imperialism of medical schools and the large medical centers— the physician currently in midlife never anticipated challenges from these sources. He never dreamed that he would someday be confronting the organizational craziness and stifling bureaucratism of bigness.

There is one other insult interacting with these other injuries: physicians sense a real decline in society's attribution of godlike qualities to them. We are all familiar with the increase in medical malpractice suits and the refusal of some physicians to practice until the costs of malpractice insurance are scaled down. The bitterness of the midlife physician toward these developments is very deep. The large majority inveigh against avaricious and ambitious lawyers who prod clients to sue unjustifiably; a much smaller number criticize physicians who will testify for such clients; and less than a handful state that it was about time that people woke up to the facts of how poor medical practice could be and how frequent mistakes were in hospital care. What is indisputable is their feeling that they have been tarnished, and they are helpless to correct the situation. Helpless! That was the last word in the language they would have thought of using to describe their futures as they entered medicine.

During the 1975 strike of medical interns and residents in some of the New York City hospitals, I interviewed two physicians from that city, both in their fifties and both in private practice with medical school affiliations and responsibilities. One physician said: "Mark my word. That is the most important strike which has ever taken place *anywhere, any time*. In one respect I have no sympathy for them because they are not dedicated to medicine. They don't work as hard as we did, not because they are lazy but because they don't see the point of breaking their necks, as we did, to learn as much as you can as fast as you can. I always had the feeling I wasn't learning enough, that they weren't teaching me all they could. My God, on my day off I would go to the hospital if I heard that an interesting case was going to be discussed. I worked like a dog, and they worked me like one, and don't think I didn't resent it sometimes. But underneath it all I was eating it up. For twenty-five dollars a month plus food and cigarettes! Today they get anywhere from ten to fifteen or more thousand per year and they are squawking. They want to be physicians and still have a good time, and that's impossible if you are really dedicated. But in another respect I sympathize with them. They work in these big, goddamned hospitals where everybody is short changing everybody else and where the individual doesn't really count. Hell, they have so many bosses they don't know who they're working for, and they usually don't know who makes what decision. About the only thing they really learn is what bad medicine is. If what is happening in medicine continues, we will all be forced to unionize, but against whom?"

The second physician gave a picture more in accord with what appeared in the newspapers: "A lot of those fellows are moonlighting and they want more time to do more of it and make more money. This business that because they work such long hours for several days the health of patients is endangered is baloney. Patients aren't getting better care today than thirty years ago. In fact, they may be getting worse care because everybody is out for himself, and no one really is in charge or wants to work. I wouldn't say this in public, but don't think that it doesn't worry me that I or some member of my family may get sick and go to the hospital. There are only two times you should go to the hospital: when you are well or you are dying. In the first case you don't need care, and in the second you probably will get care. If you are in between and you need human care, stay home and sweat it out."

A caveat is in order here. I am not trying to convey the impression that physicians currently in midlife are weighted down with the burdens of despair, discouragement, and disappointment. These feelings are in the picture certainly, but I think that the strength with which they were conveyed was in part due to the fact that the physicians were verbalizing to me, sometimes for the first time, what they had difficulty facing in themselves. Therefore, these feelings came out with an intensity that can mislead one about the balance between satisfactions and dissatisfactions. And, we must never fail to remember, the strength of these negative feelings must always be seen in their experienced relationship to what has been happening in other areas of living that, though geographically separate and on the surface psychologically separate, are integrally part of the experience of work in two respects: the changing functions that work has for the individual over the course of life, and the role of work either in adversely affecting or in compensating for what happens in different areas of relationships. Just as the physician is now aware of the fact that what happens in the larger society affects the field of medicine in very concrete ways, he or she, like the rest of us, knows that his or her experience of work very much affects and is affected by his or her experience outside of work. If our language differentiates between work and "nonwork," that is no excuse for assuming that the distinction is psychologically valid.

If my interviews demonstrated anything, it is how inordinately difficult it is for people to talk candidly about their experiences of work, especially if their work is regarded by society, as it once was by themselves, as an endless challenge on the road to wisdom and growth. In this connection the following excerpts are revealing. They are from the pioneering study of medical students, *Boys In*

White (Becker, Geer, Hughes, and Strauss), carried out in 1957 and published in 1961—somewhat after the midlife physicians I interviewed had been in medical school. The material excerpted is presented by the authors as typical of statements made by students, describing medicine as a "peerless profession" or as the subtitle of their Chapter Five says, the "best of all professions":

> After anatomy lab I stayed with Harvey Stone while he was scrubbing up. Harvey said, "You know, we were talking it over at the [fraternity] house last night. We were wondering what it would be like to flunk out of medical school. I just can't imagine it because if you went back home everybody would say you had failed." I said, "Do you think it is more important than flunking out of other schools?" Harvey said, "Oh, yes. You know medical school is a kind of little plateau; it's the very tops in most people's minds. . . . I think it would be harder to go back and face all those people talking about you than it would be to stick it out here even if you were pretty unhappy here. I don't think many people have the guts to take social pressure of that kind. We've got so much at stake here it really isn't funny" [pp. 72–73].
>
> At dinner at his fraternity house Sam Watson said he liked to test his concepts by making pictures of them in his mind. I asked him how he would feel if he flunked out. He said, "Oh, I guess I would be very angry." Then he began to think about it and said, "Well, I guess it would be pretty hard to go back home and face the people. I think that would be very difficult." I said, "Do you think it would be more difficult than flunking out of any other school?" Sam said, "Yes, I do. You see medical school is like a dream. Now if you were in law school and flunked out you could very easily go into some business course and make out just as well, but once you started in

medicine you couldn't work in any small part of medicine because you never would be satisfied. I have a picture for that. Medical school is like a stairway and I am standing on a stair and it is about three feet high and I am normal size, but I just look at this one stair. I can see the ones above but the thing I have to do is get up this step right now—this one step, and I can't really do anything about the ones above me. I think all of life is a stairway and I hope there will never be anytime when you come out on any platform at the top. I like to think that we could always look upward and never have to look down. I think we do. I think when you get to the top when you get your degree, you don't look back on what you have done, you look ahead again" [p. 73].

These are revealing statements which, taken together with the idealism the authors describe, define with crystal clarity what is meant by great expectations. Note, however, how difficult it would be for these students to tell others if they were unhappy or had failed in medical school. If you believe you are in the best of all possible professions, and society says the same thing, how can you get society to understand your unhappiness or failure?

There is, two decades after the study was done, a dated quality to *Boys In White*. This is in no way a criticism; rather, it is a consequence of the thoroughness and thoughtfulness characterizing the study. As one finishes reading the book one realizes how utterly unprepared these students (and their teachers) were for those societal changes that would change their lives. It is remarkable how insensitive medicine was to what was taking place in the world, and how unrelated it was to those changes. The students had a view of the future that was a replica of all past stereotypes: once they got out of the medical school rat race in which almost everything was prescribed for them, they would become autonomous, continuing to learn and grow according to their needs and interests, and not according to what the medical faculty thought was appropriate. Money was important to them, but by no means an overriding concern. Far more important to them was a continuing acquisition of knowledge and improvement of skills, constantly invigorating one's sense of self-satisfaction.

The picture of the medical student one gets from *Boys in White* is remarkably similar to the retrospective accounts of midlife physicians, that is, idealism, autonomy, the satisfactions of learning and growth, and a comfortable living. If side by side with this sweet nostalgia is a bitterness with the changed scene and their unwilling envelopment in it, it is a mixture of feeling not unrelated to social reality. The wound is real and deep and festering, and the discomfort is compounded by the inability, difficulty, and fear of putting it publicly into words. Physicians have long been regarded, and have regarded themselves, as possessing knowledge and skills incomprehensible to ordinary mortals. If for a long time they have known the truth to be otherwise, they have kept it a well-guarded secret.

Physicians are by no means the only ones to feel unable or unwilling to talk candidly about their experience of work. Generally speaking, any professional whose work is viewed by society as important and interesting over the course of the career, and who entered the profession in part because he or she agreed with that opinion, will tend to refrain from utterances that deny the validity of that opinion. What happens when an individual disconfirms society's evaluation? How do people react when such a highly respected professional says: "I have had enough. I no longer want to do the same thing. I want new experiences and new challenges"?

Let us take an actual instance. Robert F., forty-two years of age, was superintendent of schools in a Midwestern suburban community containing a university. He received his doctorate from a prestigious university after he had spent several years as a classroom teacher. After receiving his doctorate he became a principal, and then he was offered a superintendency elsewhere, which he accepted. He had two children, three and six years of age. His salary was $42,000 a year. (This, remember, in 1977). In the middle of the academic year, he applied to be admitted to the Yale midcareer program for school administrators. Ordinarily, this was a full-year program enrolling a dozen or so big-city school administrators whose salaries were wholly or in large part paid by a special grant to Yale. In applying to come for only one (the second) semester, Robert would have to pay his own way because all fellowship funds for that year were exhausted. He also needed to be sponsored by a faculty member, and I was asked to see if I could do so after reviewing his file. His credentials were impeccable, which was probably less important than the fact that he knew of my work and wished to study with me. And he came. After chatting for a few minutes, I asked him how come his board of education had given him a sabbatical in the middle of the year? "They didn't give me a sabbatical; I resigned."

What emerged over the course of this initial conversation was almost identical, with one exception, to what the surgeon had told me. Robert, by all criteria, was a very good superintendent and could stay on in that position for as long as he wished. His relationship with his board, staff, teachers, and community groups were cordial and smooth. The community was suburban middle class, willing to support education rather generously, and quite articulate in their respect for him, his accomplishments, and goals. There were problems, of course; the job was demanding, but all in all it was a splendid situation for someone who had dreamed of such an opportunity. So why quit, and what were his plans?

"For the past two years I came to realize that I had done what I dreamed of doing. And what I did, I did well. But I simply did not want to continue to do it year in, year out. Not that it is without its satisfactions. I had a wonderful bunch of people working with me, and I always get a kick out of helping people realize their goals. But I just didn't want to feel that I would always be doing what I have been doing. I wanted new experience and new challenges. I came to Yale to give myself a chance to think, figure out what I would like to do, and pursue some leads. I would like to be a college president or dean or something like that. The one thing I am sure of is that I want out from being a superintendent. And I realized that if I don't get out now I will never get out. I had to make the break, make the move, and start something new."

We had many long and searching discussions, but among their most fascinating characteristics was Robert's description of people's reactions to his resignation. The chronology of their reactions went like this:

1. When he told his friends he had resigned, each of them assumed he had been offered and accepted a "better" superintendency.

2. When he said he had no other job, some of his friends thought he was being coy or secretive or that for some good reason he was not at liberty to reveal what his new job would be.

3. When it finally got through to his friends and colleagues that he really did not have a new job and none was in the offing, their puzzlement was obvious and extreme. A few friends asked what the trouble was to drive him to such a rash decision. Indirectly, word came back to him that something strange had to be happening in his life to impel him to give up such a splendid job and career. His wife, of course, heard many of the same things and spent a fair amount of time reassuring friends that Robert had not gone off his rocker, and that their marriage was as secure as ever.

4. After a couple of weeks, a number of his friends, in individual discussion, expressed their admiration and envy at Robert's bold decision, bemoaning their inability or unwillingness to forge a new career. By the time he left to come to New Haven (at his own expense) almost all his friends and colleagues understood and approved of what he was doing.

I could give other instances in which successful professionals had to contend with the puzzled reactions of others to a radical shift in work or career. They are reactions in all respects identical to our reactions when the marriage of friends, seemingly secure and happy by "objective" and traditional criteria, comes apart. We are surprised, puzzled, and curious; and in short order, we start intuiting what the sources of trouble might have been. It is another story, of course, if the marriage was obviously rocky and troublesome. *That* we can understand and we even feel relieved that the marriage partners will no longer suffer from the consequences of the mismatch. But when the marriage has been "successful," we are at a loss to understand. It is no different when someone like Robert F. starts divorce proceedings from his successful job and career.

Earlier I pointed out that there has been a strange absence of studies on how highly educated, professional people experience their work over the course of time. I discussed three factors: society's positive judgment about such work, the individual professional's acceptance of society's view as he enters the profession, and the resistance of professional organizations to self-scrutiny. These and other factors make it inordinately difficult for the professional to be candid about feelings that go against society's stereotype of him and his work. As I pointed out, such feelings may engender other feelings of guilt and peculiarity that are not wholly unrealistic in light of society's reactions, with which he has identified. If, for example, Robert's wife had reacted to his plans the way his friends initially did and had continued her protestations or gone along with loud reluctance, he would have been far less secure about his decision. I have come across numerous instances of marriage breakups or deterioration in which the wife either prevailed in her objections or, if she did not, the consequences either altered the marital relationship or the couple could only resolve their differences through divorce. Today, of course, we are seeing the reverse situation: the successful housewife and mother who no longer wishes to remain in these roles seeks new experiences and challenges in the world of (different) work but whose husband and friends are uncomprehending of her experience and motives. In the past two decades numerous novels have been written on this theme, far more, I think, than were written in the past five decades about men.

Candor about one's experience of work, as well as the reactions of others to it, are very much a function of the age of the individual, as are the characteristics of the society at the time one is seeking information. Neither candor nor job satisfaction are, so to speak, platonic essences uninformed by or unrelated to the perception of society's status and direction, let alone the seamless relationship of these elements to marital status and marital-familial obligations. Candor about one's negative experience of work is intrinsically dangerous not only because of the surprised reactions of others or the articulation of one's sense of guilt and peculiarity, but also because such candor confronts one with the need or necessity for action in new directions. It has been said that at least half of whatever efficacy psychotherapy has is a consequence of the individual's decision to seek help. That is to say, once an individual has the perceptiveness or honesty or personal strength to admit to himself that he must articulate to someone else his personal difficulties—that he must act in order to gain relief from pain—he is on the road to change. And that decision is usually preceded by great turmoil. The professional who is dissatisfied with his work is in a similar (but not identical) situation: he knows he is dissatisfied, he knows he should do something about it, he is acutely aware of constraints on and obstacles to action, and he further knows that all he knows is private, and that once he says out loud to others he is dissatisfied he cannot escape the need to act. But the situation is even more complicated, because it is the rare professional who is without sources of satisfaction in his work and career, and needless to say, it is the "successful" professional who no longer is challenged by his work who has special difficulties in being candid.

Do these accounts represent a trend that is picking up steam, and if so, is it having the effect of facilitating the expression of hitherto private feelings and fantasies? The message from the popular media is clear: you should not feel guilty about changing the nature and direction of your work. Life is too short to feel confined by what you have done at the expense of doing what you can and would like to do. Look at these people, all with successful careers, who gave them up to pursue new challenges. It is not easy to do, but it can be done. The alternative is to live an increasingly hollow, dissatisfied life. This message is but another manifestation of the values and outlooks that began to take hold after World War II. Personal authenticity or self-realization, the need for new experience, the importance of growth—the language or jargon varied, but their meanings were unmistakable—became overarching values informing personal living. They were values that understandably were eagerly accepted by the generations who came to maturity after World War II, but their significance and power did not become clear until those generations experienced work in our contemporary society. It is not fortuitous that so many of the capsule biographies of professionals who gave up their careers not only emphasize the dissatisfactions stemming from the creeping restrictions on their sense of autonomy but also that the new directions they took were calculated to maximize autonomy. The feeling of entrapment, a kind of symbolic symptom of the dying, withering process, that these biographies describe are similar to what our interviews with professional people revealed.

A caveat is in order here. It has not been my intention to paint a gloomy, depressive picture of highly educated professional people in midlife, nor have I wished to describe them as having little satisfaction in their work. For one thing, to generalize about such a mass of variegated people, even restricted to those in midlife, is to indulge presumption. For another thing, as I have been emphasizing, the assumption that the highly educated segments of our population have been immune to the diseases of boredom, disinterest, and alienation from work has exempted them from close scrutiny (with the exception of those in business and industry, whose plight in bureaucratic bigness and the economic jungle was thought to be atypical of professionals in general). Finally, I have no firm basis from my own studies on which to base secure generalizations. My aims have been more modest, but nonetheless important. At the very least, I have attempted to explore if and why candor about the experience of work is difficult. My interviews and participant-observer role leave little doubt that candor about the experience of work and career among midlife professionals is understandably difficult and dangerous, not only because of the economic-familial matrix in which work and career are embedded, but because the experience of work reflects an ever changing psychological fabric in which the hopes and plans of the past, and the perception of the future, give a pattern and dynamic to the living present that render it impossible to escape the question of life's purposes and meanings—and *that* question is the most insistent and important of them all. The difficulty is further compounded by society's view of the professional, and his early incorporation of that view which, if and when they become discrepant, reinforces privacy rather than public expression of feeling.

Another of my aims was to suggest that the midlife professional who reached maturity in the 1940s and 1950s, absorbing as he did certain values and outlooks about what was important in personal living, was unprepared for or ignorant of the fact that he was living in a society characterized by a dynamic of growth, bigness, and bureaucratization that would threaten those values and outlooks. It was not that the society changed but that it had been changing in these ways for a long time. If the professional knew but ignored this, it was in large part because he assumed or was told that by having the elevated status of professional he would be exempt from evil consequences of the societal change. On a relative basis this assumption has validity, but I have suggested that this validity may be in the process of erosion, the pace of which is not determinable, if only because the problem of candor about the experience of work has been given scant attention.

The previous pages are what I concluded and wrote about in 1977. What is the picture today, twenty years later? I think I am safe in assuming that any reader of this essay knows that the health care arena in 1977 already had the features of big business and industry.

And if the reader was too young in 1977 to know that, the reader learned it in spades in the recent and still continuing debate on national health insurance. Federal and state governments, large corporations, insurance companies, health-medical corporations large enough to be listed on New York stock exchanges and to buy hospitals and group practices on an ever accelerating rate, hospitals that are buying hospitals and group practices, HMOs and PPOs and kindred acronyms that are becoming part of everyday conversation—these are the actors in a social drama that the ordinary citizen understandably cannot comprehend and that engenders the feeling of being a snowflake in a storm.[5] But it is not only the ordinary citizen who feels that way. That is the way *everyone* in the medical community feels. Indeed, for a month during the debate, and as preparation for this essay, I asked scores of physicians and friends to explain the Clinton health plan, if only because the plan was an inkblot to me. No one, but no one, could truly say they understood the plan, that is, how the many features of the plan were to be brought together and how they were supposed to work. (They understood the plan the way they understood the federal income tax law, which is why they and a lot of other people go to accountants.) Some who were not physicians supported the plan even though they admitted that their support stemmed less from understanding and more from faith and hope and anger and disgust about a medical

[5]During the debate, newspapers and other mass media published the salaries of the top layers of administrators of leading hospitals. The salaries varied from a half million to nearly a million dollars a year. With rare exceptions these people were not physicians. I shall not pass judgment on the size of these salaries. What I can and should say is that these salaries were greeted with anger (too weak a word) by the medical and allied professionals. This reaction made it clear that the growth and bureaucratization of hospitals had wrested control from physicians; *that* really was not new knowledge to them, just a form of proof positive of what had been happening in the post–World War II era. That they thought the salaries were economically and morally outrageous goes without saying. Years ago I said that the medical center was the last remaining jungle in American society. I was referring then to what may be called psychological–professional warfare. I was not as sensitive as I could have been to the economic aspects of that jungle, although those aspects were already well known to everyone who worked in the jungle.

scene that was inequitable at best and morally scandalous at worst. Uniformly, the physicians' responses conveyed feelings of impotence and anger because they saw themselves in a no-win situation.

One of the physicians put it this way: "I have read some of the stuff you have given me. When you talk about how puny so many people feel, you always use Kafka's *The Castle*. Well, for a long time that is the way physicians have been feeling. We are the peons at the foot of the mountain, and at the top—whether that top is the head honchos of the hospital, of the government, of the insurance companies—are strangers who are screwing us."

Several things are hard to exaggerate in the case of physicians (and allied professionals). They deeply resent, to indulge understatement, becoming accountants and businesspeople. (One group practice of eight specialists has fifteen clerical staff handling paperwork. That, today, is not unusual.) Their autonomy is steadily being circumscribed. They fear the private practice of medicine may be a thing of the past as they are forced, formally or informally, to become employees under the control of large organizations. They are no longer able to practice medicine the way they had one expected. They have lost a poignant degree of self-respect as well as respect from a once-respectful public. It is not unusual to hear physicians say that they would not encourage any of their children to enter the profession.

What I said and wrote in 1977 contained in muted form all of the above. What was muted then is no longer so. The public is not sympathetic, because so many who have some form of health insurance do not understand why premiums increase; the cost of medication seems scandalous to them; not all procedures and examinations are covered; they have to fill out forms that are difficult to decode; they see their physicians as well-heeled professionals many of whom lack caring and compassion (Sarason, 1985), and their experience in and with hospitals as far from satisfying.

What has happened in the health community—which, let us not forget, is a sizeable fraction of the working population—is by no means peculiar to it. If I have singled it out in this essay, it is because I consider the factors contributing to its present state no less influential among other highly educated professionals, whose great expectations about an onward and upward career of challenge, growth, and fulfillment, about work as a source of intrinsic satisfaction over the lifetime, frequently founder as they encounter life in increasingly large, impersonal organizations, or in smaller ones that are vulnerable to the economic features of our economy, features they forgot (if they ever knew it). But economics and bigness are only part, albeit an important part, of the story, because the challenge to the one life–one career imperative antedates bigness (really giantism) and the recessions of the latter quarter of this century. Indeed, one of the more explicit themes voiced by young people in the turbulent decade of the sixties (the early postwar generations) was a devaluation and even total rejection of conventional conceptions of work and "careerism," conceptions they saw as a mammoth constraint on the expression and development of people's protean nature, a form of societal tyranny inimical to their interests, needs, and potentials. If the theme was vague and couched in utopian imagery, it nonetheless was expressing open disdain for the conventional one life–one career imperative. They indicted bigness and materialism, to be sure, but it was from a stance that what people needed, wanted, and deserved could not be given them in the society in which they lived. Slotting, pigeonholing, and imprisoning people in narrow lines of work from which they could not escape was immoral exploitation. Better to remove one's self from the societal treadmill and give up illusory conceptions of the presumed benefits of "careerism"; many did by leaving their colleges and universities and starting communes in rural America.

There was a second, associated theme: buying into careerism impoverished the capacity to love, the experience of intimacy, the sense of community.

These themes of love, work, intimacy, and community were articulated by young people most of whom were highly educated and who in the prewar years would have enthusiastically embraced the one life–one career imperative. And there were many among them whose parents had divorced or who were quite aware of the escalating divorce rate or who saw their parents in a marriage they had reason to believe was unrewarding to both partners. It was not happenstance that unmarried males and females living together and the transiency of those arrangements were hallmarks of the sixties, one of the more obvious features of the sexual revolution, of the weakening of the one mate–one life imperative.[6] If Freud said that loving and working were the two major tasks in life but said nothing about working, the young people of the sixties expressed and repaired that omission in their own way. But for them there was a third task coequal with loving and working, which when absent, as they saw to be frequently the case, set definite limits to how satis-fying loving and working can be. That third task was to experience a sustained sense of community, which I cannot elaborate on here except to say that they considered the contexts of work in organi-zation as barriers to the sense of community.

That there have been changes in the arenas of loving and work-ing is indisputable. I have not argued that these changes were in some simple and direct cause and effect relationship to what hap-pened during and soon after World War II, let alone asserted that the psychological dynamics in individuals were similar in substance and force. World War II provided fertile ground for the seeds of the social change, but it was not inevitable that they would sprout when

---

[6]In her book *The Way We Never Were*, Stefanie Coontz (1992) pointed out that teenage birth rates in the 1950s set record highs unsurpassed even now. By 1955 the number of out–of–wedlock babies placed for adoption increased by 80 percent from a decade earlier. Also, tranquilizers rose from relative obscurity in 1955 to a total consumption level of 462,000 pounds in 1958 and 1.15 million pounds by 1959—a rate of increase that warrants the hypothesis that the subse-quent rate of increase in "hard" drugs had some of its psychological roots, both for younger and older people, in the decade and a half after World War II. These sta-tistics were barometers of social change about which few people were knowledge-able or the significance of which few people knew how to interpret until, of course, the dimensions of the social change became all too clear.

and in the ways they did. Social change is a process that becomes general, that goes beyond seemingly discrete areas of social life, when changes in these discrete areas coalesce, when the agendas of different groups get interconnected in a way that says, so to speak, that a sizeable part of the society is articulating a new worldview. What is inevitable is that there will be resistance to the seeds of change, and even here it is unpredictable whether the resistance will inhibit or delay their growth or unintentionally stimulate their growth.

Atomic testing, assassinations, racial conflict, the cold war, Vietnam, the civil rights struggles and movement—all these and more were factors that altered people's conception of and attitudes toward themselves, others, and the past and future of the society. And few factors were as fateful as one I did not list: the women's liberation movement, which on the surface was only about working but which, as it gained strength, could not but alter the ways in which working, loving, and family structure were, as they always were, intertwined. We are far from understanding the changes that intertwining has wrought or what it portends for the societal future for good or for bad. No partisan of the women's movement can see other than the benefits of its goals, just as opponents cannot see other than its negative consequences. If that is understandable, the fact remains that they will both be victims of the law of unintended consequences.

Social change is not like a storm we know will go away. Social change feeds on itself, sometimes slowly, sometimes with amazing speed. That is not hard to accept in the abstract. It is extraordinarily hard to accept in quotidian living, riveted as we are on the present and the near future. Nor do we have barometers of social change to suggest—and suggest is the most we can expect—that the change we are living in *may* have consequences of which we at the least should be aware. Someone said that posterity is the cruelest of critics, which meant that posterity will pass judgment on us for being unable to take seriously what should have been obvious or was not obvious because we were prisoners of faulty assumptions about our social world, which prevented us from even sensing the dimensions of social change until after the social change had occurred. So we play catch-up in the present, hoping that the future will take care of itself, that it will not stray far from becoming a carbon copy of the present. Matters are not helped by the fact that those intellectual-professional disciplines concerned with social change are so separated from each other and each comprises so many specialized subfields, making it too easy to miss the forest for the trees. Economics has no interest in loving; psychology (and psychiatry) have only a passing interest in working; loving and working are by no means near the mainstream of sociology; and now that exotic, so-called primitive, societies uncontaminated by the West are few in number, anthropology is having trouble deciding whether it should play to its archeological strengths and traditions or renew itself by applying accrued knowledge to highly developed societies such as ours. As I said elsewhere about psychology (Sarason, 1995), I have no doubt that the mind-boggling varieties of specialties that comprise the field will be judged very negatively by posterity. But that kind of specialization within specialization is true for many if not all fields. That is reason enough to be pessimistic that our understanding of social change will improve, because that can only take place by people who deserve the label generalist. Whatever their virtues, and they are not few, universities produce specialists. So, for example, specialists will never understand why and how loving, working, and community are, as they always have been, a unity in which what happens in one part has repercussions in the other parts, again for good or for bad. That, some will say is a hypothesis, not a fact. Santayana's caveat that those who ignore history are doomed to repeat its errors is also a hypothesis that, like Darwin's theory of evolution, has not been replaced by a more valid and encompassing one.

10

Artistic Expression

I exploit my friends by plying them with questions about what I happen to be writing about at the time. During the years these essays were germinating and taking shape, I asked two questions: What in your experience in the post World War II era said to you that a social change had taken place? How did you explain it to yourself?[1] Most of my friends are over fifty years of age but about a third are in their forties, with distinct memories of the sizzling sixties which they recall with a mixture of nostalgia, bemusement, and tinges of sadness. That, of course, was in striking contrast to most of my older friends who saw that decade as a semidisaster that was and largely still is not explainable by them. The one thing they had in common, in the sixties as well as today, is what they called the generation gap. But the word gap is misleading, a kind of euphemism for what I have very good reason to say in regard to both age groups was family warfare.

There was one and only one "signal" of change that everyone mentioned and it happened to be one in which I have long been

---

[1] I shall say nothing about the answers to this question. I asked it primarily to see how the answers were social-historical in nature. With very few exceptions they were not. The ahistorical stance was distinguished by its absence, although every one of my friends is a knowledgeable observer of the social scene. Some of what they said about the social scene then and now is reflected in some of the previous essays.

interested and about which I have written (1990a). I refer to the arts generally, although the unanimous agreement of my friends centered on music—popular music. What my older friends said could be paraphrased this way: "I have always liked the romantic, June-moon songs of the thirties, forties, and fifties. Bing Crosby, Frank Sinatra, Perry Como, Ella Fitzgerald, and Peggy Lee were my favorite singers. "Stardust," "And the Angels Sing," and "Dancing in the Dark" were the kinds of songs I loved to hear the big bands play. The Hollywood musicals were superficial, contrived affairs but the music was glorious. So was the dancing of Fred Astaire and Ginger Rogers. Don't get me wrong. I didn't like all popular music, but none of it was an assault on my ears. Rock and roll was an assault to the point where I didn't even try to comprehend the words. What truly mystified me was that my teenage children and their friends gobbled it up. They knew the kind of music my wife and I liked and the records we bought, popular and classical; that kind of music was not foreign to them. Along comes rock and roll and they couldn't get enough of it. How did it happen and why? I don't know. It all seemed to erupt so quickly, out of nowhere."

Another of my older friends said essentially the same thing but with a different emphasis (paraphrased, of course): "I knew something was changing when Elvis first began to appear on TV. It wasn't Rock and Roll. It wasn't a blast of sound. It had a distinctive beat. If you closed your eyes the music *qua* music wasn't offensive; it was simply uninteresting to me, it moved me not at all. As for the words of his songs, they were not of the June-Moon genre but they were about young love, with the difference that they not only were not what I call romantic but they were much more sexually explicit, and if I had any doubt about that they vanished as I watched the sexual suggestiveness of his bodily contortions. Look, I remember in my teens when I [a male] and the girls I knew shouted, screamed, and stomped when Sinatra came either to the Palace or the Roger Sherman in New Haven. When the Messiah comes He will not get a more enthusiastic welcome, even though there will be no entry charge. Sinatra *sang*, he did not *cavort*, but there was something about the combination of music, words, skinny frame, together with a facial expression containing hints of softness, purity of feeling, and *vulnerability*, that made me want to be like him and made the girls want to embrace him, and more. To teenagers, Elvis was not vulnerable, he was *invincible*; he was not a forlorn *victim* of unrequited love, he was a parading conqueror; he did not *imply* sexuality, he *demonstrated* it. So when I saw him and how live audiences and TV viewers reacted to him, it reminded me of how my generation responded to Sinatra. But in our case the older generation saw us as ebullient juveniles with too much energy. To them our reactions represented no threat to their values or standards. In fact, they liked the songs he sang. But to me Elvis' rise to celebrity told me the world was changing." (I have italicized some words because I distinctly remember how each was given special emphasis by my friend, an unusual feature of his way of talking.)

These are very familiar stories. It was one of the older women who somewhat rounded out the picture: "We were enthusiastic about the music and those who sang the romantic ballads but we were not rebellious. We were attacking nothing or nobody in a social or societal sense. We were middle class in values to the core. What you have to remember is that I grew up at the end of the Depression and during the war years. What we wanted and needed was music that said love and hope would see us through, that come what may we could not give up on love and hope. You could say it was unrealistic, that we lived in the world of our fantasies, but that is very wrong. We knew there was something screwy about the real world but we also knew we needed, truly needed, what those songs conjured up in our imaginations. They were moments of satisfaction, even joy, in days when suffering, war casualties, and the like were constant reminders that all was not right in the world. It was not that our heads were in the sand, but that our hearts needed love and hope to keep us going. We had few, if any, feelings of alienation. Popular music did something positive for me in no way different from what listening to Tchaikovsky's Pathetique symphony does to me, not that I am putting them in the same league as music."

Let me now paraphrase what my younger friends said: "I can't explain why Elvis had such an impact on us, and the word impact is too weak. What the words said, the striving beat and pace of the music, the way he dressed, those pelvic movements, those piercing and leering eyes, the curl of his mouth—we had never seen anything like that before. There were a lot of things we hadn't seen before but this was in a class by itself. I really don't know how to explain it. Was it that we wanted to feel excitement? That to us he stood for a freeing sexuality? For abandon? For rebelling against the inanities coming out of Hollywood and Tin Pan Alley? I really do not know." And then, as an afterthought, one person added something all my friends said by the time our conversation ended: "Didn't Elvis come to our attention when the drug and hippie culture began to be noticed, the protests against atomic testing, the 1954 desegregation decision and the civil rights movement?"

What the afterthought suggested was that the new sound of music and its quick acceptance by young people was about more than music. It was, in my opinion, a reflection of the strength of an emerging need for new and unrestraining experience. I do not offer that in any narrow psychological sense, as if a psychology of the individual could explain what was truly a social or group or generational phenomenon. It was not, initially at least, a need to rebel against a state of affairs. It was a going toward or fastening onto what appeared to be outlets for self-expression, for new experience. That need showed up in different ways in different individuals at the same time that what they had in common via TV was being able *literally* to see and hear happenings, events, and personalities to a degree never before possible. If there was a "compliance" factor in them, the society and its media were also "compliant."

If they were primed for Elvis, he primed them for the Beatles, as well as for Bob Dylan, Joan Baez, and other folk singers with their themes of social protest, parental insensitivities, and young people as victims. Clashes over desegregation; atomic fallout in Pennsylvania's Three Mile Island nuclear power plant; the Berlin Blockade; the Cuban Missile Crisis; the assassinations of a President, his brother, and Martin Luther King Jr.; urban riots and fires (in Newark and elsewhere); and the buildup in Vietnam the consequences of which for young people did not need to be spelled out for them— these events and more were *seen and heard* by young people, with two effects. The first was that their need for self-expression and new experience quickly became embedded in a truly rebellious stance toward the world as they saw it, a world in which there was no place for such needs. The second, a variant of the first, was a coalescence of different groups—white and black, young and old, men and women, those of varying sexual styles—that could justifiably be called a "freedom" movement, a freeing from what is to what should be. The response to the sound of the new music did not remain an encapsulated phenomenon. What young people saw happening in the world made that encapsulation impossible to continue. The response to Elvis was a barometer of a change, but that barometer was interpreted largely in narrow, ahistorical, psychological terms, that is, it was another instance of how youth have always devised strange ways to get their kicks, to give expression to longings characteristic of the growing-up process, a process of *sturm and drang* in which fads and fashions come and go. If only because it is hard to be completely wrong, such an explanation has a kernel of truth. But it was an unproductive and misleading kernel precisely because it ignored the seeds of social change spawned by World War II and its immediate aftermath, that Elvis and the response to him was not taking place in a social vacuum. That it was otherwise did not become clear until several years had passed and the coalescence process was complete.

The coming and going of "new" music is a distinctive feature of the twentieth century. Early in this century Schoenberg and his followers proclaimed and wrote what they predicted would be the music (serial music) of the future. Although it was and is warmly greeted in some musical quarters, the unassailable fact is that the listening public's response was and is not warm, to indulge understatement. It "speaks to and touches" few people, regardless of age, education, class, and devotion to classical music. And that is the point: if new music does not "move" people, whatever the reasons, it will have a quality of social preciousness that reduces its significances for and potential impact upon the social scene.

Following World War II, John Cage and his students achieved a degree of notoriety for their new music, which made Schoenberg's music seem traditional, conventional, old hat. There has been no compliance factor in and from the social scene. In recent decades we have seen the creation and development of "minimalist" music written for the symphony orchestra and the opera. If it has received a more favorable but by no means enthusiastic response from musicologists and musical critics, no one denies that the public is underwhelmed. The argument can be made that the public is not ready for such new music; it has been schooled, so to speak, to stay with the traditional and the familiar; but who can deny that what is true now may not be the case for future publics to whom the music will appeal? The answer, of course, is perhaps, maybe, who can tell? But that is my point: future publics may respond more favorably not because their auditory systems have changed but because a lot of other things in and out of music have changed. Jazz, ragtime, and the blues have a long history in our country and until the early decades of this century they were predominantly heard in the black community, although they were heard by and impacted on white composers of popular music. Beginning with World War I and in relatively short time that impact became more general here and abroad. It was not that readiness had been created but that social changes made that music have individual and social meanings for people it had not had before. There was no simple cause and effect relationship.

Showboat, produced in 1927, was the first musical to deal with an important, conflictful social issue. It was by conventional standards a hit: the music was glorious, the acting and singing superb, especially Paul Robeson's rendition of "Old Man River." But in no way did the social content of the show influence others to deal with social themes. That did not take place until after and because of World War II. *South Pacific, The Sound of Music, The King and I, No Strings, West Side Story, Most Happy Fella* and other musicals dealt with racial, ethnic, social, or political themes. People came to these musicals in obvious droves with different psychological sets than their earlier counterparts.

What about Gershwin's *Porgy and Bess*, written before World War II? Is that an exception to what I have just said? Generally speaking, the critics recognized its contribution as music and drama. A good deal of the music became popular apart from knowledge of the story itself. The fact is that *Porgy and Bess* did not have a long life on Broadway, and before World War II performances of it were very infrequent. That changed dramatically after World War II and in two ways. First, groups began to perform it in regions where it would have been impossible before the war. Second, the public wanted to and indeed went to see it. (If memory serves me right, there was but one recording made before World War II. There were at least six after the war.) Third, when *Porgy and Bess* opened, musical critics judged it, as music and drama, a notch above a Broadway musical. Was it opera? No. Would it ever be performed in an opera house, let alone become a staple in the repertory? Pretentious nonsense. It has turned out otherwise. The critics assumed that the racial situation as they experienced it would not change, that there would always be a limited public who would want to see and appreciate it, that the conventional criteria for what was or was not an opera would not change, that the likes of the Gershwins, writers and composers of "pop" music, could not have written something deserving of the label "opera." And today, music critics and music snobs cannot make up their minds whether Bernstein's *West Side Story* and *Candide* should be called operas or musicals.

I am no musicologist. I have no credentials whatsoever for

passing judgment on the innovativeness, structure, and skill of a musical work, popular or classical. But one thing I and every reader know, and no musicologist can deny: the initial response to music has an affective quality or component. You are not indifferent. You may like the music, you may dislike it, you may be puzzled, and shades in between, but your response is never an indifferent one. Depending on temperament, knowledge, and interest, when you begin to analyze the music, diverse ideas and images may come to the fore, that is, the initial affective component may be transformed or replaced by purely cognitive processes or, not infrequently, the affective component may become more clear. Regardless of the affective component, and not necessarily because of it, you may seek to hear or play it again, in which case you may find that you are changing your "liking and disliking" judgment, which always has an affective *component* (it is a component of a complicated gestalt, it is not *a* response but part of one). Individual variations in response to a piece or genre of music may be enormous. However, when that music is "new" or appears to be so and elicits a very positive affective response in a significant segment of the population—and a contrary one in other segments—to the point that individual variations obviously have no explanatory power, we are then dealing with a social phenomenon for which an individual psychology has a "missing the forest for the trees" effect. To those who like the music it is a revelation; to those who do not it is an abomination they hope is transitory. It may or may not be transitory, but in either case the explanation has to go beyond individuals (the trees) and look at the social context (the forest). The response to Elvis, the Beatles, and similar folk were social phenomena the significance of which as a barometer of a social change were not sensed until after the social change was plain to see.

I have emphasized the need for novelty and new experience as a need that gained a good deal of strength and saliency in the post World War II era. That emphasis was not in the service of reductionism, as if invoking that need explains everything or most of everything. It does not. It is a factor the importance of which has not been given the recognition I think it deserves. As I have tried to demonstrate in previous essays in this book, its presence and strength are a part, and only a part, of other manifestations of social change, such as loving and working, divorce, or drugs. I say this to bring attention to a distinctive feature of what has happened since Elvis. And what has happened is nothing less than a somewhat bewildering array of adjectives to describe different types of musical sounds of different performing groups. Rock and roll, hard rock, heavy metal, porno rock, and rap are only a few of the labels given to and/or promoted by different groups, each seeking to sound and be distinctive, to be new. In the prewar years there were also many bands each of which had a distinctive sound, such as, Tommy Dorsey, Benny Goodman, Glen Miller, Guy Lombardo, Artie Shaw, Charlie Spivak, Duke Ellington, and so forth. The need to create a new sound in popular music is not peculiar to the postwar years. The difference between the periods is twofold: the pace at which a new sound becomes popular, and the age of those who exemplify the new sound and the age of those who are its intended audience. The big bands appealed to all age groups, and that is clearly not the case for the music I am talking about: music by (and for) young people eager to be seen as novel, even if that means provoking and shocking the audience, and doing it with the knowledge of what the intended effects should be. The use of MTV—its format, content, implicit and explicit messages—are wholly in line with what I have, in part at least, described and attempted to explain.

In the visual arts (painting and sculpture) the story is both similar and different. It has always been the case that visual artists have been aware of the long history of their craft. At any one time, and however much some artists may have been disdainful of current art, they have been respectful of that history and have placed its artists in the pantheon of greatness, even when they have had no intention of emulating them. They also have known that some of the greats did not get the recognition they deserved in their lifetimes, and they have believed that a similar fate was likely for them, that is, the conventions and styles of art were not easily or quickly overcome either by the artistic establishment of the time or by a public taste that establishment had cultivated. Generally speaking, artists have a sense of a long history, quite in contrast to the case of popular but not classical music. So, when the visual artist rebelled it was not out of disrespect or with the goal of consigning the past to oblivion or as a denial that there was much in the past that could and should be enjoyed in the present. They went their way in their time and they deserve our respect. We live in different times and we have to go different ways. Different times, different styles, content, rules, and goals. If anything is true about the music I discussed earlier, it is that its writers, performers, and promoters are ahistorical in stance, as is their audience, and they regard any music and any performers from more than forty years or so ago as not worthy of their attention and ears. Some might argue that it has always been the case that young people are intent on creating a new world, on departing from the conventions of the time. That, I would agree, is somewhat (only somewhat) true, but it is a difference that makes a big difference when that departure occurs at a time when a lot of other changes are occurring in the society, of which that departure is both effect and cause. It is not just that they are young and trying to find a place in the societal sun, that they neither know or are interested in the past, or that their enamorment with the new music is disparaged by many in older generations, but rather that their music has not, like many fads and fashions, gone away; it expresses and conveys messages by no means absent in other age segments of the society. It has been more than music *qua* music. It was and is an important social phenomenon, a barometer of an ongoing social change. When history becomes less and less a feature of more and more people, does that play no role in the content and pace of social change?

Reams have been written about how the art scene in this country changed after World War II, and rather quickly. The shift of artistic gravity from Paris to New York did not take long at all. What was called the New York School was a heterogeneous group each member of which had his or her own style but all of whom proclaimed a break from the past that contained strands of which they were aware. It was a very sharp break, as was the break that Elvis represented.[2] In what follows, I restrict myself to trying to cast light on two questions: What might be said about their motivations and attitudes in regard to their abstract-expressionist paintings, a label that critics seized on? How might one explain why ten years after the war they were on their way to becoming celebrities, and with each passing year their prices went up to the thousands, then to the hundred thousands, and then to the millions?

Let us begin with the term that abstract-expressionists applied to the members of the New York School. They eschewed the idea that the external reality, and the expression of ideas and feeling by the artist, required the use of recognizable forms, such as nature, people, and other recognizable things. The millennia-old tradition of representational painting—however it had changed and whatever its indisputable glories—was exhausted, no longer adequate in this modern world to give expression to the artist's outlook, goal, and role. What was required was that the artist employ "pure" form and color to express his or her ideas and feelings about self and the world. Pure form and color, and only those two, were the basic materials of the artist. In the past those basics had been used by artists to represent what conventionally is called reality; in one way or another the viewer could recognize, instantly, who and what was being represented, such as a person, an aspect of nature, or an identifiable activity. When one looked at Michelangelo's *Pieta*, or a Pissaro country

---

[2]Elvis's reception was as if an unpredicted, startlingly glowing meteor came into sight. But as Elvis apparently knew or sensed, he brought together features of music and its performance that were features of music he grew up hearing in the black community (Guralnick, 1995).

scene, or Picasso's *Guernica*, one saw familiar, cultural content. Commitment and devotion to representation of "reality" were no longer productive for what the abstract-expressionists wished to convey to the viewer. They sought other ways artistically to comment on the world.

I do not regard it as of minor significance that these artists stood for new ways to give expression to their outlooks and feelings. However, the word "new" is a form of understatement. Cubism had been new earlier in the century, and if its way of representing reality was strange (at least initially) to most viewers, the paintings contained recognizable objects, albeit in a "distorted" way. If the viewer found the paintings strange, the titles the artists gave to their paintings were helpful in making sense of which objects were being represented from a new perspective. The abstract-expressionists did something more radical; they rejected representational painting. (As a "school" or a group, there was variation among them, but in general how I have characterized them is accurate.)

Historians have said that changes in the style and content of art herald a larger social change, that is, they are barometers, very early ones, of a social change. Whatever the status of that assumption, and I think it is largely true, it is also the case that artists have clearly believed that over the course of history they have played such a prodromal role. They want to believe it is true, and I say that without any intention of disparagement. When the artist paints, he or she is expressing a point of view, a message, that is intended to have meaning for the viewer, that is, to enlarge the viewer's experience, to engage the viewer in a silent dialogue. If the artist has no control over how the viewer reacts, interprets, and judges his work, the artist knows that his ideas, concepts, and feelings were part of the process of creating, that is, he did not do it for the hell of it, so to speak; he knows that the work reflects his thinking, feelings, experience, *and* a desire to express and communicate them in ordered form.

The label "abstract-expressionist" is a revealing one in that it clearly indicates that these artists sought to express themselves—to express their ideas, feelings, and outlooks—by abstract use of form and color, and one source of their intention (among others) was a strong need to depart from a tradition the virtues of which had been exhausted. Most if not all of these artists came to maturity before World War II and early in their careers their works were in the traditional style. Their departure from tradition began to occur during World War II, which began almost two years before the United States entered the war.

Correlations do not permit statements of cause and effect. I am suggesting two things, the first being more clear than the second. The first is that historically artists have seen themselves and have been seen by others as free spirits whose work and lifestyle could not be judged by conventional standards. They were apart from society and frequently in conflict with it. They were unpredictable; you could always count on someone in the artistic community to come up with something new, strange, and controversial. (The history of Greenwich Village well illustrates this point, and not only in regard to visual art.) That was especially true in the first half of the twentieth century, a fact that was obvious to and salient for the abstract expressionists. To characterize the art of the twentieth century as a conscious and persistent searching for and embracing of new forms of expression, both personal and conceptual, is to state the obvious.[3] From that standpoint the appearance and use of abstract-expressionism should be no great surprise, although it does not explain why it appeared when it did.

That brings me to the second point. If artists have seen themselves apart from their society and are so seen by others, it is in part

[3]It has long been the case in the major cities of the world (such as Vienna, Paris, London, and Berlin) that the art and science communities were not socially and intellectually isolated from each other. Generally speaking, artists respected not only the accomplishments of scientists but their moral-psychological ethos: past knowledge and methods were not sacrosanct, exploring the new and the strange was.

because works of art frequently have been negative (but not always) commentaries on the societal scene. Coming to maturity when they did, these artists saw the war years as the last gasp of a world that was unredeemable and the traditions of which were no longer adequate to depict the self-defeating craziness of that world. I am not suggesting that the abstract-expressionists woke up one day and said, "I need and will create a new artistic form and expression that will enable me better to represent my reality, my outlook on the world, and that will speak in a compelling way to the viewers' need to understand self and the world better, a world that does not allow truly personal expression and that bombards the viewer with representations of reality that are corrupting." It does and did not happen that way. Each artist, in his or her way, struggled against obstacles from within and without to develop a new way literally of expressing himself or herself, and if that meant departing from and rejecting artistic traditions in a most radical way, so be it. A dying old world required a new art, not one that continued to be representational.

It should be apparent that I am trying to be descriptive and not judgmental. My point is a simple one: abstract-expressionism is incomprehensible if when and where it happened is not part of the explanation. And by "where" I mean America and New York, not in a weary, war-ravaged Europe, in a world of power where the center of gravity had shifted to the United States, and in the case of art that meant New York, a shift that Hitler's Nazi Germany had started in the several years before the war when refugee artists began to become noticeably part of the New York scene. The work of no artist is exempt from the influences of place, regardless of whether that artist is traditional or not. And that was the case for the abstract-expressionists, who were living at a time (during and in the years immediately after the war) when a complex social change was occurring, when everyone yearned and hoped for a new and better world, and the word new says it all. The past had to be overcome, and nothing illustrates that stance more clearly than the rise to prominence of the abstract expressionists.

How do we explain that prominence? It is not to suggest that most of the general public warmly embraced that art, which they viewed as mystifying, "unrealistic," solipsistic, and another instance of artists for whom to be regarded as shockingly avant-garde was a badge of distinction. But in some quarters these artists received a more favorable reception because their works were congruent with their own need for a new art in a new world. The new art "spoke" to them. One source of support came from younger art critics (such as Clement Greenberg and Harold Rosenberg) whose articles and reviews appeared in places read by the intellectual and artistic communities, which meant they were being read by faculty (and their students) in numerous colleges and universities where the size and emphasis of the humanities, especially art and literature, burgeoned and who were receptive to new ideas and trends, a receptiveness that was no less true in other disciplines. It was not that the past was irrelevant but that it *had to and should have been superseded*; that was a clear component of the campus zeitgeist, one that students and faculty were primed to accept. As I said in previous essays, the social change that began during the war and became clearer soon after it was accompanied by an influx of students, graduate and undergraduate, for whom new ideas and outlooks, far from holding terror, were food for thought. And those students were greeted by an increasing number of instructors not much older than they were.

Another source of support were art gallery owners, some of whom were established and influential and willing—for entrepreneurial-economic reasons, to satisfy personal aesthetics, out of a sense of professional obligation, or for a mixture of all these—to display and promote the new art. Gallery owners (then) were not noted for their risk taking, but when they read the critics, whom they usually knew, and when some wealthy and nonwealthy individuals showed an interest in the new art, they were not about to look a potential gift horse in the mouth.

It is the second word in the label "abstract-expressionism" that I am emphasizing, because I believe it suggested and encapsulated the importance that many people felt should be given to the need of personal expression, for new experience, for new outlets, needs that played a role in the meteoric rise of psychoanalysis and existential philosophies after the war. A personal anecdote is relevant here. It was near the end of World War II and I was walking somewhere in and around midtown Manhattan. I passed a store with the name Gallery (or museum) of Non-Objective art. I walked in, picked up and read a flyer on a table by the entrance. The first sentence read: "Non-Objective Art is like nothing else in this world; like music it means nothing." The point was, the flyer went on to say, that the artists represented in the gallery intended no concrete visual representation of culturally familiar human forms, scenes, or things. These artists were giving expression in a particular formal way to a very personal stance. The obligation of the viewer was to use the work of art, its color, line, and composition, as a stimulus to a process in the viewer of identifying and expressing the meaning the work held for him or her. This was, of course, mystifying to me, but the accuracy of the flyer was totally confirmed when I saw the art. It was like no other art I had ever seen. Compared to it, cubism was an obvious representation of the world as we literally see it. There was nothing in my background, knowledge, and experience to allow me to react other than with total bafflement. That this art would within a decade gain an acceptance and celebrity by a significant part of the art world (in galleries, museums, and even some of the mass media) was a possibility well beyond my imagination. That it might be a barometer of change was ludicrous. Many people still react the way I did, but today those people see it as but one of many changes indicative of a larger social change.

As was the case with Rock and Roll and its subsequent, sizable, variously labeled descendants, the abstract expressionists were followed by an even greater number of art trends, "schools," sects, each seeking to be new and different, each clamoring for a place in the artistic sun and public attention. Somewhere in a magazine an art critic noted and bemoaned this metastatic feature by saying that it was hard to keep up with "the new art in the new week." And more than one art critic or art historian, none of whom had been adverse to earlier post World War II art, have judged much of the later art as a form of self promotion and not art. No one has written more devastatingly about this than Hilton Kramer, who has been editor of *The New Criterion* since its inception in 1982. If you read issues from that journal from 1982 to today, you will find many examples of what I have meant by a coalescing of discrete barometers of social change.

Music and visual art have always, of course, been means of personal expression. Those means, again of course, have always reflected absorption of features of time, era, and place. In the May 29, 1995, issue of *The New York Times* there is a review of *Walt Whitman's America: A Cultural Biography* by David Reynolds, whose aim it was to tell the story of how Whitman "absorbed his country and how he tried to make his country absorb him." He quotes the following that Whitman wrote in 1891: "No great poem or other literary or artistic work of any scope, old or new, can be essentially considered without weighing first the age, politics (or want of politics) and aim, visible forms, unseen soul and current times, out of the midst of which it rises and is formulated." That statement is crucially true and explanatory for the arts in post World War II America. It is no less relevant for other arenas of social activity in which different groups redefined themselves in the effort to display a form of expression quite different from that they displayed before World War II or that which the society had allowed them. The personal is always social (Whitman's "midst"). World War II gave rise to a new "midst" containing new seeds for personal and social change and it did not take long for the seeds to grow and then coalesce to make it clear that a social change was occurring and is continuing in ways and at a pace that should give pause to those whose picture of the future is not markedly different from that of their present. That stance is to me understandable in those born, say, thirty or forty years ago. It is not understandable to me in those who, like me, go back farther in time, and that includes many in the social sciences who should know better and for whom the verdicts of history will not be kind.

11

. . . .

Power Relationships in Our Schools

The purpose of this essay can be put in the form of three questions: Granted that our public schools have changed in numerous ways reflective of a larger social change, why have educational
outcomes been so inadequate? Why, unlike in other arenas, has the
social change hardly altered power relationships in schools, an alteration that is one of the hallmarks of social change? If educational
outcomes remain at the level they are, or get worse, is it likely that
the playing out of the post World War II social change will take on
new, destabilizing features?

The defining feature of a national revolution is in the intention
and achievement of a cataclysmic break in the allocation and dis-
tribution of political power. That feature is transforming, pervasive,
the polar opposite of anything that can be called cosmetic. Battles
are fought, lives are lost, existing institutions may be abolished, a
new future is proclaimed. No major institution is exempt from the
necessity or pressure to change in accord with the revolution's
intents. The American, French, Russian, and Chinese revolutions
are, of course, clear examples the consequences of which are still
with us. The Nazi revolution in Germany is a deceptive exception
because Hitler came to power through "legal–constitutional"
processes. But before Hitler was literally handed power peacefully,
his paramilitary forces had already demonstrated their willingness
and capacity to be disruptive and to murder. Once he was installed

in power, the revolutionary dimensions of his ideology and goals became evident (a fact that was but should not have been surprising, because Hitler did precisely what he had long said he would do. In that respect Hitler was the most consistent of revolutionaries.)

Concepts like revolution and social change may appear to be tautological in that both are intended to signify a pervasive alteration in an existing state of societal affairs. It could be argued that the main difference between the two concepts is that revolutions are inevitably bloody, but like eras of social change, the two are similar. In regard to revolutions, historians ask three questions: What were the precursors and why were they hardly or not at all recognized or appropriately weighted? How did these discrete precursors-barometers come together to give force to the social change? Was the bloody overthrow of the existing order inevitable or was it avoidable? Those are clear questions, but books are still written on each of the revolutions because new evidence or new conceptions suggest overlooked precursors or that the interpretation of the interaction among traditional precursors gave a distorted picture. If predicting the future is risky business, making organized sense of the past has its problems. That is no less true when a social change, like that in the post World War II era, is neither initiated nor continued by a revolution. I would argue that in such instances the problem is in many ways more difficult because the alterations in power relationships are so frequently "silent" and their accumulating and interactive strength difficult to recognize and label. And even when recognized, those alterations may appear not to be of such a degree as to justify saying that the essential character and purpose of social institutions have changed. So, for example, in the post World War II era the university has changed in several ways.

1. Demographic changes in the number and cultural diversity of students decreased the power of the faculty-administration in relation to students.

2. Power relationships among university departments changed in the direction of increasing the power of the sciences in relation to the humanities.

3. The most dramatic and consequential change was that an external force, the federal government, became, for the first time, a controlling force in university affairs, that is, the university was no longer, financially and otherwise, the independent entity it had been before World War II. *That* was a momentous change, far more obvious in consequences than the changes suggested by points 1 and 2.

To readers who entered college in the past twenty-five years, these are not changes; "that is the way things are." To someone like me who went to college in the thirties, followed by three years of graduate school, and then began to teach in the university in 1945, the changes in the university are remarkable. Let us imagine that we could collect, read, and analyze all addresses of university presidents to incoming freshmen classes and to graduating seniors. I would bet and give very attractive odds that the changes I noted above are rarely mentioned, let alone seriously discussed. The addresses would contain the message that indeed the world has changed, that the university has an obligation to respond to those changes, and that the university is changing but in ways completely consistent with its values, purposes, and traditions. There is truth to these assertions, but a very partial truth and most of the presidents no doubt know that. They do not or cannot talk openly about how the university has changed and is continuing to change in worrisome ways. As one president said to me in a moment of anguish and candor (I paraphrase): "The university is still a cultural treasure but, unlike the national debt, which increases in size, the value of the cultural treasure is slowly decreasing. Yes, we will probably muddle through, but we have already been muddied. The university has changed and it is illusory to say otherwise. The good old days were not all that good, but that is no basis for equating change with progress."

The issue here is not whether you agree or disagree with the judgments of this former president, but rather whether you accept the fact that changes in power relationships—in the culture of the university—have occurred. I put it that way because, generally speaking, people have no barometers to signal that a change has occurred that may or may not continue in strength or pace. Barometers, like thermometers for body temperature, register changes. Whether you regard those changes as good or bad, temporary or not, depends on two factors: previous experience with a particular barometer, and the relationship of that barometer with other barometers. A temperature of 101° unaccompanied by changes in other barometers of bodily function may cause you to conclude "this too shall pass." But if it is accompanied by a yellowing of the eyeballs, a whitening of the stool, and depleted energy, your physician will start to worry about hepatitis. The significance of a single index can be murky indeed. It is the interrelationships among several indices that counts, and even then their significances for the future may be unclear. In regard to the university we have had no such barometers except for those at such a macro level as to be unrevealing if not misleading, such as growth in size of faculty and student body, the addition of new facilities, more and larger research grants, increase in number and size of publications, increase in endowments, and creation of new centers and institutes. If we are interested in the hows and the whys of institutional change, and if we regard, as we must and should, alterations in power relationships as crucial features, those barometers are of little use.

Here is an example, one that has hardly been—and if noted, not weighted—in discussions of university changes. Imagine that it is the decade before 1960 and a student sees the dean of the college to tell him (very few hers) that he wants to take a year's leave to travel or to think and reflect on his future plans or to work for the year in a setting that interests him. In nine out of ten cases, and in some universities it would be ten out of ten, the student would have been told that his request was most irregular and even unacceptable, that the college would not go along with a request it deemed not in the student's academic-educational best interests. The dean might not say it but he would certainly think that that student lacked the appropriate motivation, that he was immature and irresponsible, that he did not want to grow up. Leaving all of this aside, the fact is that very, very few students would have had the courage to make the request either to parents or the dean. You went to college for four consecutive years and that was that. No fooling around with a hiatus. (Medical leave was, of course, another story.)

By the mid sixties, taking a year off "to find yourself" had become desirable, acceptable, and frequent. That change did not come about because college authorities had decided on their own that taking a year off could be intellectually, socially, and educationally enhancing. It came about because students had become more assertive and militant about university rules, regulations, and government and about a lot more outside of the university. The university had rolled with the punch, so to speak, and in so doing underlined the fact that power relationships had changed. The point is not whether you look favorably or not on that particular change but how that change relates to and interacts with other changes in and out of the university. And however you regard that coalescing of changes, you are not exempt from the obligation to respect two interrelated laws: there is no free lunch and there are always unintended consequences.

One more example: In the university there are power relationships and power relationships, which is to say that a few of these relationships, when altered, truly change the character-culture of the university. What makes it difficult to generalize about the universities is that they vary considerably (in the present and past) in these crucial relationships. One of these relationships involves students and faculty (including administration) and the other involves faculty and administration. Both are important but the latter far more than the former because when that relationship undergoes change, the percolating consequences are more widespread and longer lasting. In any complicated, socially stratified institution, power relationships between layers of the hierarchy have their uneasy features. You could say that adversarialism is built into such institutions, at times silent or muted, at other times openly expressed. No one at all knowledgeable about the university will deny the adversarial undercurrents or features of the faculty-administration relationship. And no one (like me) who has spent his or her post World War II years in university arenas is in doubt that when those relationships tilted, as they did, in the direction of greater power to the administration, the basic character of the institution began to change. When the faculty begins to see itself as having decreasing power over educational policy and decisions, the process of the psychological disengagement from the university and its students has begun.[1] It is a cumulative but slow process of institutional change, which may not be recognized as younger faculty, not possessed of memories of earlier times, join the ranks.

The tilt toward increased power of administration is what has been happening in the university; the "top-down" style of governance is more frequent, although universities differ in pace and explicitness of the tilt. For the purposes of this essay it is not relevant whether or not you approve of the tilt. If it is obvious that I do not approve, it is not because I believe that faculty always exercises its powers in wise let alone exemplary and visionary ways. That has not been and will not be the case. Faculty no less than administration can be self-serving, obtuse, irresponsible, and even blind to its different roles in society. But over time they have served to check and balance each other, and the locus of academic responsibility has been clear. Generally speaking, those checks and balances have

[1]When shortly we come (finally) to the object of this essay, the public school, the disengagement process among teachers will be a central point.

begun to erode in many colleges and universities and, if I am right, the verdict of history will not be a favorable one.

My argument is a simple one: if you want an institution, any institution, to change, then you must seek to change the power relationships between what are the equivalents of faculty and administration. You may make other changes that are far from trivial, but if the faculty-administration type of relationship is not altered, the basic character of the institution—that characteristic which if altered has the most pervasive consequences—is likely to survive.

With that as prologue, let us turn to the public schools which have so clearly reflected the post World War II social change, whose inadequacies no one denies and which are an increasing source of societal anxiety into which billions of dollars have been poured in the effort to improve or reform them, and the results, generally speaking, have been nil and by conventional criteria may continue to reflect a worsening of the situation. I used to say that in regard to improving our public schools the more things change the more they remain the same. I now sincerely but reluctantly believe that things will not remain the same; they will get worse.

Why have schools been intractable to change? I have discussed that question in a number of books and I cannot even briefly summarize my answers here. Suffice it to say, as in the case of the university, whatever changes have occurred in our public schools have their origins in World War II. The population explosion, the 1954 desegregation decision and its aftermath, the civil rights movement, the women's liberation movement, demographic changes among students and faculty, the 1975 Education for Handicapped Children's Act, and federal subsidies and programmatic support for schools—each of these, singly and interacting, changed diverse features of our schools, changes which nevertheless produced no improvement in educational outcomes. This is not to say that the culture of the school did not change in discernible ways, but rather that the improvement of educational outcomes was intractable regardless of the intended goal of these changes, a goal about which there was never any mystery or doubt.

How do we explain this intractability? Why is the goal of improving educational outcomes so elusive? Was there something missing or overlooked or avoided in all of these efforts? Was it that these efforts rested on an egregiously mistaken conception of the role of institutional power relationships in sustaining a state of affairs insuring intractability? Let us examine chronologically the different efforts at institutional change, that is, the diagnoses that are powering them.

1. Very soon after the end of World War II it became apparent that cities, especially the larger metropolitan areas, did not have and could not generate the funds necessary to respond adequately to the consequences of the "baby boom." In addition, the marked increase in juvenile delinquency after the war was seen as connected to inadequate school facilities and resources. This led to a momentous decision representing a break with national tradition: the federal government would have to become a factor in public education. That was the beginning of a steady stream of federal support for old and new programs targeted at underserved groups. It is fair to say that it was never the intention of the early legislation to change schools in any significant way. The diagnosis was that money was the problem and the solution; there was nothing fundamentally amiss in the traditions, structure, and culture of the institution we call a school or school system. Give it more funding and it would do the job as well as it had done in prewar days. Few people noted that beginning in the late nineteenth century there had been articulate critics of the public schools who saw the public school as an antieducational rather than an educational institution.

2. Science-technology played a crucial role in winning the war. The need for scientists and engineers would be greater than ever before. That meant that schools, especially high schools, would need to offer a broader spectrum of courses in addition to those in the nonscience areas. This could not be efficiently done or fiscally

possible in our smaller high schools. What was called for was the "comprehensive high school" which would be larger, broader in coverage, and cost-effective. In brief, the high school would be bigger and better; the organizational chart would be more differentiated and complicated. The internal dynamics of the high school were not an object of scrutiny and change. So, for example, there was no discussion about possible adverse educational and personal effects on students and teachers in large, bureaucratic institutions. As in point 1, history was ignored.

3. Beginning in the mid to late fifties a note of criticism aimed at educators was sounded and with each passing year it got louder and shriller. The criticism was that what was basically wrong with our schools was that teachers had an inadequate grasp of the subject matter they taught. As a result, students had a very superficial, misleading, and nonproductive grasp of subject matter, thus shortchanging them in respect to the world of ideas, intellectual skills, range of interests, and career paths. These criticisms came from academics (including presidents of prestigious universities) who looked upon teacher colleges and schools of education as little better than trade schools. At Yale, for example, the president eliminated (with faculty approval) its graduate department of education and replaced it with a master of arts program for would-be teachers in which pedagogy took a distant second place to learning, indeed being steeped in, subject matter. Those kinds of programs proliferated. The criticisms were by no means new, but now it was more assault than criticism. Put starkly, the message or diagnosis was that whatever was wrong with our schools would be taken care of by better-educated teachers. Change the personnel and the system, the school culture, and outcomes would improve. You did not have to change anything else. It was a conception of institutional change grounded in unreality and powered by wish fulfillment. What was indisputable was that dissatisfaction with our schools was picking up steam. The pressure for change was mounting and the 1954 desegregation plus the orbiting of the first space satellite by the Soviet Union in 1956

dramatically increased the pressure for change in our schools, as it also increased the federal role in education.

4.   The first explicit challenge to existing power relationships in schools was the successful attempt, beginning in the late fifties, by teacher unions to gain recognition as bargaining agents for its members. Heretofore, salary, working conditions, school hours, and nonclassroom duties were determined by boards of education and the top layers of administration. The single teacher had the power of one person, which is to say that for all practical purposes the teachers had no power. Militant unions, with a good deal of public support, changed that asymmetry. Teacher salaries were scandalously low, as was morale, two factors that forced teachers to overcome their resistance to joining a labor union. Needless to say, the centers of power in schools fought this development. Today, those in schools who are responsible for making educational policy make sure they read the union contract before proclaiming a policy, and of course union leaders examine those policies to determine their implications for teacher remuneration, hours added to the workday, seniority considerations, and more. Although the union contract inevitably has indirect effects on the substance of educational policy—fiscal matters always do because resources are always limited—the fact is that any union is primarily and exclusively concerned with matters of pay and working conditions, not policy, which is the prerogative of management. Goals, curriculum, evaluation criteria and procedures, initiation or elimination of programs, the organization of the school, length of class sessions, rules governing suspension and expulsion, and more are off-limits in collective bargaining. However, in one very important respect the unions claimed, and initially received, a good deal of public support on the basis that raising teacher's salaries would improve educational outcomes, if only because it would stem the flight of teachers out of the profession and attract the most able people to the profession. Again, the diagnosis of the inadequacies of public schools was that there

was nothing basically wrong with schools that money would not discernibly improve. It was an argument for the status quo.

5. The aftermath of the 1954 desegregation decision, interacting as it did with a militant civil rights movement, gave rise to the second challenge to existing power relationships in schools. "Community control" became a rallying cry, especially in our cities, where racial and ethnic minorities were most vocal and militant. In essence, several changes were demanded. First, the racial-ethnic composition of school personnel had to reflect better the racial-ethnic composition of the community. Second, that kind of change should also be reflected in the racial-ethnic composition of boards of education, who were ultimately accountable for the workings of schools and their educational outcomes. Third, schools should no longer remain socially insensitive, encapsulated enclaves; if war was too important to be left to the generals, education was too important to be left to the professional educator. Who should have the power to do what for whom and for what purposes? Who owns the schools? However clear the challenge to existing power relationships within the school and between the school and the community, it was unclear why the sought-for changes would improve educational outcomes. Just because you change power relationships, it does not follow that educational outcomes will necessarily be improved. In what ways would classrooms change? In what ways would relationships among and between layers of the educational hierarchy change? In what ways would schools become more intellectually and personally stimulating to students and teachers? In what ways would schools take seriously what has been learned about the nature and contexts of productive learning? These questions were never raised because the diagnosis rested, as in the case of subject matter discussed in point 3, on the assumption that changing personnel was the answer to the inadequacies of our schools. And the failure to raise these questions precluded recognition of the possibility that answers to these questions suggested alterations in

power relationships far more radical and transforming than changing personnel.

6.   There have been three revolutions in American education
in which each impacted on every school. The first was the requirement of universal, compulsory education. The second was the 1954
desegregation decision. The third was the 1975 Education for Handicapped Children legislation, which essentially said that schools
must educate *all* children regardless of physical or psychological
handicap. Up until that legislation was passed, schools were relatively free to refuse to accept handicapped children or, when they
did accept some, to segregate them in special classes. The law not
only made refusal illegal, it also said that every effort should be
made to "mainstream" these children, that is, to accommodate them
in the regular classroom, in the "least restrictive environment." The
passage of that law is inexplicable apart from the fact that over the
years a volcano of resentment had been building up in the parents
of these children toward schools they regarded as mammothly insensitive to their needs and plight. That explains the "civil rights" part
of the legislation, which in an amazingly detailed way prevents
schools from making or changing a handicapped child's program
without the participation and approval of the parent. *That* was an
alteration in power relationships, embodied in law, but not applicable to "normal" children. Someone who helped write that legislation said to me, "We wanted to make damn sure that parents had
rights at least coequal with those of school personnel." Generally
speaking, however, and despite the intent of the law, *in practice* the
parents are not coequal.

7.   As the years went by and long-sought improvements were
neither attained nor on the horizon, proposals heretofore given
short shrift began to receive serious attention. One was vouchers to
parents, which would enable them to place their child in any private or parochial school. A second was "charter schools," that is,
schools financed by public funds but for all practical purposes unen-
cumbered by rules and regulations of state departments of educa-

tion. A third was "privatizing": local boards of education literally giving a private corporation responsibility for administering some of its schools, and in the case of the city of Hartford it was the entire system. Whatever the articulated justification for these actions, they were acts of desperation because nothing previously had made a difference. In one or another way they were reactions to the perception that schools as they are have features inimical to innovation and change. What those features were was by no means clear, but in each case it was implicit that the culprit was a stifling educational bureaucracy. (So, for example, as I write these words the governor of New York has made it clear that he would like to eliminate the State Board of Regents and dramatically cut the size of the state department of education.) If explanations of past failures were at best murky, the rationale for why these new actions would bring about the desired change was somewhat less murky but nevertheless murky. As best as I can determine the rationale is that schools are allergic to change, aversive to innovation and risk taking, and the new actions will avoid or dilute these features. The fact is that schools *have* changed, sometimes reluctantly to be sure, in response to past criticisms. Indeed, one could legitimately argue that they have been unusually and unduly accepting of new programs and curricula promising school improvement. Why then have the results been so discouraging? Is it possible, even likely, that past efforts rest on conceptions of institutional change that are incomplete or downright wrong in whole or in part?

The intractable issue goes far beyond schools in that there are other barometers of social change that lead one to suggest that if the intractability continues, the public schools may well become far more socially explosive and destabilizing than ever before. It is not unwarranted alarm to say that our schools are like time bombs waiting to be ignited. And what may trigger that explosion is that our cities have been and will continue to be politically dominated and controlled by racial-ethnic groups.

After World War II the term "urban problem" gained wide

currency. Fifty years later that term, while still applicable, masks what may be better termed a crisis. As the cities become the domain of social-ethnic groups, as their political leaders are frustrated in their efforts to improve educational outcomes, as demands for more financial support from the political leaders of the majorities outside the cities are seen as inadequately responded to, or even in the unlikely situation that those demands are met and *yet* educational outcomes do not improve—all of this taking place in an era in which literacy and electronic-technological sophistication at some minimally acceptable level is necessary and below that minimum the individual can only get jobs at or below the poverty line—crisis is not an unlikely scenario for each aspect of which the barometers spell trouble ahead. This is not an extrapolation from what is now the case because these barometers of an ongoing social change are discrete, that is, each refers to separate social, political, economic, or psychological (violence, crime, drugs) phenomena. If those barometers are discrete, it is their increasing *interactive* effects that are the basis of my scenario. To anyone knowledgeable about our urban schools those interactive effects are plainly evident there.

One thing is not evident, however, about the urban schools, and for two reasons: the appropriate barometer has not been devised, and no one in or around those schools will say publicly what they say privately: that the bulk of urban schools, especially middle and high schools, are lost causes. Why they feel that way is really not relevant here. The brute fact is that they feel that way. And that feeling is fed by puzzlement both about why past efforts have been feckless and what could be done that is not a rerun of the past.

Beginning in 1965, orally and in print, I predicted the steady decline in the educational outcomes of our schools. The reasons were several and one of them was the discrepancy between the rhetoric of reform and privately expressed judgments about the success of reform efforts. What the general public has not grasped is that there is substantial evidence that the policies proclaimed by educational policy makers (boards of education, superintendents and their immediate staff) have little or no impact on what happens in classrooms, a point well developed by Edward Pauly in his book *The Classroom Crucible* (1991). I cannot discuss in this essay the basis for my unfortunately accurate prediction, but I can assure the reader that changing schools is a very complicated affair both conceptually and practically and I do not claim to have covered all related factors. Kenneth Wilson's recent book *Redesigning Education* (1995) is a major contribution to how we should conceptualize school systems, their relation to universities, professional development, and the spread of tested and productive educational practices.[2]

So why the intractability? As I have discussed in my writings, there are two parts to my answer. The first is that reform efforts have left untouched existing power relationships *within* the classroom, *among* layers of the school system's hierarchy, *between* the schools and the university where educators are selected and prepared, and *between* school and parents-community. Absent changes in those power relationships, there is then no basis to expect that what has been learned—and a good deal has been learned—about the nature of and contexts for productive learning can be applied in our schools. Changing power relationships is a necessary (but not sufficient) condition for establishing contexts of productive learning for

---

[2]Other books by Wilson will be forthcoming. A Nobel Prize Laureate, he is someone from the "hard" sciences who has truly immersed himself in the educational reform literature and looked with fresh eyes on what we call the educational system, examining the features it contains that are obstacles to systemic change. He has given examples of ongoing educational programs illustrative of how paradigm shifts can begin to alter the system; he does not oversimplify the social-cultural context with which the system transacts and in which it is imbedded; and he recognizes (wonder of wonders) how mindlessly obtuse and arrogant is the stance, "If you will only do and think the way we in the hard sciences have thought and done, the problems can be solved," yet he uses compellingly the history of science and technology to cull principles that are very much relevant to conceptions of educational change in its cultural, institutional, and individual aspects. And again, wonder of wonders, his thinking forces him to arrive at a time perspective for change that is truly realistic in that it avoids the excesses and pitfalls of wish fulfillment. And finally, he asserts that changes in our schools cannot occur independent of changes in the university.

students *and* teachers, not *only* students. *Teachers cannot create and sustain contexts of productive learning for students if those contexts do not exist for teachers.* That I regard as a glimpse of the obvious, but it is not the first time that the obvious (and its implications) is not taken seriously. Schools as we know them are direct lineal descendants of schools created, structured, and administered to indoctrinate (I use that advisedly) children of the large waves of immigrants who came to this country in the nineteenth century and early decades of this century. It never was in the minds of the citizenry or the educators of those days to base pedagogy on a conception of individuality and productive learning. School was a place to tame and socialize foreigners, and to do it in a *"fiscally efficient"* way, which is why classrooms of fifty and more students were by no means unusual and some high schools had as many as or more than five thousand students. (The use of student "monitors" arose as a "creative" response to size of classrooms.) Granted that classrooms today are smaller (but average number of students is again rising), it is still the case that the pedagogical rationale—when, why, and how students experience learning that is intrinsically interesting and self-sustaining—has not changed and will not change under existing power relationships. Musicians say that the Beethoven Violin Concerto is not for the violin but against it. Schooling is not for productive learning but against it. (Achievement test scores are a barometer of learning, but that is *not* to say that they are barometers of productive learning. Someone said that achievement test scores are excellent baselines for determining the rate of subsequent forgetting, a rate that I am sure the reader will agree is speedy and fits their experience in schools.)

There are revealing exceptions to what I have just said. If twenty years ago it had occurred to me (as it did not) to devise barometers of school change having to do with power relationships I might have noted that two types of "messages" began to be heard in the educational community. One was about structuring the learning experience of students in terms of the rationale for cooperative learning, a rationale that gives more power and responsibility to students instead of the traditional "whole class" method where all wisdom, knowledge and instruction emanate from the all-controlling teacher. There has been a good deal of research on cooperative learning, much of it of good quality, justifying the conclusion that it is superior to the whole-class method both by intellectual and social criteria. Despite this, on a percentage basis cooperative learning takes place in a minuscule number of classrooms. I know of no school system where as a matter of policy cooperative learning is strongly encouraged (not mandated) and which makes it possible for teachers to learn and implement its rationale, which on the surface appears relatively uncomplicated but implementing it appropriately is not. Cooperative learning involves a dramatic change in power relationships in the traditional classroom; it cannot be carried out in cookbook style, although it sometimes is, with the result that the disparity between letter and spirit of the approach is glaring. Similarly, I do not know (that is, there may be exceptions) of a preparatory program for teachers that exposes them to cooperative learning to the degree that they can use it at some minimally acceptable level of competence when they start solo teaching. What would occasion surprise would be if teachers warmly and willingly embraced an approach that required a change in the traditional relationship between teachers and students that they had been taught was right, natural, and proper. Cooperative learning is no panacea but it is a challenge to customary power relationships in the classroom, a challenge that school systems and training programs either do not recognize or that they successfully resist. In the past twenty years there have been hundreds (perhaps thousands) of reports about school reform by commissions and task forces. I have read a fair number of them, most of which have the virtue of making sleeping pills unnecessary. I can recall none that discusses power relationships in the classroom. Nevertheless, the interest in and research on cooperative learning are barometers of a slowly increasing dissatisfaction with existing contexts of classoom instruction and learning.

The second exception is a more explicit challenge to existing power relationships, and on the level of rhetoric it has gained much wider acceptance than cooperative learning. It is a barometer of change that, at least on the level of rhetoric, seeks to change power relationships in an entire school and school system. Briefly, the challenge can be put this way: the inadequacies of our schools derive in large part from the fact that educational policy and the rules and regulations they spawn are the domain of a bureaucratically oriented school system hierarchy who are either not knowledgeable about or who do not have to confront the day-to-day issues and problems of a school's personnel; as a result, teachers feel impotent to articulate policies and make alterations they deem necessary to improve the quality of the educational experience of students; existing power relationships effectively inhibit creative thinking and strengthen risk-aversive attitudes; therefore, in order for teachers to be held realistically accountable for educational outcomes, they should have the most power to determine how a school should be structured and administered, why and how resources will be allocated, and how a school should be related to those outside the school who have a stake in the school, such as parents. The most popular term for this challenge is "site-based management." It is fair to say that there have always been a few schools where the *spirit* of the challenge has been manifest although the *letter* of the challenge has been absent. It is also fair to say, based on my inevitably limited experience, that in the increasing number of instances where site-based management has been adapted or proclaimed as a policy, it is the exception rather than the rule that does not deserve the noun charade, that is, the letter and spirit of the challenge are aspects of game playing; the "right" kinds of things are said, new forums for discussion and decision making are created, but no one is in doubt that "power" resides where it has always resided.

I bring attention to these exceptions not because they are barometers of institutional change that are a basis for optimism—they are not—but because they signify a degree of recognition of the view that no significant improvement in educational outcomes can be expected unless there are changes in the existing governance structure of schools *and* the classroom. Those changes, as I said earlier, are necessary but not sufficient prerequisites for improved educational outcomes because there is a prior question: power for what overarching conception of the purpose of schooling? Changing power relationships means just that: power relationships have changed. If those changes are not in the service of a clear and concrete conception of productive learning, we end up confirming that the more things change the more they remain the same. Cooperative learning begins to address the question; what passes for site based management does not. That prior question, I fear, will not get raised, let alone seriously discussed, as frustration with the inadequacies of our schools will predictably increase and will lead people to become more apathetic at the same time they become more receptive to the idea that the public schools as we have known them have outlived their usefulness.[3]

Relevant here is an interesting contrast between universities and the public schools. The two major purposes of the university are to contribute to knowledge and to convey that knowledge to students. Earlier in this essay I noted that since World War II both purposes have been directly and indirectly influenced by alterations in power relationships. However, despite these changes, and indeed as a consequence of these changes (government and foundation support, competition, and considerations of status and prestige) there has been no change in the university's commitment to scholarly and

---

[3]The reader who believes that our suburban schools are enclaves of productive learning betrays an appalling ignorance of those schools. Equating high achievement test scores as indicative of productive learning is as justified as equating income with happiness.

research activities. If anything, that purpose and commitment became stronger, and exposed what had long been the case: in the selection and promotion of faculty, teaching effectiveness was (is) a distant second as a criterion to those of quantity and quality of scholarly and research publications. In practice, the overarching purpose of the university is to create and sustain those conditions and facilities that enable the individual faculty member to discharge that overarching purpose. It is an instance in which despite changes in power relationships in the institution the commitment to an overarching purpose has been maintained, even gotten stronger, not infrequently to the detriment of the quality of teaching. And protecting that commitment has been possible only because the bulk of faculty and administrators agree with the overarching purpose, which at least in faculty decision making meetings is articulated in the most clear language. Whether you agree with that priority is not relevant here; the point is that it is strongly held, articulated with clarity, and its consequences for practical action and judgment are taken seriously (which is not to say they are not without problems, but that is another story). In regard to our public schools, there is no such agreement about an overarching purpose, a purpose which if not given the top priority makes other important purposes far less than attainable. Today, for all practical purposes, the purpose of schools is to insure by use of conventional achievement tests that students have absorbed a body of knowledge and that they possess certain academic skills. Even so, school personnel are far from agreement about such a purpose and evaluation methods, although for the most part they do not offer any alternative, and they are aware that the school system is organized, directed, and judged by how well students perform on tests. It is the absence of an alternative overarching purpose, about which there would be agreement and the practical consequences of which would be relatively clear, that explains why I have emphasized in my writings that changing power relationships is a necessary but not sufficient condition for improving educational outcomes. Absent a compelling overarching purpose, changing power relationships will not, cannot, impact on educational outcomes. That, unfortunately, is the story of past and present school reform efforts. They lack an alternative vision and purpose. They are not informed by anything like serious acceptance of productive learning.

Let me be concrete. For the past several years I have said to and asked of a number of groups the following: Schools have a number of major purposes. However major these purposes they are not coequal in importance. What is the one overarching purpose of education? When your child is graduated from high school, what is the one characteristic you want your child to have? As I said, there is more than one major purpose, but is there one you value the most, regardless of whether he or she is headed for college?

I have put that question to groups of parents and educators. The first reaction is one of silence. People are not in the habit of scaling the purposes of schooling. Almost always I have had to break the awkward silence by saying, "Let me give you my answer. When a child is graduated from high school, I want that child to continue to want to be curious about and to want to learn more about self, others, and the world. If that curiosity and degree of motivation stamp him or her, then the school has done well its most important task." In every discussion that has followed, no one ever, even subtly, disagreed with what I said. In all groups, but particularly groups of educators, the participants articulated observations and opinions supporting what research has concluded: As you go up the grades students experience the classroom and school as a boring, stifling, uninteresting place, a form of legally sanctioned child abuse. With rare exceptions schools are not places for capitalizing on and sustaining the curiosity, awe, and wonder they possessed when they started schooling. Until this state of affairs is generally recognized and seriously confronted, none of the desirable purposes of schooling stands a chance of being realized. I said that in 1965 and there has been no reason to alter that judgment and prediction.

The post World War II social change invaded and altered the

university and the public school, and in very important ways. In regard to the university, those changes have not all been beneficial, depending on your point of view. Nevertheless, what the university regards as its overarching purpose has been minimally weakened, if at all. And I hear no cries from the general public that that overarching purpose should take a back seat to any other purpose. In regard to the public schools, however, the cries for change are loud, clear, persistent, and insistent. The public wants and demands institutional change. What the public does not grasp, what frustrated politicians (I do not use that word pejoratively) do not comprehend, what the educational community has failed to articulate is that there is no agreed-upon overarching purpose which, if not realized, rules out the realization of all other purposes. The university knows what central purpose it protects. The public school does not have such a central purpose to protect. If it protects anything, it is the status quo. It has learned nothing from its past and it has no conceptual basis for an alternative future.

The name Edward Deming has become a familiar one in the American private sector and in university business schools. In Japan, Deming has the status of a secular saint because it was he who after World War II persuaded Japanese industrial leaders to base their efforts to rebuild a shattered economy on the basis of his rationale for total quality management, the results of which we are quite familiar with. It took the catastrophe of a total defeat in war for the Japanese to consider alternative ways of rebuilding. Stated all too briefly, Deming's rationale had three crucial aspects: power relationships within the organization would have to change, workers as resources would have to be redefined, and the driving force suffusing and controlling all steps in policy formulation, decision making, and production would be *quality of product*, not quantity or even profit margin. Quality product and customer satisfaction were inseparable considerations. While this was going on in Japan, their counterparts in the United States proceeded to disregard, as they had almost always done, both quality and customer satisfaction. It was

Henry Ford who said that you can have any color Ford you wanted as long as it was black.

If Deming has become well known in the United States, that does not mean that what he stands for has been warmly embraced and appropriately implemented in other than a small number of companies. Institutional change is not simply a matter of accepting new ideas or rationales. What is required is that degree of understanding that prepares you to withstand the predictable sturm and drang that is a consequence of a new overarching value (quality, not quantity) that is organizationally radical in its requirements. The ultimately most productive "bottom line" is *quality* of outcome.

There are a few people in the educational community who have seen the significance of Deming's rationale (and accomplishments) for the direction that educational reform should take. And they make it clear that the driving power in such reform is what I have called a riveting on productive learning, on the social contexts that are necessary to arouse and sustain a combination of intellectual curiosity and striving, a sense of personal worth and growth, and a commitment to the educational enterprise. Those are not "pie in the sky" generalities, empty of substance, and impossible to "measure." I have seen schools, pitifully few in number, which to a pessimist like me were sources of inspiration. They were what they were despite many obstacles the school system in which they were embedded presented. I said "were" because some of them succumbed to the traditions and pressures of the system.

A note for the historical record. Everything I have said was said by John Dewey a hundred years ago. Dewey never really systemized what his ideas meant for how schools and school systems should be organized. Dewey was crystal clear about what productive learning meant for the classroom, but he never directly confronted how that classroom could be created and survive in a system he knew was antithetical to productive learning. Before or since, no one more than Dewey foresaw the potentially destabilizing and socially divisive effects of an educational system and process in which productive learning was not the overarching purpose. *All of the ingredients in Deming's systematic rationale can be found in one or another of Dewey's writings. Also, as few people today know, beginning early in this century Dewey became the secular saint in the Japanese educational community.*

Hundreds of volumes have been written about the post World War II social change. In very few of them is there serious consideration of the possibility that future historians will conclude that the failure of the public schools to change consistent with the ideas of a Dewey and Deming contributed mightily to social upheavals. Absent that change, it is a prediction I am reluctantly forced to continue to make.

12

. . . .

Cities and Schools

I have no intention in this concluding essay of offering a scenario about how social change will be played out. I have tried to point to some (not all) of those aspects of the social change, especially those that seemed to me to have had their origins or reinforcements in the war years. In so doing I was quite aware that although today those aspects are, to me at least, clear and even compelling, I should not assume that they will be of equal significance in how the social change will get played out. That will be an assessment that future historians will make, and even those assessments will undergo change as one worldview is supplanted by a new one. But, like every reader of these essays, I am not indifferent to the social change. Some things strike me as more important than others for the future. And, again like every reader, I have values and hopes about what that future should be. But not everyone shares my values and hopes. Some view the social change as an unmitigated disaster, a defeat of their values and hopes. Some view it as the dawning of a new world in which their values and hopes stand a chance of realization. And then there are those who do not know what to think, how to judge the tomorrows by the todays. If a poll taker asked me into which of the three categories I put myself, honesty would require that I say "all of the above."

Why is part of me in the unmitigated disaster category? My succinct answer—a full answer would require a book—is that the

American melting pot, far from melting, is getting colder, its elements more encapsulated and rigid, the magnetic force that might
keep them together losing its potency, as if each element is governed by different principles. That is the way I view the social scene
sometimes. The need or desire to "melt" is far weaker than it has
ever been. The rhetoric, of course, says otherwise, but it is largely
empty rhetoric.

Why is part of me in the second category? My succinct answer
here is that America has become dimly aware that it is hoist by its
own social-moral-political petard. The Declaration of Independence
and the founding Constitution of 1787 proclaimed the primacy of
two interrelated obligations. The first was the obligation of the individual to strive to become what he wants to become. The second
was that the individual has obligations to the collectivity, that is,
to participate as a member of that collectivity in ways and on the
basis of laws and principles that harmonized the obligations, to self
and the collectivity, after they conflicted. The founding fathers were
amazing realists. They had no illusions about the perfectibility of
people. They knew most of what needed to be known about the
negative and positive consequences of power, individual or collective. They devised rules of the game governing relationships among
the individual, groups, and the larger collectivity. You could write
two histories of the United States. One would be a seamy history of
failures that ignored the spirit and letter of the two documents. The
other would be a glorious history of successful efforts to put flesh on
the bones of those documents. The post World War II social change
has contributed to both histories.

Of one thing I am sure: however the social change develops,
what will be fateful will be what happens in and to our cities and
their metropolitan surrounds. Crime, violence, racial unrest and
conflict, drugs, gangs, unemployment, a growing underclass—all of
these and more are associated in the minds of the public, inside and
outside cities, with a sense of impotence and anxiety. Impotence
because nothing that has been tried seems to have been even min-

imally successful and no one has faith that much can be done, especially at a time when the public has been made aware that federal and state governments are forced to reduce their budgets, except in regard to beefing up police departments and building new prisons. The anxiety is more personal and focused: cities are not safe places, especially after working hours.

The above paragraph was written the day before (June 4, 1995) I watched the segment on CBS's "Sixty Minutes" about crime and corruption in the New Orleans police department specifically and in the city in general. If what the viewer was told was 50 percent valid, it mightily reinforced the already accepted public view that cities were hopeless dens of iniquity and social disorganization. One of the interviewees, a former policeman who is in jail for bank robbery, said that the picture the interviewer (Mike Douglas) had been given by others was a gross understatement. For people who believe that our cities are out of control, that they are indeed intractable to remedial efforts, the program was proof positive for that belief.

The program was about police and political corruption. The mayor and police chief plaintively (and pathetically) "defended" themselves by saying that the problem in New Orleans is no different than it is in other cities, although they literally could say nothing in response to the question: "But why does New Orleans have the highest crime rate in the country?" Police commissioners elsewhere have been more insightful and forthcoming in that they say something like the following: "We draw our officers from the different and many groups in our cities, groups disadvantaged or heretofore discriminated against by our department and society generally. The bulk of people in these groups, whatever their problems and grievances, do not resort to criminal behavior, although it is all around them: sex, violence, drugs, you name it. Like it or not, that's the pool from which we have to select. So we get some who are rotten apples, and police work being what it is in the cities plays to their worst inclinations. Police departments reflect cities, their best and worst features, and their worst features are on the front page of the newspapers everyday." The CBS program targeted the police. What it said about cities was virtually nil, leaving many viewers to conclude, I am sure, that reforming police departments would have more than a transient effect. The history of police departments, at least in the post World War II era, says otherwise.

I have no doubt that in regard to our cities there are historians who will say, "So what else is new? It has always been the case that cities have been cauldrons of social unrest, social disorganization, crime, counter-cultural trends and groups, changing lifestyles, and foreign or rural or religious or political immigrants or refugees giving voice and force to new ideas. Granted, this was a mixed bag with pluses and minuses, costly in lives, fortunes, and happiness, at the same time that out of those cities came ideas and social movements that shaped the modern world. Whatever is progressive in the modern world—the idea of religious and political freedom, individual rights, the importance and right of self-expression, even the freedom of science to go where it has to go—had their origins primarily in cities. Cities changed the larger society, not vice versa. Of course, our cities today are worrisome, but that does not mean that the consequences of what is happening in them will over the long run be more socially negative than positive. On a historical-actuarial basis you have to bet that over the long term the positive will outweigh the negative. The actors are different today, the script is different, and the audience is not local but global; but the themes are what they always have been: equality, justice, fraternity."

Historically, actuarially, what the historian says is not without justification, which is why I would tell the poll maker to put me in all three categories. But, there is always a but, I have nagging thoughts. The first is that the historian believes that humanity has been on an upward course of progress, notwithstanding the fact that this has been the bloodiest century ever, that today there are forty plus wars going on on this earth, and that there are groups and countries seeking to possess unprecedented weapons of destruction. You do not have to be a nihilist or cynic to be unable to embrace visions of "progress." Was World War II like World War I? Would a World War III be like World War II? The stance "this too shall pass" is not convincing whether applied to war or to our cities. If our cities have never been tranquil places, they contain today a degree of destabilization, of open-group conflicts, of generational gulfs of violence, that is opposite of static.

Very soon after World War II we began to hear about the "urban problem" and juvenile delinquency. Efforts to deal with these issues were undertaken and with each passing decade—to say each passing year would not be hyperbole—the amount of expenditures increased at a very fast clip. The result was that in 1994 Congress passed the largest crime bill ever, much of it for new prisons and more policemen. Congress proclaimed, and much of the public believed, that the legislation would reduce crime and quiet the fears of people, promising that they would have a safer existence. Why what has been tried before and failed should have a discernibly more successful effect this time—it *may* have some effect—escapes me. The fact is that the legislation revealed that Congress did not know what else to do except to do a lot more of the same. It was not the first time in the post World War II years that America wanted to believe that our most troubling social problems could be "solved" by throwing money at them, confirming Mencken's quip that for every important problem there is a simple answer that is wrong.

The small state of Connecticut has the highest per capita income among the states. Its three largest cities are well in the top ten of cities of their size for the number of people at or below the poverty line. I have lived in and around New Haven for almost half a century, and I have familiarity with Hartford and Bridgeport. That these cities have changed racially, ethnically, and economically is something I have witnessed in more than a visual sense because in the decade of the sixties I was actively and daily a part of the "war on poverty"—indeed, the federal war on poverty was heavily influenced and shaped by the programs an activist New Haven mayor had initiated for his deteriorating city. Remnants of these efforts, for all practical purposes, do not exist. What does exist is a news-worthy crime rate, a flourishing drug industry, the buildings of the two major department stores (Macy's and Malley's) empty and boarded up, a self-defeating tax rate, and an embittered white, black, and Hispanic citizenry. (The story in Hartford and Bridge-port is very similar.) The flight from New Haven began after the war, its loss of population has been steady.

So what else is new? One is the pervasive belief that the city is unrescuable, a belief that people are not able or willing to state pub-licly although in private conversation that is what they say. More than a few white people blame the attitudes, outlooks, values, and lifestyles of the blacks and Hispanics, and some quite agree with the "Bell Curve" explanation, unaware that that explanation was even more explicitly articulated when their immigrant parents or grand-parents came to this country. At best these people will say, "If our parents and grandparents made it on their own, that is what blacks and Hispanics have to do." That is what an undetermined number of those in these racial groups also believe—although few will say it out loud—but even they believe what almost all in these groups believe: white people do not comprehend the obstacles these groups face, the racism (subtle and otherwise) that exists, the force of a his-tory the crippling consequences of which are psychologically in the present, and that the price the larger society has paid will pale before the price that will be paid if things go on as they are. The bitterness is not disguised, the need to hope is not quite extin-guished, and the fear that their young will fall victim to crime, drugs, and violence is strong.

What is new are the interactive effects of the belief that the city is intractable to improvement, and the perception by these racial-ethnic groups that that belief is a self-fulfilling prophecy. The inter-active effects are those that the youth in these groups inchoately perceive, that is, you do not get the goodies of this world by fol-lowing the rhetoric of the larger society.

An interesting and instructive aspect of the New Haven story concerns the Yale–New Haven relationship. The brief way of describing it is that until relatively recently Yale was in but not of New Haven. Yale's constituency was not New Haven. Yale considered itself a national university and the sources of its endowment testified to that. If New Haven was nothing like a gift in the eyes of Yale, the university considered itself an unalloyed gift to the city. New Haven was proud of Yale but psychologically and socially its citizens saw Yale as in another world, as halls of Ivy which they would never see from the inside except when one took the guided tour when one heard of its wondrous resources and the accomplishments of its renowned faculty. There were sources of tension, of course, due mostly to exuberant, impulsive students. From the standpoint of the two officialdoms town-gown relations were cool but cordial. Communication was clear, at least from Yale's standpoint: New Haven has its tasks and purposes, and Yale has its tasks and purposes, and they did not overlap.

Beginning in the 1930s and accelerating during the war years, Yale found itself largely bordered by a growing black ghetto. This poor and not very pretty city initially suggested, requested, and later demanded that the university, which was located in the Broadway–Forty Second Street area of New Haven (although the university looked like Park Avenue), should in lieu of its tax exempt status make a yearly contribution to the city, which provided the university with police, fire, and other services. Yale declined to do so. By the early 1960s the black ghettos had increased, its leaders had became more militant, and one of the objects of its anger was Yale, which they saw as very rich, very aloof, and unconcerned with the needs of the city. They were not proud of Yale, they were disdainful of it (New Haven was one of the Black Panther strongholds). The sixties have been called the sizzling decade. That was glaringly the case in New Haven and therefore at Yale.

The story is a complicated one, parts of which I have related elsewhere (1988). Perhaps the most "objective" way of suggesting what happened is to state that with each passing year Yale's budget for security exponentially escalated. Yale became a fortress surrounded by a hostile city whose racial-ethnic composition had dramatically changed. Only in the last few years has the Yale leadership confronted the fact, the brute fact, that what happens to New Haven predictably will impact on the university. Yale has taken steps, largely financial, to demonstrate its desire to be helpful and supportive. The overall outlook varies from murky to gloomy.[1] That is the opinion of many people. For reasons I shall give in a little while, my outlook varies from gloomy to dangerous. (I know I am an old man and all that may suggest but I developed and wrote about my outlook when I was much younger. I have been wrong about many things, but not about our cities.)

One more thing about the New Havens of this world: by any criterion of performance their schools are deplorable. Beginning in 1965, I have written and explained why this is so, why it has to be so (Sarason, 1965). In my earlier writings I managed to suppress or modulate the depths of my pessimism, but in successive publications I could no longer hide what I truly believed, which is why I titled my 1990 book *The Predictable Failure of Educational Reform*. I predicted that failure a quarter of a century before.

In what follows I am in no way suggesting that our cities will be "saved" by radically changing schools as we have known them. It is much more complicated than that. *But I consider it axiomatic that our cities will not be desirably changed apart from radical educational change.* It may surprise readers to be told that that axiom is being accepted by an increasing number of educators who have been driven by experience to conclude that money is not the primary problem. Few will say that out loud when the public is listening, but in private conversations and in the quiet of their nights their view is a hopeless one and most have no alternatives to suggest. Of course, there

---

[1]The Yale–New Haven story is by no means idiosyncratic. There are many colleges and universities in urban areas where the story is similar, if not identical. It is also similar to the situation of many hospitals and medical centers.

are schools in scandalously inadequate facilities with immorally sparse resources, that is, situations that should not be allowed to exist. Unfortunately, it does not follow that with spanking new facilities those schools will in the future produce better outcomes, except minimally, if that. There are many confirming instances, the most notable of which is Kansas City, Missouri, and that is notable because of the amount of money the city and state had to expend to comply with court orders.

I cannot here go over ground I have covered in my previous writings, and I cannot assume that other than a few readers are familiar with my work. Nor can I assume that readers will have been aware that some of the most troubling aspects of the post World War II social change were early or plainly seen in our schools. What was happening in our cities was happening in our schools. The early warning signs were there, but just as Yale paid no heed to what was happening in New Haven, the diverse professionals grouped under the rubric the "public policy disciplines" were incapable, indeed uninterested, in schools. That is also true for the social sciences generally; historically they have never considered schools to be central to their interests and purposes. How do parents raise and influence their children? What are the nature and consequences of social class? How do we explain deviant behavior? How does personality "arise" and develop? How do people make decisions? What is intelligence and how do we determine the relative strengths of heredity and environment? How does being in this or that group affect an individual's behavior? Can we identify the conditions in which attitudes get changed? These (and more) are important, legitimate questions. Most of them are potentially productive for what happens to the children and the adults in schools, but you would not know it from reading the literature in the field. Nor would you know that in the university the bulk of the disciplines look down on department or school of education as something that no one would miss if they went out of existence, that is, granted that schools need personnel and that society (or the state legislature) requires us to

prepare those personnel, we do not have to like it, let alone participate in that preparation. In intent and principle that is the way
Yale saw New Haven. I am not picking on Yale (for which I have
much to be grateful) because the conditions I am discussing are true
nationally.

Am I suggesting to people in the university that they drop what
they are doing and start studying schools? Of course not, just as I
would not suggest to Yale that it devote its considerable material
and intellectual resources to the rescuing of New Haven. No, what
I am suggesting is that the social sciences specifically and the university generally, explicitly and publicly justify what they do as contributing to the public good and welfare. How and when that
contribution will be manifest are far from predictable; that is guaranteed by the complexity of the problems being studied. But "we"
do not do what "we" do for the hell of it. "We" want to contribute
to the kind of society that "we" are and/or that we want to become;
"we" want to be able to discover how the ills and problems of individuals and/or the society can be explained and ameliorated even
if the knowledge "we" gain is seen as radical, upsetting, or discom-
bobulating to conventional ways of thinking and acting.

I agree completely. But what if what I (and others) have said
about schools and our cities is approximately correct? What if our
cities continue to deteriorate in specified ways? Are they already so
far down the slippery slope that will lead to social conflict and
upheaval with consequences that even those who look favorably on
such upheaval will have cause to regret? And what if I am right that
efforts to "save" our cities, past and present, have failed and will fail
if our schools are not literally transformed?

In this century there have been three times when many of the
people I am addressing willingly redirected the contents and methods and sites of their work, with the result that in two of the
instances their fields forever changed in ways that the verdicts of
history have judged positively. World War I and II are two of the
instances. The perception that the country was faced with threats

to its goals and values was a spur to the change. The third time was not an event but the decade of the sixties when every major social institution was affected by and forced to deal with open conflicts centering on race, civil rights, poverty, and the cities, generational gulfs, and schools that were clearly inadequate and racially segregated. Many in the academy sought to be "relevant," a word that was a rallying cry of militant youth clamoring for change. With the best of intentions many members of the academic community sought to be helpful and in diverse ways. The verdicts of history have not been positive. Indeed, for many of the participants, their participation exposed them to the "real world" in ways that were the basis for their conclusion that they would do well to retreat, to leave the scene. They learned a lot about the messiness of the real world, the inevitable destabilization that accompanies social change, and the inadequacies of the theories and research in their fields either for understanding or coping with the social change. It was an orderly retreat to a more familiar and protecting setting. If they learned anything it was that the important problems in this real world are not capable of a once-and-for-all solution; those problems do not go away, they fester, and these participants hope and pray that the social change will not affect them personally and professionally in the future as it did in the past. I am not being critical. They were simply unprepared, as they are unprepared now, for how to think and deal with those problems. And yet, although many of them will not say it publicly, they are plagued with the feeling that things are out of control, they may get worse, and where is all this taking us? In these respects these academics are no different than a general public distrustful of those with power and authority, puzzled by the failures of past remedial efforts, fearful and condemning of what they hear, see, and read about daily crime in cities—all of this feeding the belief that what Myrdal before World War II called "An American Dilemma" is showing signs of becoming "The American Social Earthquake." And the signs are coming from the cities and their schools.

In an all too brief way I shall give the core of the complex argument that schools as they are (and have been) have to be literally transformed. That core is not all that complex, but if taken seriously the consequences are far more than complex. The transformation that core requires has to start now, but its fruits will not be apparent except over several decades. Anyone who thinks that schools can be transformed in a matter of a few years is like those in 1954 who believed that school segregation would be a thing of the past in five, ten, or fifteen years. Famous last words.

1.   We have learned a lot about the contexts that facilitate productive learning, and by productive learning I mean the motivation to acquire knowledge and skills in ways as to motivate the individual to want to learn more. Productive learning is far more than an exercise of memory, or of acquiring knowledge and skills with the aim of satisfying the requirements of others (read adults) at the expense of personal significance. As Dewey said a century ago, knowledge is external, knowing is internal, a sense of personal possession.

2.   To foster productive learning, you start with where the child is: his or her interests, questions, curiosity. Ignore those aspects, start where *you* want to start, "pour in" what *you* want the child to learn, pace that instruction according to a predetermined curriculum and the pressure of the school calendar, ignore the inevitable and brute fact of individuality—proceed in that way and you have a prescription for making wanting to learn a sometime thing, if that. The modal classroom is a dull, uninteresting, boring affair both for students and teachers, and for children in our city schools that is an understatement. As they go from the elementary school to the larger middle school to the even larger high school, wanting to learn is near extinction, as is the sense that someone has recognized and taken their individuality into account. Absentee rates climb as does the dropout rate. For young people, wanting to read makes as much sense as wanting to learn math, or science, or history.

3.   It was *never* in the minds of those who promoted compulsory education that the aim of education was to respect, nurture,

and exploit a child's individuality, that is, to enter his or her world as the educational starting point *from which that child can begin to enter and comprehend your world.* The purpose was to tame and socialize. However schools have changed since then, schools are still primarily places where you start not with where the child is but where the teacher wants or expects that child to be. The classroom is organized on the basis of the top-down theory of management and production. The classroom, school, and school system reflect that way of thinking. How teachers regard children is the way school administrators (principals, assistant superintendents) view teachers, and at the apex of the pyramid is the superintendent and the board of education, seen by all below it as kin to Kafka's Castle.

4.   Children today, more than ever before, know there is a fascinating world outside the school building. They not only know that, they want to understand and be in that world. The encapsulated classroom in the encapsulated school is a mammoth barrier to capitalizing on children's interest for their intellectual-educational growth and sense of competence and worth. What children want to learn and experience, what they can learn to experience, should never be the *sole* basis for the organization and purposes of the educational program. But to say that in no way justifies ignoring what children want, can, and should learn and experience in a variety of sites outside the school.

That is as bare-bones a statement of the core as I can write. Others before me have said similar things. The point is that once that core was accepted and taken seriously, the transformations our schools would have to undergo would become as obvious as they are complex, and it would begin to be clear why so few people disagree with that core at the same time they regard its implications as the stuff of which fantasy is comprised. The fact is that you can find a classroom here and a school there—some of them in the ghettos of our cities—where they have taken that core seriously. (In my experience they have with rare exceptions been elementary schools.) And it is also the case that these occasional classrooms and schools have done what they have done despite the school system and not because of it, so that when their creators and sustainers leave, stultifying tradition takes over.

What about our suburban schools? The reader would be quite wrong in concluding that they acknowledge and take the core seriously. They do not. The most comprehensive and scathing assessment of the American high school was made in the thirties by a group of educators who knew the game and score (Aiken, 1942). Their critique is as applicable today as it was then. When in the late fifties and sixties there was a wailing and bemoaning of the failures of our schools to nourish and sustain student interest in science, it was as if that earlier assessment had never been made. Suburban schools are only minimally (if that) different from city schools in their organization, administration, and conception of learning. Generally speaking, the graduates of those schools no longer possess the awe, wonder, and curiosity—or the desire to learn—they had when they began schooling. Some readers will find that hard to believe, in which case I can only offer two suggestions. First, start reading, an activity that is no longer fashionable for high school students. Second, visit these schools, talk to teachers and students, sit in classrooms, determine the frequency with which students appear interested, engaged, intellectually alive, and so on, as opposed to just going through the motions.

Suburban schools do not contain the social dynamite that is in our city schools. And that, of course, is my point. As long as too many students in our city schools see their schools as not for them, as having nothing to do with life as they know it outside of school, as directing them to a future that is not theirs, as making "learning and education" empty of personal significance, those schools are contributing, albeit unwittingly, both to the destabilization of cities and to the defeat of attempts to improve them; if they once were the effects of social change, they are now a cause of it, and in a worrisome way.

Am I an alarmist? A prophet of gloom and doom? An old man indulging nostalgia for the good old days? I grew up in Newark, New

Jersey. I knew there was a *contained* black ghetto and the word I italicized tells the story: "That's the way it is, and that is the way it will be, however unjust I may feel it is in light of my radical political views." That Newark would change beyond recognition in the next three decades was a possibility that could not occur to me. That after the war there would be riots in the previously all-white Belmont Avenue section, and that part of it would have burned to the ground—*that* was the stuff of nightmarish fantasy. That the state of New Jersey in 1994 would seek to take over a scandalously inadequate Newark school system—*that* would have been fantasy to pre World War II me.

In regard to our cities, the post World War II social change has exposed the size and potency of the social dynamite in our cities. If it has exposed that dynamite, the many well-intentioned efforts to diffuse it have failed, and nowhere is that failure more egregiously clear than in our schools. In 1994, Walter Annenberg made the unprecedented gift of half a billion dollars to our largest cities to change and improve their schools. In his brief talk explaining why he was making the gift he was refreshingly clear that he was mightily anxious about the increasing degree of violence and group conflicts that are daily fare in so many schools. Annenberg deserves more than a few brownie points in a heavenly existence. Unfortunately, neither he nor President Clinton, who was standing next to him when the gift was announced, know the educational game and score. Money is not, initially at least, either the problem or the solution. The post World War II social change has been a pervasive one, which is not to say that its effects have been uniformly positive. In the matter of our schools, especially city schools, the social change has had negative consequences, if only because nothing has discernibly altered the core, the rationale, the philosophy, call it what you will, of schools.

References

Aiken, W. A. *The Story of the Eight–Year Study with Conclusions and Recommendations*. New York: HarperCollins, 1942.

APA Working Group on Investigation of Memories of Childhood Abuse. *The National Psychologist*, 1994, 3(6), 7.

Becker, H. S., Geer, E., Hughes, E. C., and Strauss, A. L. *Boys in White*. Chicago: University of Chicago Press, 1961.

Beckett, S. *Waiting for Godot*. New York: Grove Press, 1954.

Blankenhorn, D. *Fatherless America*. New York: Basic Books, 1995.

Coontz, S. *The Way We Never Were*. New York: Basic Books, 1992.

Dershowitz, A. Commencement Address, Brooklyn College. Brooklyn, N.Y.: *Brooklyn College Magazine*, Winter 1995.

Dollard, J. *Criteria for the Life History, with Analysis of Six Notable Documents*. New Haven, Conn.: Yale University Press, 1935.

Engelhardt, T. *The End of Victory Culture*. New York: Basic Books/HarperCollins, 1995.

Guralnick, P. *The Last Train to Memphis*. New York: Little Brown, 1994.

Kerouac, J. *On the Road*. New York: New American Library, 1957.

Kinsey, A. C., and others. *Sexual Behavior in the Human Male*. Philadelphia, Pa.: Saunders, 1948.

Klinkenborg, V. "The Ideal Family on Film." *The New York Times*, Arts and Leisure Section, January 29, 1995.

Lynd, R. S. *Knowledge for What? The Place of Social Science in American Culture*. Princeton, N.J.: Princeton University Press, 1970.

Lynd, R. S., and Lynd, H. M. *Middletown: A Study in American Culture*. Orlando, Fla.: Harcourt Brace Jovanovich, 1956.

Lynd, R. S., and Lynd, H. M. *Middletown in Transition: A Study in Cultural Conflicts*. Orlando, Fla.: Harcourt Brace Jovanovich, 1982.

Maynard, J. *Looking Back. A Chronicle of Growing Up Old in the Sixties*. New York: Avon Books, 1972.

Nisbet, R. *Social Change and History*. New York: Oxford University Press, 1969.

Nisbet, R. *The Degradation of the Academic Dogma*. New York: Basic Books, 1971.

Pauly, E. *The Classroom Crucible*. New York: Basic Books, 1991.

Reage, P. *The Story of O*. New York: Grove Press, 1965.

Reik, T. *Surprise and the Psychoanalyst*. New York: Dutton, 1937.

Reik, T. *Listening with the Third Ear: The Inner Experience of a Psychoanalyst*. New York: Farrar, Straus & Giroux, 1983. (Originally published 1948.)

Reynolds, D. "Review of *Walt Whitman's America: A Cultural Biography*." *The New York Times*, May 29, 1995.

St. Jorre, J. de. "The Unmasking of O." *New Yorker Magazine*, August 1, 1994.

Salinger, J. D. *The Catcher in the Rye*. New York: Bantam Books, 1968. (Originally published 1951.)

Sarason, S. B. *Psychological Problems in Mental Deficiency*. New York: Harper & Row, 1949.

Sarason, S. B. *Work, Aging, and Social Change*. New York: Free Press, 1977.

Sarason, S. B. *The Culture of the School and the Problem of Change* (2nd ed.). Longwood, Mass.: Allyn and Bacon, 1983.

Sarason, S. B. *Schooling in America: Scapegoat and Salvation*. New York: Free Press, 1983.

Sarason, S. B. *Caring and Compassion in Clinical Practice*. San Francisco: Jossey-Bass, 1985. (Republished in 1995 by Jason Aronson, 230 Livingston Street, Northvale, N.J.)

Sarason, S. B. *The Making of an American Psychologist*. San Francisco: Jossey-Bass, 1988.

Sarason, S. B., Davidson, K., and Blatt, S. *The Preparation of Teachers: An Unstudied Problem in Education*. Cambridge, Mass.: Brookline, 1989. (Initially published in 1962.)

Sarason, S. B. *The Challenge of Art to Psychology*. New Haven, Conn.: Yale University Press, 1990a.

Sarason, S. B. *The Predictable Failure of Educational Reform*. San Francisco: Jossey-Bass, 1990b.

Sarason, S. B. *Letters to a Serious Education President*. Newbury Park, Calif: Corwin Press, 1993.

Sarason, S. B. *The Case for Change: Rethinking the Preparation of Educators*. San Francisco: Jossey-Bass, 1993.

Sarason, S. B. *Psychoanalysis, General Custer, and the Verdicts of History*. San Francisco: Jossey-Bass, 1994.

Sarason, S. B. *You Are Thinking of Teaching?* San Francisco: Jossey-Bass, 1994.

Sarason, S. B. *Parental Involvement and the Political Principle: Why the Existing Governance Structure of Schools Should Be Abolished*. San Francisco: Jossey-Bass, 1995a.

Sarason, S. B. *School Change: The Development of a Personal Point of View*. New York: Teachers College Press, 1995b.

Schorske, C. *Fin-De-Siècle Vienna*. New York: Knopf, 1980.

Skinner, B. F. *Walden II*. New York: Macmillan, 1948.

Spock, B. *The Common Sense Book of Baby and Child Care*. New York: Dell, Sloan, and Pearce, 1946.

Tocqueville, A. de. *Democracy in America*. New York: Vintage Books, 1945. (Originally published 1845.)

Wilson, K. *Redesigning Education*. New York: Henry Holt, 1995.

Wright, S. "Review of Guralnick's *Last Train to Memphis*." *The New York Times*, Sunday Book Review, October 30, 1994.

Zigler, E., and Muenchow, S. *Headstart*. New York: Basic Books, 1992.

Zigler, E., and Styfco, S.J. (Eds.). *Headstart and Beyond*. New Haven, Conn.: Yale University Press, 1993.

Index